Living in the World:
CULTURAL THEMES FOR WRITERS

NATIONAL GEOGRAPHIC LEARNING

WADSWORTH CENGAGE Learning·

Australia • Brazil • Japan • Korea • Mexico • Singapore • Spain • United Kingdom • United States

Living in the World:
Cultural Themes for Writers

Publisher: Monica Eckman

Acquiring Sponsoring Editor: Kate
Derrick

Development Editor: Danielle
Warchol

Editorial Assistant: Marjorie Cross

Media Editor: Cara Douglass-Graff

Brand Manager: Lydia Lestar

Senior Content Project Manager:
Corinna Dibble

Executive Director of Design:
Bruce Bond

Art Director: Bethany Casey

Manufacturing Planner: Betsy
Donaghey

Rights Acquisition Specialist:
Ann Hoffman

Production Service and Compositor:
Integra

Text and cover design: Bruce Bond
and Bethany Casey

Cover Image: O. Louis Mazzatenta/
National Geographic Stock

For product information and technology assistance, contact us at
Cengage Learning Customer & Sales Support, 1-800-354-9706.

For permission to use material from this text or product,
submit all requests online at **www.cengage.com/permissions.**
Further permissions questions can be e-mailed to
permissionrequest@cengage.com.

Library of Congress Control Number: 2012950115

ISBN-13: 978-1-285-07197-8
ISBN-10: 1-285-07197-2

Wadsworth
20 Channel Center Street
Boston, MA 02210
USA

Cengage Learning is a leading provider of customized learning solutions with
office locations around the globe, including Singapore, the United Kingdom,
Australia, Mexico, Brazil and Japan. Locate your local office at **international
.cengage.com/region**

Cengage Learning products are represented in Canada by Nelson
Education, Ltd.

For your course and learning solutions, visit **www.cengage.com.**
Purchase any of our products at your local college store or at our preferred
online store **www.cengagebrain.com.**
Instructors: Please visit **login.cengage.com** and log in to access
instructor-specific resources.

Printed in the United States of America
1 2 3 4 5 6 7 16 15 14 13

Table *of* Contents

Narration

Definition & Classification

Comparison & Contrast

Cause & Effect

III. GENRES

Personal Narrative

Travel Writing

Science Writing

Investigations & Exposés

Cultural & Historical Surveys

Introduction:
Writing with *National Geographic*

To "cover the world and all that is in it" has been the aim of the National Geographic Society since its founding in the late nineteenth century. Now, in the early decades of the twenty-first century, this world continues to grow ever larger as the boundaries of what is known and knowable keep expanding and encompassing ever more far-flung places and peoples. From its inception, the *National Geographic Magazine* has furthered this enlarging of the world and our understanding of it in the very process of investigating its discrete features, and with articles drawn from recent editions, this reader follow suit. Its contents speak to *Living in the World* today and take writing as an essential means for exploring it.

What, you may ask, does sitting in a classroom have to do with living in the world? The two can seem so antithetical. The world just beyond the campus sometimes feels so very removed from the world in it. Yet, there's always a way to connect simply by reading and writing. Even in the most confined circumstances, there's nothing to prevent us from going out and exploring.

Take the word "explore" itself, which is a verb, and a very active one, too, though not necessarily in the sense of physical exertion or any strenuous bodily activity at all. Definitions include to investigate, study, analyze, examine; to travel over new territory with the aim of discovery; to search out, to seek out in order to ascertain. You don't need a space suit or a deep-sea diving outfit to do any of the above. Sturdy boots, a reliable canoe, or well-tempered camel may be helpful, but not strictly necessary. A map that shows a point of entry to an ice field in the Arctic or a dense jungle in the Amazon is useful, but only up to that point. In essence, curiosity is all it takes to explore. But to share an enthusiasm for intellectual adventure with an audience, to convey the delights and the fruits of the quest in writing–these do take skill and practice. What better way to gain proficiency than by learning from those who spend their lives exploring?

The contributors to *National Geographic Magazine* are consummate professionals. Attuned to some of the most pressing concerns of our times, they also bring new challenges and new wonders to light in their work. Yes, many are journalists by training; others are not. All might be considered authors of innovative, observant nonfiction writings. They are also well versed in a variety of styles and genres. Thus, some of the articles here could be said to belong to the category of travel writing: take, for instance, an account of a solo journey down hundreds of miles of a river in a kayak, which happens to provide an excellent example of narrative, too. Investigative reporting that reveals the extent of slavery throughout the world today is more than an exposé; it's a call to action. So are features on over-fishing the seas and over-working the land. At the same time, you'll find science writing on such ineffable qualities as beauty and mysterious feelings as love. Nor is the cold, hard reality of money out of the question, especially not when it takes the enchanting and dangerous form of gold.

A global food staple such as rice makes for a broad field of investigation. Think of all buzz in the topic of caffeine, too. While on the subject of food, you and your fellow students could probably produce an anthology of pizza, treating everything from the cultivation of the wheat that goes into the crust to the selection of toppings heaped on it. An array of rituals, from county fairs to Celtic rites, also figures in this reader. Some will be familiar; some will be foreign; a few will be downright strange. But then the very alien qualities of such ceremonies can prompt reflection on the meaning of those you observe in your world and their influence in defining who you are.

While world cities, from ancient times to the present and even beyond, furnish abundant interest for the world traveler, armchair or otherwise, the many ways that we shape our cultural and physical environments and they shape us form a vital topic. You could say this is one of the most fundamental concerns of National Geographic. At the same time, the singular individual recounting unique experiences is also amply represented in the pages of the magazine, and this reader's samples of personal narratives could certainly inspire you to seek out a voice to compose your own. Meanwhile, no survey of living in the real world would be complete without including its imaginative realms. Fairy tales also fall within the purview of the magazine, and a fascinating account of their enduring allure is included in this reader as well.

You will also find pictures, and many of them. The most instantly recognizable feature of the magazine has always been its stunning photography. From the cover image that is invariably framed in that iconic yellow rectangle all the way to the very last page, the pictures tell stories in their own right, and understanding what they are saying is as critical to understanding the substance of the article in which they appear as the text. In fact, one of the articles in this collection focuses precisely on the stories that were told, along with those that were not, in images of the American Civil War, and thereby calls attention to ways in which illustrations present specific points of view, even arguments in themselves. How we respond to representations, in other words, is a critical concern of the contributors to the magazine, as well as its editors. So, in and of itself, is the power of the written word, which is the subject of another feature article included in this collection, and brings us to the heart of this book.

As all of us who write anything know, without asking ourselves the right questions before we begin to write, our thoughts remain unfocused and shadowy. "What is my main purpose?" "Who is my intended audience?" "How do I organize what I want to say?" "What's the right word or phrase?" These are all questions that should be answered before you write your paper. The main purpose is the reason you're writing the paper; it can be trying to persuade someone to believe your argument, providing them with facts and figures to supplement your research, or describing the similarities or differences between two items. Your audience is also important since your writing style will differ depending on who is reading. For instance, a personal narrative about your childhood is going to sound much more informal compared to a research paper aimed at an academic audience.

Both of these concepts are key to starting your paper, but the other key concept is organization. Organizing your thoughts will make it easier to write your paper. Start by jotting down everything you want to say and work your way up to creating a formal outline listing the order or your major points. Finally, with precisely the correct expression, a concept crystallizes; without it, there's likely to be just a blob. While this reader calls for careful consideration of language, it also takes language itself as a primary tool for analysis. Working with definitions of words, with their literal and figurative meanings and implications, can further critical thinking and writing about any given topic.

Most writers, regardless of their topic or writing style, rely on the same strategies. All of the rhetorical strategies defined below will appear in the readings throughout this text. However, it should be noted that while all of these modes are important, they won't show up in every piece of writing.

RHETORICAL MODES

- **Exposition:** Using description, ideas, and evidence to explain and analyze information.

- **Persuasion:** Influencing a reader's opinion or attitude through discussion, argument, or solid use of facts.

- **Description:** Creating a visual of a person, place, situation, or object so that the reader can imagine what is being described.

- **Narration:** Providing a timeline – usually chronological – of the events that occur in the essay or story.

- **Definition & Classification:** Definition explains terms, issues, and topics the reader might be unfamiliar with. Classification places information into specific categories or ranks.

- **Comparison & Contrast:** Discussing the similarities and differences between two or more subjects, ideas, people, locations, or objects.

- **Cause & Effect:** Exploring the reasons (cause) behind an event or occurrence and discussing the results (effect).

Definition is a primary strategy suggested by the writing prompts that accompany the articles. Techniques of comparison and contrast are logical extensions, as well as suitable for a multicultural range of perspectives. To follow links of cause and effect is just as critical as examining similarities and differences in this extensively interconnected world. Although *Living in the World* is not a writing guide, it does pay attention to rhetorical modes and to ways in which certain kinds of subjects bring certain kinds of thinking and writing to mind. As the brief tour of this reader indicates, the articles selected not only represent a wide variety of genres, from the personal narrative to the poised argument, from the descriptive report to the analytical essay, but also suggest opportunities for trying them out.

The questions that follow the selections fall into three broad categories. The first, Critical Responses, can include anything from gut reaction to considered reflection. Here, the style of an article is emphasized as much as the content, especially regarding the stylistic choices writers make that affect both what is communicated and how the communication is received. This section also invites discussion of broad themes and controversial issues broached in the articles, generating ideas that lead to essays.

The section on Writing Topics offers more direct guidance, with questions specifically focused on eliciting critical analysis of an aspect of an article or of a closely related subject. While suggestions for close readings of images, separately and in relation to the text, lead to a variety of possibilities for expository essays, ones that take a well-reasoned stand on controversial issues are also encouraged, as are those that draw connections between National Geographic topics and our day-to-day lives.

The section on Further Explorations includes invitations to do just that – explore. It offers openings for following interests arising from the articles, individually and in groups. It provides opportunities for engaging in collaborative activities that bring different points of view into contact with one another. And it opens possibilities for pursuing research and writing as means for making a way in the world.

Ultimately, the life of the classroom and the life of the world turn out to be not so distinct after all. The boundaries between the dorm room and the world beyond the campus are not at all fixed. There's no limit to exploring.

Preface

Living in the World is a thematic reader, its selections drawn from contemporary archives of the *National Geographic Magazine* and arranged according to topics that emerge from feature articles themselves. Both highly focused and universally resonant, some of these topics include crucial staples such as food, essential activities such as work, and fundamental emotions such as love. Some topics also offer local and global perspectives on distant isolated places and teeming urban cores, old rituals and new customs, aboriginal habitats and futuristic ones. In all these selections, one of the great strengths of *National Geographic Magazine* comes to the fore: the extent to which figures are as familiar as they are foreign, so that even as articles prompt us to recognize and engage with ways of life that are remote, they also help us notice habitually overlooked aspects of our day-to-day lives and bring a new awareness of how many diverse ways there are of living in the world.

Although many of the twenty-four articles collected in this reader are examples of superb journalism, journalists are by no means the sole contributors. Kira Salak, for example, holds a doctorate in English and writes award-winning fiction and nonfiction, in addition to adventuring alone to some of the most desolate and dangerous places in the world. To be sure, her travels and writings are unique, and yet in their very path-breaking quality they are also characteristic of many National Geographic explorations. Like Salak, the writers represented here are notable for the intellectual as well as the physical risks they take. Crossing multicultural boundaries, they have stories to tell, insights to offer–and have a talent for doing so exceptionally well. As models for composition and exploration in the fullest sense of the word, their work can animate the classroom and send students out into the world asking questions, seeking more.

Another instantly recognizable feature of *National Geographic* is also abundantly represented in this reader: this, of course, is the spectacular photography. While gorgeous in themselves, the images not only illustrate the subjects they cover, but also present specific points of view, even make their own arguments. Together, photos and text are mutually enhancing and mutually informing. At the same time, a discrepancy between word and image occasionally surfaces, demonstrating a productive tension between the writer's and photographer's point of view, a provocative difference in their combined visions.

Enhancing visual literacy is thus as crucial an aim of this reader as encouraging cultural awareness and curiosity. What is brought into the frame and the foreground? What is relegated to the background or given no place at all? These questions are critical to the reading of any text, visual or verbal or both, and they figure prominently in all the pedagogical materials accompanying the articles. For the convenience of the student and instructor, brief explanations of rhetorical modes are included in the reader. Writing prompts further involve students in processes of defining, comparing, analyzing, synthesizing, evaluating, and formulating new questions above all. In addition, prompts also encourage writing in various genres, whether the genre is a personal narrative or a descriptive essay, a profile of some stranger or a position staked in an absorbing debate. In all cases, questions direct students to pay attention to the strategies they employ in writing and thus to reflect on their aims and audiences throughout. A rhetorical table of contents, organized according to purpose, mode, and genre, supplements the thematic table of contents for this reader.

More details about the design of the pedagogical apparatus can be found in the general introduction. A brief tour of feature articles can be found there as well. In addition, each of the main sections of the reader is preceded by a brief synopsis of the articles included under that heading and suggests how they are related to one another. An **Instructor's Resource Manual** will also be available for download on the Instructor's Premium Website. This manual will have a summary of every reading and examples of answers for the questions asked at the end of each reading. Lastly, while a reader such as this does not presume to be comprehensive, in the interest of inclusiveness and variety, the text of some articles has been edited, and some accompanying images have been excluded. It is hoped that the necessity for such abbreviations in no way detracts from the feature articles themselves and that, on the contrary, they will only be augmented by the range and diversity of this collection.

ACKNOWLEDGEMENTS

Extensive thanks go out to the following professors who provided crucial feedback during the development process of *Living in the World*: Heather Akers, *University of Alabama Tuscaloosa*; Michael Alvarez, *Pima Community College*; Carolyn Ayers, *Saint Mary's University of Minnesota*; Leslie Bai, *Long Island University Post*; Aishia Bailey, *Virginia State University*; Lisa Beckelhimer, *University of Cincinnati*; John Bennett, *Lake Land College*; Laura Bolf-Beliveau, *University of Central Oklahoma*; Julia Chavez, *Saint Martin's University*; Sherry A. Cisler, *Arizona State University*; Andrea DeFusco, *Merrimack College*; Zana Easley, *Pima Community College*; Benjamin Emery, *Central New Mexico Community College*; Tyler Farrell, *Marquette University*; Allison Fetters, *Chattanooga State Community College*; Benjamin Fischer, *Northwest Nazarene University*; Catherine Fraga, *Sacramento State University*; Rebecca Gidjunis, *Eastern University*; Charlotte Gordon, *Endicott College*; Tami Haaland, *Montana State University-Billings*; John Haught, *Wright State University*; Thomas Henry, *Utah Valley University*; Kristina Holland, *Brevard College*; John Hyman, *American University*; Ekaterini Kottaras, *Pasadena City College*; Kim Lacey,

Saginaw Valley State University; Ken Lindblom, *Stony Brook University*; Stephanie Masson, *Northwestern University*; Matthew Masucci, *State College of Florida*; David Mead, *Palm Beach State College*; Trista Merrill, *Finger Lakes Community College*; Dorothy Minor, *Tulsa Community College, NEC*; Robert Morace, *Daemen College*; Jason Nado, *Marquette University*; Nancy Nanney, *West Virginia University at Parkersburg*; Alicia Nitecki, *Bentley University*; Kelly O'Connor-Salomon, *Russell Sage College*; Ashley Oliphant, *Pfeiffer University*; Leon Raikes, *Maine Maritime Academy*; Elizabeth Remsburg-Shiroishi, *Golden West College*; Donald Richardson, *Phoenix College*; Sorina Riddle, *Davidson County Community College*; David Salomon, *Russell Sage College*; Lisa Sandova, *Joliet Junior College*; Rebecka Sare, *Polk State College*; Jimmy Smith, *Union College*; Susan Todd, *Jefferson College*; Hunter Vaughan, *Oakland University*; Amy Watkin, *Concordia University*; Amy Wilson, *Central Methodist University*, Dianna Winslow, *Rochester Institute of Technology*.

Additionally, *Living in the World* would not have been possible without the help of our editorial team. Thanks must first go to Lyn Uhl, Editor in Chief, and Monica Eckman, Publisher, for their unwavering belief in and support of the partnership with National Geographic Learning and in this project. Kate Derrick, Acquiring Sponsoring Editor, and Danielle Warchol, Development Editor, with the assistance of Leslie Taggart, Senior Development Editor, worked closely together with Tanya Holloway to make the many content and design decisions that shaped this reader. Thanks must also go out to Wendy Perkins for her wonderful visual literacy contributions as well as Leila Hismeh, National Geographic Learning Associate Manager, Jen Shook, National Geographic Coordinator, Bruce Bond, Executive Director (Design), Bethany Casey, Senior Art Director, and Marjorie Cross, Editorial Assistant.

As one can imagine, it took several brainstorming sessions to finally arrive at a set of readings, images, and design with the cohesiveness necessary for a Freshman English Composition reader made up entirely of content drawn from National Geographic. It is the hope of the editorial team that the essays, the images, and the writing suggestions and critical thinking questions will excite, inspire, and move your students to want to read more, learn more, and to write about *Living in the World*.

© JAMES L. STANFIELD /National Geographic Image Collection

80°

70° Monday
Sunday

Date Line

ARCTIC CIRCLE

60°

50°

Haida Gwaii
(Queen Charlotte Islands)

BRITISH
COLUMBIA

C A N A D A

**Outer
Hebrides**

Galway
IRELAND

Bremerton

WASHINGTON

40°

Sacramento Valley

Spencer
IOWA

New York
N.Y.

Northampton
MASSACHUSETTS

Cordoba

CALIFORNIA **U N I T E D   S T A T E S**

30°

TROPIC OF CANCER

20°

Lake Placid

FLORIDA

Tecún Umán

GUATEMALA

SENEGAL

10°

0° EQUATOR

**Amazon
Basin**

P E R U

B R A Z I L

La Rinconada

10°

20°

TROPIC OF CAPRICORN

WINKEL TRIPEL PROJECTION, CENTRAL MERIDIAN 0°
SCALE 1:106,897,000
1 centimeter = 1,069 kilometers; 1 inch = 1,687 miles at the equator

0   500   1000   1500   2000   2500
KILOMETERS

0   500   1000   1500   2000   2500
STATUTE MILES

30°

Date Line

Sunday
Monday

60°

ANTARCTIC CIRCLE

70°

80°

90°

90°

80°

70°

ARCTIC CIRCLE

60°

50°

Sunday
Monday

Date Line

40°

don, ENGLAND

● Hesse
GERMANY

OM

S

● Prejidor

ANY

BOSN. &
HERZG.

● AZERBAIJAN

Dazhai ●

● Ise
JAPAN

ITALY

30°

USIA

● Kalamáta
GREECE

C H I N A

ZHEJIANG

Alexandria ●

● Punjab

● Sarabit el
Khadim

TAIWAN

TROPIC OF CANCER 20°

Dubai ●

Dhaka ●
BANGLADESH

MYANMAR
(BURMA)

EGYPT

UNITED
ARAB
EMIRATES

Kolkata ●
(Calcutta)

● NIGER

INDIA

● Manila

● SUDAN

PHILIPPINES

10°

A H E L

Kerala ●

DEMOCRATIC
REPUBLIC OF
THE CONGO

EQUATOR 0°

I N D O N E S I A

ANGOLA ●

Bali ● ● Sumbawa

● MALAWI

10°

20°

TROPIC OF CAPRICORN

30°

ANTARCTIC CIRCLE 60°

70°

80°

90°

PART 1
Exploring with *National Geographic*

Porters carrying goods through the Everest region of the Himalaya Mountains in Nepal.
© 2001 MICHAEL S. LEWIS/National Geographic Image Collection

This opening section begins with feature articles by two *National Geographic Explorers,* Kira Salak and John Dau, whose lives could hardly be more different. Whereas Salak was born and raised in the heartland of the United States and earned a Ph.D. in English, Dau was one of the "Lost Boys of Sudan," a victim of horrific conflict who could not read the "U.S.A." logo on a t-shirt he was given in a refugee camp. Now, however, he is pursuing higher education in the States and bringing his knowledge and care back to Africa. Salak, on the other hand, ventures to remote places constantly, pushing cultural boundaries in order to write and writing in order to continue exploring.

This human urge to transcend boundaries, actual and imaginative, is central to the next article on the enduring "Power of Writing" and the one following, which focuses on the creation of fairy tales as a significant real-world activity ("Guardians of the Fairy Tale"). How pictures tell stories is the emphasis of "A Sketch in Time," which offers some critical tools for reading images from the past, while "Tale of Three Cities" goes back in time and forward into the future, offering another model for exploring.

ARTICLES IN THIS SECTION:

A visual literacy section will appear at the end of the chapter.

MYANMAR'S
RIVER OF SPIRITS

By Kira Salak

Photographs by Steve Winter

MYANMAR'S RIVER OF SPIRITS

A daring and accomplished explorer and an award-winning author of both fiction and nonfiction prose, Kira Salak has undertaken many ambitious and perilous expeditions, including an unprecedented journey as a lone woman kayaking hundreds of miles down the Irrawaddy River of Myanmar. Engaging in her own distinct ways with the life of the river that flows through the strife-ridden country, Salak witnessed age-old rituals that have remained as constant as the current, as well as experiencing economic and political conflicts that currently riddle the land.

Than Swe Thant, a laborer, bathes in the Irrawaddy River near Mandalay.

The spires of Buddhist shrines float in the mist at Bagan on the Irrawaddy. The former royal capital is a tourist draw in a country where travel is tightly controlled.

IN A COUNTRY FILLED WITH STRIFE, THE IRRAWADDY IS A SOURCE OF HOPE FOR THE BURMESE PEOPLE. IT IS WHERE THEY WASH, WHAT THEY DRINK, HOW THEY TRAVEL, WHERE THEY PRAY.

The name "Irrawaddy"... translate[s] as river that brings blessings to the people.

I've always believed the best way to know a river is to paddle it, to feel its undercurrents and speed, to take in the changing nature of its banks. I wanted to explore the romance of Myanmar's Irrawaddy River, which has stirred the imagination of some of the world's greatest writers, such as Kipling and Orwell. The name "Irrawaddy" is an English corruption of Ayerawaddy Myit, which some scholars translate as "river that brings blessings to the people." But it's less a river than a test of faith, receding during the country's dry season until its banks sit exposed and cracking in the sun, only to return each spring with the monsoon, coming to life, flooding fields, replenishing the country with water, fish, and fertile soil. The Irrawaddy has never disappointed the Burmese. It is where they wash, what they drink, how they travel. Inseparable from their spiritual life, it is their hope.

So I set out to experience the Irrawaddy, the historical lifeline of Myanmar, paddling my first 340 miles in a kayak. The waters are icy cold to the touch as I get in my inflatable red kayak near Myitkyina and shove off into the brisk current, the soft blue waters winding with patient certainty toward distant hills. Shelducks, lounging in the shallows, take to the air, their ruddy feathers gleaming in the sunlight. Civilization quickly passes as I leave Myitkyina behind me, and save for the solitary gold panner digging into a sandbar, I have the spread of river and sky to myself.

The peace around me belies Myanmar's recent history. Today the country is notorious as the place where Nobel Prize winner Aung San Suu Kyi has been under house arrest for 10 of the past 17 years. It is a totalitarian state controlled by a group of ruling generals who in 1989 changed the name of the former British colony from Burma to Myanmar, a version of its precolonial name. In 1990, Suu Kyi's National League of Democracy (NLD) won more than 80 percent of the seats in national elections. The ruling junta, refusing to relinquish power, ignored the election result and clamped down on all opposition groups; in

Adapted from "Myanmar's River of Spirits" by Kira Salak: National Geographic Magazine, May 2006.

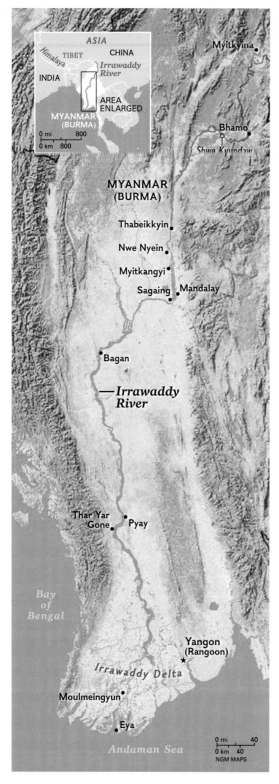

From its lofty source near the Tibetan border, the Irrawaddy
flows cold and undammed for its 1,300 miles.
Source: National Geographic

2003 dozens of Suu Kyi's backers were reportedly killed or injured during the "Black Friday"
attack by government supporters. Meanwhile,
human rights reports have cited evidence of
killings and torture as hundreds of thousands
of villagers in ethnic communities have been
forced to abandon their homes and relocate
to deny insurgents a civilian base. Last year,
U.S. Secretary of State Condoleezza Rice con-
demned Myanmar as one of the world's six
"outposts of tyranny."

Surely it is this troubled history that follows
me along the Irrawaddy as I make my long
journey to the sea, and that offers an explana-
tion for why my government guide, Jiro, who
follows behind me each day in a motorized
boat, tells me I shouldn't talk to anyone about
politics or religion. Surely it helps to explain
why large swaths of the country are off-limits
to tourists, who are kept to a well-trodden
route leading from the capital of Yangon to
Mandalay to the temples of Bagan. To devi-
ate from this route—to paddle a kayak down
a river—arouses suspicion.

Jiro, 33, works for the Ministry of Tourism
and will be filing reports on me with police
or military intelligence posts along the river
for the next five weeks. He is an amiable and
gregarious man who got married days before
I arrived. He knows this isn't how I envisioned
the trip, but there's nothing he can do. We strike
a compromise: He keeps his boat far away so I
can paddle with the illusion of being alone.

Gratefully, the Irrawaddy knows nothing
of politics. It is 1,300 miles of indifference to
such things. No matter what happens, I can
count on it to carry me along, as if the river
were a metaphor for the teaching that guides
the 89 percent of Burmese who are Buddhists:
All that arises, passes away. These waters
speak of glacial beginnings in the snow-
covered peaks of the Himalaya below Tibet.
They have surged through jungle-covered
highlands to emerge in the sun-scorched
plains of central Myanmar, where they will
continue to the ocean, releasing finally into
the Andaman Sea.

Docked beside one village, I find a small, lavishly decorated shrine on a wobby bamboo raft—the first of a handful of such shrines I will see along the river. Inside is a bronze statue of Shin U Pa Gota, the "saint" of all waters. Local villagers have left offerings of flowers, rice cakes, and locks of hair at his altar. According to legend, Shin U Pa Gota grew up a troubled boy until the Buddha visited him and brought him instant enlightenment. From that moment, he spent his time meditating in the Irrawaddy.

He is the saint of boatmen, of fishermen, of anyone who relies on the river. Bowing before him, I hope he is the saint of kayakers, too. In another day or two, the villagers will set the raft loose so it can continue down the river, bringing blessings to the next village that takes it in. I wonder if the raft will make it all the way to the end of the river. I can hardly imagine that end for myself now, the river opening wide, taking me into limitless blue waves.

Past the town of Bhamo, my paddling becomes a pilgrimage, each bend in the river, each rise of a hill promising the sight of a bright white pagoda pointing heavenward. Riverside temples smell of sandalwood incense and jasmine flowers. Bells on pagoda steeples tinkle in the breeze. The river winds past pristine 800-foot-high cliffs leading to Shwe Kyundaw—Golden Royal Island—where thousands of stupas rise from a tiny island barely half a mile long.

I park my kayak on a sandbar near white steps that rise from the water's edge. Everything is strangely silent. No one is around; to the Burmese people, the Golden Island is an unspeakably holy place on the Irrawaddy, where the Buddha himself is said to have pointed, announcing that an island would arise. And not just any island, but a place where a pagoda would be built along with 7,777 stupas, each to contain a relic from his own body after he died. The Golden Island

rose as prophesied, and more than 2,500 years later the promised stupas still stand, crumbling from the heat and dust of eons.

An old man in saffron robes greets me with a smile and a bow. He is the head monk, the Venerable Bhaddanta Thawbita. At 82 years old, he looks as much a relic of the ancient island as its stupas. He has lived on the Golden Island his entire life, beneath its arching bodhi trees and golden pagoda. During World War II, he watched as Japanese soldiers hid among the stupas, prompting Allied Forces to bomb the entire island. Two buildings survived the damage completely unscathed: the main temple and a crypt where four sacred statues—depicting the Buddha's previous incarnations—are kept, each believed to contain his actual blood.

They are considered such holy objects that in 1997 General Khin Nyunt—since ousted from the ruling junta—decided he wanted to move them from the island to a special temple in the capital. Thawbita strongly cautioned him against it. Witnesses later described how at the moment Nyunt reached the river with the statues, the sky grew dark and a violent storm began. Terrified, the chastened general promptly returned them.

Busy with visiting locals, Thawbita has his assistant monk, 67-year-old Ashin Kuthala, guide me into the temple. I expect the statues to be stored deep in a vault, far from visitors, but instead they rest on silk sheets inside a gilded cage just a few feet from passersby. I find their close proximity a rare gift. I gaze at the large padlock on the metal door. I ask Kuthala if he ever opens the door to the cage.

"Only for VIPs," he says. "For prime ministers, heads of state."

"Oh." I study the statues. I press my case. Kuthala takes a moment for consideration—and then goes to get the keys.

He asks me to sit on the floor just outside the chamber. Unlocking the door, he goes inside and

Worn-out monks' robes are reincarnated as sails on taxi boats at Pyay.

brings out one of the statues. Holding it, he asks me to pray. He places the statue on top of my head and begins reciting something from scripture. My eyes brim with tears. I'm lost in time.

The dry zone of central Myanmar, though one of the country's most populated regions, receives fewer than 30 inches of rain a year. The land is brown and parched, patches of cactus providing the only green. Each day the heat reaches at least 115°F, dust clouds blooming at any suggestion of wind. It's next to impossible to stay hydrated, my only shade being the four-inch brim of a hat. As I paddle, streams of barges overloaded with old-growth teak logs come at me like leviathans;

it's a wonder there are any trees left. The river, passing numerous towns, becomes covered for miles with raw sewage.

As I kayak through floating trails of excrement, I am bolstered by the memory of a local woman named Than, 35, whom I met squatting on the rocky shore near the town of Myitkyina. Her wiry forearms were burnished a coffee brown from the sun, and she wore a dirty sarong around her tiny waist. All day long she raised a mallet over a pile of rocks before her, cracking them into halves, then into fourths, to sell to the roadbuilders. Her two-year-old son, naked and with a bloated belly, stood nearby; her two daughters, ages three and twelve, helped gather the rocks. I asked how long she'd been doing such work.

"Ten years," she said. There was no bitterness in her voice. Just the crack of her mallet on a new stone.

Since 1996 the Myanmar government has sponsored a campaign to encourage tourism, but there's been much debate in the West about traveling to this country. Suu Kyi advises against it, arguing that tourism funds the government's oppression; other Burmese exiles believe tourism creates much needed jobs for local people and provides foreign witnesses to internal conditions. Shortly after I'd arrived in the country, I shared a taxi with a stranger in Yangon who suddenly started telling me about his support for Suu Kyi and his expectations of the collapse of the country's military leadership. There seems to be a need among people to talk to someone—anyone— from outside the country. To tell the world about a hidden, deep suffering. Unwittingly, I find that I am viewed less as a tourist than as a witness.

As I pull my kayak onto the shore of the tiny village of Myitkangyi, children gather nearby, mouths agape. When I take a step toward them, they run off, screaming. I think of how I must look—bush hat and sunglasses, my face coated with white sunscreen. I remove as much of it as I can. A sole child remains, a toddler of about three, who, to judge from the screams of an older boy hiding behind a boat, hasn't the good sense to avoid strange white women arriving in kayaks. When I turn my back, the older boy leaps out and seizes the child, dragging him to safety.

The children look skinny; UNICEF reports 32 percent of Burmese children under five years of age are malnourished. I take out a bag of candy from my backpack and hold it out to the children. "I come in peace," I say. An adult approaches and encourages them to snatch a piece of candy. Before long, my bag is empty.

Myitkangyi is a primitive village. It has no electricity or running water, no motorized vehicles, no telephones or paved roads. Everyone lives in thatch huts on stilts, and the only ground

He is the saint of boatmen, of fishermen, of anyone who relies on the river.

transportation is by oxcart. Like most villages along the river, it is self-sufficient, with its own blacksmith, carpenter, and wheelwright.

I pitch my tent on a sandbank across from the village, and adults wander over to sit on their haunches and study me for hours. When I eat dinner in the boat, word goes out. Soon a large crowd has gathered, sighing in unison as I open a can of Coke, exclaiming if I drop something.

The local fishermen are a bit more used to outsiders. A few scientists have recently come to the tiny village to witness an unusual ritual: using dolphins to help catch fish. To San Lwin, 42, a fisherman who shows me the practice the following morning, there is nothing remarkable about this. His father taught him to fish with dolphins when he was 16; the practice has been passed down for generations. Lwin's face, bronzed and creased from the sun, expresses a sort of reverence as he studies the silver waters for sight of a dolphin fin. "If a dolphin dies," he says, "it's like my own mother has died."

We reach the area of the river where Lwin says the dolphins congregate. Classified as critically endangered, only about 70 Irrawaddy dolphins are left in the river that gives them their name. Lwin and the other men tap small, pointed sticks against the sides of their canoes and make high-pitched *cru-cru* sounds. Several gray forms, gleaming in the sunlight, arch through the water toward us. One with a calf by her side spits air loudly through her blowhole.

"Goat Htit Ma!" Lwin yells, pointing at her and smiling. "She's calling to us!" Goat Htit Ma has been fishing with them for 30 years, Lwin says.

The fishermen splash their paddles to tell the dolphins they'd like to fish together. One dolphin separates from the group and begins swimming back and forth in large semicircles. It submerges again, reappearing less than ten feet from our canoe, its tail waving with frantic urgency. Lwin winds up and tosses

continued on page 14

Black floats mark nets at the river's mouth, where each haul brings in a few more cents and vital protein. Despite its fishing grounds and rice fields, Myanmar is one of Asia's poorest nations.

continued from page 11

a lead-weighted net over the spot where the dolphin has shown its tail. The net spreads in the air like a great parachute, quickly sinking beneath the water. As Lwin slowly pulls it in, numerous silver fish flap in the strings. Lwin says the dolphins help themselves to any fish that escape the nets.

We are following the dolphins upriver when we pass some gill-net fishermen camped along the shore. This is one of the biggest threats to the Irrawaddy dolphin: Long nets are stretched across sections of the river to catch anything and everything that passes by—including dolphins.

The fishermen call to us. "Do you want to see a big fish?" they ask. They produce a six-foot-long *nga maung-ma*, or catfish, its head a foot and a half wide, its great whiskers three feet long. The orange-and-white body, dotted with black spots, glows in the sunlight, a masterpiece of creation. Tomorrow they'll take it to Mandalay and sell it for a small fortune: 45,000 kyat or 55 dollars—about a quarter of the average Burmese's yearly income.

As we begin paddling after the dolphins again, I ask Lwin to wait.

"I'd like to buy the catfish," I say.

The gill-net men laugh at the idea, but when I show them the 45,000 kyat, they hand over the fish. My plan is to reach the deep channel on the opposite bank so I can set it free. For centuries, Buddhist monks living along the river have cherished these giant catfish; at the monastery near Thabeikkyin, monks told me they hand-feed giant catfish during the rainy season. And now Lwin, a Buddhist, eagerly embraces my plan to free the fish, noting the karmic merit I will accrue. But my sudden desire to save the fish's life is a simple matter: I just don't want that great orange fellow to die.

Numerous spirits live along the river, and worshipping them has become big business. Traveling the lazy way for the rest of my trip—by motorized boat—I stop near a small village called Thar Yar Gone to witness a *nat-pwe*, or spirit festival. Inside a large thatch hut, musicians play loud, frenetic music before a crowd

of rowdy onlookers. On the opposite end of the hut, on a raised stage, sit several wooden statues: *nat*, or spirit, effigies. I pass through the crowd and enter a space underneath the stage, where a beautiful woman introduces herself as Phyo Thet Pine. She is a *nat-kadaw*, literally a "spirit's wife"—a performer who is part psychic, part shaman.

Only she isn't a woman—she is a he, a transvestite wearing bright red lipstick, expertly applied black eyeliner, and delicate puffs of powder on each cheek. Having traveled to the village by oxcart, smears of dirt covering my sweaty arms and face, I feel self-conscious before Pine's painstakingly created femininity. I smooth my hair and smile in apology at my appearance, shaking Pine's delicate, well-manicured hand.

The cult of the nats is Myanmar's ancient animist religion. In the 11th century, King Anawrahta established the Theravada school of Buddhism as Myanmar's primary religion. When his attempts to eliminate nat worship, considered a form of occultism not accepted by Buddhist scriptures, proved fruitless, he decided to adapt it instead, creating an official pantheon of 37 spirits to be worshipped as subordinates of the Buddha. The result is that many Buddhist temples in Myanmar now have their own *nat-sin*, spirit house, attached to the main pagoda.

Though people still worship spirits outside the official pantheon, the 37 enjoy a VIP status, with traveling troupes of dancers, singers, and musicians reenacting the human stories of the spirits' tumultuous lives and violent deaths. But nat-kadaws are more than just actors; they believe that the spirits actually enter their bodies and possess them. Each has an entirely different personality, requiring a change in costume, decorations, and props. Some of the spirits might be female, for whom the male nat-kadaw dons women's clothing; others, warriors or kings, require uniforms and weapons.

To most Burmese, being born female rather than male is karmic punishment indicating grave transgressions in former lifetimes. Many

Burmese women, when leaving offerings at temples, pray to be reincarnated as men. But to be born gay—that is viewed as the lowest form of human incarnation. Where this leaves Myanmar's gay men, psychologically, I can only imagine. It perhaps explains why so many become nat-kadaws. It allows them to assume a position of power and prestige in a society that would otherwise scorn them.

Pine, who is head of his troupe, conveys a kind of regal confidence. His trunks are full of makeup and colorful costumes, making the space under the stage look like a movie star's dressing room. He became an official nat-kadaw, he says, when he was only 15. He spent his teenage years traveling around villages, performing. He went to Yangon's University of Culture, learning each of the dances of the 37 spirits. It took him nearly 20 years to master his craft. Now, at age 33, he commands his own troupe and makes 110 dollars for a two-day festival—a small fortune by Burmese standards.

He outlines his eyes with eyeliner and draws an intricate mustache on his upper lip. "I'm preparing for Ko Gyi Kyaw," he says. It is the notorious gambling, drinking, fornicating spirit.

The crowd, juiced on grain alcohol, hoots and shouts for Ko Gyi Kyaw to show himself. A male nat-kadaw in a tight green dress begins serenading the spirit. The musicians create a cacophony of sound. All at once, from beneath a corner of the stage, a wily-looking man with a mustache bursts out, wearing a white silk shirt and smoking a cigarette. The crowd roars its approval.

Pine's body flows with the music, arms held aloft, hands snapping up and down. There is a controlled urgency to his movements, as if, at any moment, he might break into a frenzy. When he talks to the crowd in a deep bass voice, it sounds nothing like the man with whom I just spoke. "Do good things!" he admonishes the crowd, throwing money. People dive for the bills, a great mass of bodies pushing and tearing at each other. The

My eyes brim with tears. I'm lost in time.

melee ends as quickly as it had erupted, torn pieces of money lying like confetti on the ground. Ko Gyi Kyaw is gone.

That was just the warm-up. The music reaches a feverish pitch when several performers emerge to announce the actual spirit possession ceremony. This time Pine seizes two women from the crowd—the wife of the hut's owner, Zaw, and her sister. He hands them a rope attached to a pole, ordering them to tug it. As the frightened women comply, they bare the whites of their eyes and begin shaking. Shocked as if with a jolt of energy, they start a panicked dance, twirling and colliding into members of the crowd. The women, seemingly oblivious to what they are doing, stomp to the spirit altar, each seizing a machete.

The women wave the knives in the air, dancing only a few feet away from me. Just as I am considering my quickest route of escape, they collapse, sobbing and gasping. The nat-kadaws run to their aid, cradling them, and the women gaze with bewilderment at the crowd. Zaw's wife looks as if she had just woken from a dream. She says she doesn't remember what just happened. Her face looks haggard, her body lifeless. Someone leads her away.

Pine explains that the women were possessed by two spirits, ancestral guardians who will now provide the household with protection in the future. Zaw, as the house owner, brings out two of his children to "offer" to the spirits, and Pine says a prayer for their happiness. The ceremony ends with an entreaty to the Buddha.

Pine goes under the stage to change and reappears in a black T-shirt, his long hair tied back, and begins to pack his things. The drunken crowd mocks him with catcalls, but Pine looks unfazed. I wonder who pities whom. The next day he and his dancers will have left Thar Yar Gone, a small fortune in their pockets. Meanwhile, the people in this village will be back to finding ways to survive along the river.

continued on page 18

At a raucous spirit festival in Pyay, a transvestite named Tun Thein plays the role of a spirit's wife, a conduit to the supernatural. Participants thrust cash at her, hoping for good luck.

continued from page 15

A well-dressed man in glasses is frowning at me. I am on the dock of the last major town on the Irrawaddy, in the delta region where greenery has replaced the desert scrub of the dry zone. The banks are crowded with teak vessels painted in hues that mimic the tropical landscape. But we have a problem. Someone forgot to list Moulmeingyun on my special permit. So I am here illegally. Much of the delta is off-limits to tourists. Did I journey nearly 1,300 miles on the Irrawaddy to have to turn back now, only one day from my goal?

I have been with Jiro long enough to know when he is nervous. He stands straighter; he makes obsequious shows of respect. I feel terrible that my trip has turned into such a headache for everyone. Gone from Jiro's face is the joy from his recent marriage, replaced with anxiety and exhaustion.

We're told we won't be able to camp along the Irrawaddy tonight; instead, we will stay in the town's guesthouse. It is not a choice. We head there immediately, and the receptionist ushers me to a concrete-walled cubicle that's stiflingly hot, reeking of urine, the bedsheets stained with blood and dirt. I sit on the edge of the bed to wait while Jiro reports to the police. After a while the heat drives me outside, and I have just reached the street when the receptionist comes after me, shouting that I must return to my room. When I do, I find a grim-looking man stationed in a chair outside my door, glaring at me. It's clear I am not to leave my room again.

I am trying to accept having to end my trip in Moulmeingyun, when the local authorities inexplicably change their minds: They will allow me to go to the sea. We speed off in a motorboat before dawn, the town vanishing into the darkness behind us. As we travel down the last few miles of the river, the sun rises as pure orange light over the mangrove swamps and jungle. We arrive at villages where the people cluster around me, eager to know who I am, where I have been. The children hold their palms together reverentially to receive my offerings of candy.

We travel farther until the river suddenly breaks open to the sea. Sunlight dazzles the churning waters, my thermometer reading 119°F—the hottest day of my trip. The heat is staggering, as if the weight of the white sky is about to collapse. We putter slowly toward a distant spit of land crowned with a golden stupa: Eya village. The last village on the Irrawaddy.

As we dock beside a white beach, I trade the sight of the Irrawaddy for the aquamarine waves of the Andaman Sea. Palm trees rustle in the breeze. Canoes dot the water, where men dive for scallops. They are Eya's biggest moneymaker—the shells ten times more valuable than the meat; each ten-pound sack, sold as fodder to chicken farms, will net the equivalent of 12 cents.

All the people I meet in Eya—young and old—say they have never seen a white person. From their thatch huts raised on stilts, they climb down to get a good look at me. They have seen a man from China a few times, they say, but never someone who looks like me.

Though the Myanmar coastline was largely spared by the great tsunami of 2004, Eya's residents tell me that it did strike their village. An old woman, her eyes wide, describes the great waves coming and everyone in Eya fleeing inland. "But no one died," she says. "The Lord Buddha protected us."

As I walk through the village, down its narrow spit of land completely exposed to the sea, I miss the security of being on the Irrawaddy, which, for all its heat and mercurial moods, felt like the safest place of my entire trip.

"We have a beautiful life," the woman says. "We can get money from the Irrawaddy *and* the sea."

And they have a special job, too: The residents of Eya rescue the Shin U Pa Gota rafts that manage to make the long journey down the river and put the statues inside a special shrine in the village. Perhaps Shin U Pa Gota wasn't meant to enter the sea.

Nor am I. I'm ready to go home. I get in the motorboat, and we return to the Irrawaddy.

Critical Responses

1. What are the main economic features of the Irrawaddy River? What are its spiritual characteristics? In what ways are these complementary? How, more broadly, does the river shape the culture—and vice versa?

2. What political obstacles does Salak confront in her journey? How do they affect her voyage through Myanmar?

3. The raft that serves as a shrine to Shin U Pa Gota, the "'saint' of all the waters," appears and reappears several times in the narrative. What is the raft doing on the river? What does it represent, actually and metaphorically?

4. What is the dominant mood of each of the photographs that accompany the article? How do these images complement the narrative—and vice versa?

Writing Topics

1. Salak refers to herself as a "witness." What does this term suggest about her attitude toward the world through which she moves? How is being a witness different from being a spectator or an observer?

2. The idea of "transport" is also important here, both in the physical sense of transportation from one place to another and in the emotional sense of being transported, or carried away. How do these meanings resonate and relate to one another in the narrative?

3. Salak herself is conspicuously absent from the photographs that accompany the feature. What do you make of this absence? Does it detract from the story or contribute to it? How, and why?

4. Touring, traveling, exploring—these ways of encountering unfamiliar places, while related, are at the same time quite distinct. How would you define each one, in itself and in relation to the others? What values does each imply? Which term or terms best describe Salak's venture, and why?

Further Explorations

1. Imagine undertaking a journey to some strange place by yourself. Where would you choose to go and why? What would be the attraction for you, and the challenge? What would you hope to gain from the experience? What might you have to offer afterwards?

2. What's in a name—specifically, the name "Burma" and the name "Myanmar"? After investigating the history of the country, consider which name is preferable, from whose perspective, and why.

JOHN DAU: A SURVIVOR'S STORY

By John Dau with Karen M. Kostyal

JOHN DAU:
A SURVIVOR'S STORY

One of the thousands of refugees who came to be known as the "Lost Boys of Sudan," John Dau endured harrowing dangers and deprivations for over a decade. A child himself, he acted as a leader of other children, and then was among the first of the Lost Boys to make his way to the United States. For 16 years, Dau was either on the run from Arab Militia and the Sudanese Army, from wild animals, from starvation and thirst—or living in refugee camps. In 2001, he was among the lucky few chosen to immigrate to the United States, a place he had never heard of until he learned to read at the age of 17. In the following profile, author and editor Karen M. Kostyal collaborates with Dau to tell the story of his perilous journey through the war-torn country and of the people he never left behind in heart or in mind.

One of the many images taken from John Dau's trip to visit the Duk County Lost Boy's school in South Sudan.
John Dau

John Dau has done a lot of living in his 34 years. One of the "lost boys of Sudan," he's now a father himself, with a new life in the U.S.

"LOST BOY" SEEMS A STRANGE MONIKER FOR JOHN DAU. AT 34 AND AN ELEGANT SIX FOOT EIGHT, HE'S HARDLY A BOY. BUT HE'S PROUD OF THE NAME— "LOST BOY OF SUDAN," TO BE EXACT. DAU IS ONE OF THE THOUSANDS OF AFRICAN MALES IN SOUTHERN SUDAN ATTACKED IN THE 1980s AND '90s BY THE ARAB SUDANESE GOVERNMENT IN THE NORTH.

When I think of Sudan, I like to remember life in my village. The land there was good, with plenty of water and grasslands for the cattle and goats that my people, the Dinka, survive on. But in 1983, when I was ten, the troubles began. Sudan's Arab president, Gaafar Muhammad Nimeiri, declared that Sudan would become a Muslim state and that sharia law would be the law of the land. But we did not want this. So John Garang, a Dinka, formed the SPLA, the Sudanese People's Liberation Army, to resist the government. We Africans were the true Sudanese, he said, not the Arab colonialists who had come into our land from the north. SPLA recruits trained in Ethiopia, but sometimes they came to our village.

We children could hear the adults talking in worried tones of fighting near us, villages attacked. Soon refugees began coming to our village. We welcomed them, and my father, who was the village leader, helped feed them, even slaughtering our cows for food. We began

> We children could hear the adults talking in worried tones of fighting near us, villages attacked.

to hear the adults say that the Arabs were killing Dinka boys particularly, so that the boys would not grow up and join the army. We grew very scared. My mother started cooking small meals, because food was scarce and because she said our stomachs must get used to less food. She told us that if the village was attacked, we, her children, must hold hands tightly, so we would not get separated as we ran.

One night as I slept—it was August, the rainy season, in 1987—I began to hear a dull thumping that seemed to be slapping me in the ear. In my sleep it was just something annoying, but then I woke up and scrambled outside the crowded hut I shared with other children. Everyone was running, and the sky was lit up by mortar blasts. I saw my father run past, so I ran after him. The women and children were

Adapted from "John Dau: A Survivor's Story" by John Dau with Karen Kostyal: National Geographic Magazine, January 2007.

JOHN DAU: A SURVIVOR'S STORY 23

running and crying. I could hear bullets, *zzzz-ing zzzing*, whistling past us. I can still hear that sound. I thought that the end of the world the Bible talks about was here.

I kept running, following my father, out of the village into the bush. And then he kneeled down in the tall grass, to watch for soldiers, and I caught up to him, and it was not my father. It was our neighbor Abraham. He told me to be very quiet, and he grabbed me and we crawled through the tall grass to the bush. I was so scared. "Where is my family?" I asked. "They are coming, they are coming," he said, and he pulled me by the arm and made me keep running, dragging me along with him. I could hear Abraham's heart pounding.

At dawn we met a woman and her two girls from our village, and we joined them, heading east toward Ethiopia, where we thought we would be safe. My knees were scraped from falling as we ran, my feet were bloody, and I was naked, because I had left the village that way. None of us had taken anything as we fled. No food, no cooking pots. We ate almost nothing—wild roots, a pumpkin from a farmer's field. At night the mosquitoes would torment us as we tried to sleep.

Then, one day, a group of militia ambushed us. The men grabbed Abraham, forced him to the ground, and began beating him with a stick, telling him to give them money. He had no money, so they took his shirt and left him in the dirt, his back bloody. I felt lucky, because they had not killed Abraham. I do not know why they let him live.

We kept going, now heading southeast to avoid the militia, but on the seventh day, we ran into another militia. Again, they beat Abraham, and this time they beat me, too, over and over on the head with a stick. While they were beating us, they abducted the woman and girls. That was the last time we saw them.

Now, there were just the two of us with our wounds. We had to keep moving, following narrow footpaths through grasses so high

they were over our heads. We stole pumpkins from farmers' fields when we could, but often we just chewed grass stems to help our hunger. We would listen for the sound of frogs, then follow that sound to find water pools. We were very careful when we went near water, as that is where others would come, including Arab militia. Abraham taught me how to stay almost submerged in the pools, with my head far back, so that only my nose would be above the water level to breathe. It was good he taught me this, because once Arabs did come to swim and relax at a river we were in. They never saw us.

What horrified me most was the night. I was afraid of wild animals, leopards and hyenas, and it was very, very cold, about 40°F. I had no clothes or covering to stay warm, so I would sleep close to Abraham.

It went on like this for several weeks, until we got near a town called Pibor Post. Here we met another group of refugees, this one with two men and 17 boys, all of them naked like me. The youngest was only about five or six. We joined them, and that gave me new life. I felt like I had comrades. Of course, being in a bigger group also caused problems. Now it was mid-October and getting drier and drier. We had a hard time finding food for so many of us, and it was much harder to move without being seen. We began walking at night and sleeping in the forest during the day. We started sending out a boy and an adult on reconnaissance before we moved on. We lost one adult that way, and a boy also disappeared. We thought maybe a leopard got him.

We were in the territory of a hostile tribe called the Murle, most of whom were cooperating with the Arabs. As the season grew hotter and drier, food became harder and harder to find. We were getting very weak, but we kept going, toward a river called Kangen. When we got there, the riverbed was dry. No water, and hot, hot sun. We were so thirsty, and we were starving. At one point, Murle hunters killed the second man from our new group, leaving Abraham as the only adult.

We moved on, looking for water. We were crying, because we were so thirsty, but no tears came. We wanted to stop, give up, but Abraham kept pushing us to move on, saying we would find water soon. When we did not, some of the boys refused to go on. At last, we found a muddy pool, threw ourselves into it, and ate the mud, just for moisture. It had been days since we had water to drink. Our tongues were swollen, our skins gray, we couldn't talk. Abraham urinated into a little container and gave it to me to drink. Now only four of us boys were left with Abraham. Along the path, we saw dead bodies, sometimes vultures eating them. I prayed, I sang Christian songs in my mind to ask for water. Then on the second day, we came to a swampy area and ran into it and drank and drank.

Once we had water, we focused on our hunger. We found tortoises and roasted them. That was the first time I had eaten protein since I left my village. We also collected grasshoppers and threw them into the open fire to cook. We spent three weeks there in those Kangen marshes, trying to regain our strength.

Then we continued on, finally crossing the border into western Ethiopia. This was the home of the Anyuak people, and most were pro-SPLA, so they helped us, giving us maize to take with us.

When the SPLA had come to our village, they had mentioned a camp near the Sudan-Ethiopia border called Pinyudu. That was where we had been heading all along. Finally, in late November we made it there. We had spent four months trying to reach it.

But Pinyudu was not good. Refugees were pouring in, and local Ethiopians were trying to help them; the UN did not arrive till several weeks later. I was selected leader of a group of 200 boys, and we had to take care of ourselves. We had almost nothing to eat—just a small amount of fortified cereal—and no shelter. It was so hot, as high as 116°F.

The ground burned our feet as we ran from tree to tree for shade. Soon, cholera hit the camp, and life became very bad. My boys were dying all around me. I was trying to help them, but I could not. If they became sick in the morning, they could be dead by afternoon. We dug shallow graves in the dirt with sticks and our hands, just a few inches deep, to bury them. But their limbs became stiff after a few hours and poked up out of the ground. At night hyenas would come and eat the bodies. Some of the boys began to act crazy. They could not take the horrors. It was a terrible time.

After the cholera epidemic, other diseases attacked—measles, chicken pox, whooping cough. They killed a lot more boys. I don't know why I survived, maybe it was something that God planned.

Then, slowly, the camp became organized. My group grew to 1,200 boys, and we built mud-and-thatch shelters. We were given clothes, too. I had a T-shirt with some symbols on it. Years later, when I learned to read, I realized the symbols said U.S.A. We were taught how to dig latrines and began getting more food, even milk. We would leave the milk in the hot sun until it curdled, something we Dinka love. Still, some boys would leave the camp, and locals accused them of raiding fields and orchards. Some boys were abducted by Anyuak; we heard they used the boys' bodies to trap leopards for their skins.

After four years at Pinyudu, adults at the camp told us we must flee, because the camp was going to be attacked by locals. The only choice was to cross back into Sudan. We figured out a way to make backpacks out of meal sacks and pieces of plastic to put food in. Then we all left the camp together, 27,000 of us, almost all boys, walking down a narrow path single file. The line went on for days.

When we got to Gilo River, it was very full and strong, and we could see crocodiles waiting away from shore. We were gathered there on the riverbank when suddenly Ethiopian rebels attacked, firing on us. I dived into the river and began swimming as hard as I could. Another boy dived almost on top of me, but he could not swim well, and he clutched at me. I tried to help him, but I didn't have the strength, and the river was forcing us both under. I had to leave him. Somehow, I made it to the other side. We lost about 9,000 boys and a few men that day on the Gilo River. But 18,000 of us, mostly Dinka boys, had made it back to our homeland.

John Dau's ordeal was far from over. The lost boys spent nine months in the SPLA-held town of Pochala, until the Sudanese government began bombing the town. Dau left with 1,200 boys, and little adult supervision, and fled south toward Kenya. For the next six months, the boys suffered starvation, thirst, and ambushes and bombing attacks by the Sudanese government. Some 800 boys eventually made it to the massive Kakuma refugee camp in northern Kenya. Dau spent the next ten years there. In an outdoor classroom, he was taught reading, English, math, geography, history, and civics. He's now working on a bachelor's degree at Syracuse University, and he's established a fund to build the Duk Lost Boys Clinic in southern Sudan. Many of his friends and family remain in refugee camps in eastern Africa.

Critical Responses

1. Given Kostyal's role in producing this profile, why might Dau's story have been presented as a first-person narrative rather than in a question-and-answer interview format?

2. Taking this question further, how would you characterize the tone of this article? How does it affect your response?

3. With over a decade of horrific suffering compressed into just a few pages, much is necessarily left out of this narrative. What, however, is gained by the brevity?

4. Graphic details are also few and far between, and there's certainly no dwelling on the ordeals undergone by John Dau and the Lost Boys of Sudan. Does this matter-of-factness draw you in or keep you at arm's length? Look at specific passages carefully as you formulate your response.

Writing Topics

1. What are some of the main characteristics of a leader? Which did Dau exhibit while in Sudan? What about since his departure?

2. Who is Abraham in the Bible and the Qur'an? How do stories of this prophet and patriarch resonate in Dau's narrative?

3. Why did the children of Sudan become segregated into "Lost Boys" and "Lost Girls"? After researching the circumstances that led to this segregation, investigate the girls' fate, insofar as you can.

4. If you could interview John Dau or any of the Lost Boys who survived, what questions would you ask and with what aim?

Further Explorations

1. Looking at your own life as a journey, describe the route that brought you to where you are and the route that you may take moving forward.

2. Besides the documentary film *God Grew Tired of Us* (2007), there are several shorter National Geographic videos that focus on experiences of John Dau and other Lost Boys of Sudan (search online for "Sudan" at http://video.nationalgeographic.com/video/places). Whether on your own or in class, view them and share your impressions, focusing on differences between your worlds and seeking out commonalities.

THE POWER OF WRITING

By Joel Swerdlow

Photographs by Cary Wolinsky

THE POWER OF WRITING

Definitions of the word "writing" are limited; they include "to form or delineate with an implement;" "to score, draw, depict, engrave." The uses of writing, on the other hand, are legion, and so are its powers. Tracing forms of writing that emerged over five thousand years ago, Joel Swerdlow looks at ways that they have shaped and been shaped by civilization from ancient times to the present.

Echoing Egyptian hieroglyphs and composed of 400 separate photographs, this illustration presents a riddle in the form of a rebus. The names of eight pictured objects suggest the sounds of other words that together form a simple declarative sentence. Clues appear throughout the text of this article, where the names of the objects are written in various languages.

WRITING

BY JOEL SWERDLOW

PHOTOGRAPHS

BY CARY WOLINSKY

The article's byline (above) was inked onto grains of rice in India.

HANDMAIDEN TO HISTORY, CHRONICLER OF THE MIND AND THE HEART, WRITING IS HUMANKIND'S MOST FAR-REACHING CREATION, ITS FORMS AND DESIGNS ENDLESS. THE WORDS YOU ARE NOW READING WERE WRITTEN ON A COMPUTER EQUIPPED WITH SOME 800 STYLES OF TYPE.

YET THE PURPOSE OF WRITING REMAINS UNCHANGED: TO CONVEY MEANING, WHETHER PLAYFUL, MUNDANE, OR PROFOUND.

Chinese state security officers arrested Wei Jingsheng, an electrician, on March 29, 1979. Among his major crimes: writing essays arguing for democracy. Wei, who would spend 18 years in jail and become a prominent symbol of the power of the written word, was placed in the Beijing detention center.

Chinese authorities feared Wei, recognizing that writing has an almost magical power: Words on paper, created by ordinary citizens, have overthrown governments and changed the course of history. So powerful is writing that the beginnings of civilization and history are most often defined as the moment cultures develop it. Anthropologists can only paint outlines of ancient societies that had no writing;

> **Words on paper, created by ordinary citizens, have overthrown governments and changed the course of history.**

a written record provides the human details—history, belief, names and dates, thought, and emotion.

No other invention—perhaps only the wheel comes close—has had a longer and greater impact. Writing helped preserve the three major monotheistic religions, whose believers the Koran refers to as "the People of the Book." The transformation of language into written words has immortalized passion, genius, art, and science—the letters of St. Paul, the poems of Li Po, the humor of Aristophanes, the treatises of Maimonides.

Adapted from "The Power of Writing" by Joel Swerdlow: National Geographic Magazine, August 1999.

THAI
"eye"

Much of writing's power comes from its flexibility. Ever since the Sumerians began keeping records by impressing cuneiform signs on clay tablets 5,000 years ago, humans have searched for the ideal tools to portray words. They have chiseled symbols in stone and bone and have written on leaves, bark, silk, papyrus, parchment, paper, and electronic screens. This skill, once known only to a few professional scribes, grew into mass literacy: Some five billion people can read and write today, about 85 percent of the world's population.

From its beginning as recordkeeper to its transformation into one of humanity's most potent forms of artistic and political expression, writing reveals the power of innovation.

But the story of Wei proclaims writing's greatest power—its ability to move hearts and minds.

His cell measured four and a half feet by nine feet. Authorities kept the light on at all times. No one, not even his guards, was allowed to speak to Wei, and he was not permitted to read or write. His requests for paper and pencil were ignored.

To understand how writing evolved, I visit Sarabit el Khadim, a flat-topped, wind-eroded mountain of reddish sandstone in the southwestern Sinai Peninsula of Egypt. Here, in a turquoise mine dug by Egyptians almost 3,500 years ago, is one of the earliest examples of a phonetic alphabet. Avner Goren, an Israeli archaeologist who supervised excavations in the Sinai for 15 years, is leading me up a steep trail, with narrow ledges and a drop-off to rocks far below. Near the top, we stoop to enter a dark hole.

"What do you think?" Goren asks, pointing to a wall about six feet in front of us. Carved into the stone are crude sketches of a fish, ox head, and square, remarkably different from the Egyptian hieroglyphs found else-where at the site.

The simplicity of these marks belies their significance. I move closer, as if proximity will reveal their magic. The people who made these signs were among the first to use characters each of which represented one sound—an alphabet. These alphabetic symbols had acrophonic values, with each representing the initial sound of the object depicted. The picture of the square—a house—thus stood for the *b* sound because the word for house was *beit*.

If these ancient writers were not Egyptians, who were they? After British archaeologists explored Sarabit el Khadim in 1905, some scholars argued that they were Israelites fleeing from Egypt with Moses about 1250 B.C. But similar writing as old or older was discovered in present-day Israel in the 1930s, so most researchers now believe that this alphabet was invented in Canaan, a region between the Jordan River and the Mediterranean Sea. Most likely, Canaanites who were brought in to work the mines left these messages.

Egyptian scribes had to master hundreds of symbols. I tell Goren that alphabetic writing must have seemed much more attractive to those scribes. "Probably not," he says. "About 30 of the symbols in Egyptian hieroglyphs represent single sounds, just like the alphabet. They knew about using symbols to represent sounds. To the Egyptians the Semitic writing may have looked too primitive to be significant."

That night, as we lie in sleeping bags at the base of the mountains, Goren warns against

MIXTEC PICTOGRAM
"bee"

seeing an alphabet as "superior" to pictographic writing. "If you came from outer space and wrote a report, you'd give the alphabet high marks," he says. "It's flexible and easy to learn. But what actual effect did that have? There was no mass literacy until after the development of the printing press in the mid-15th century."

But alphabets, it seems to me, changed the way people thought. The-oretical science, formal logic, and the concept of time as a straight line moving from past into future came from societies with alphabets.

From a small patch in the Middle East the notion of one symbol per sound spread around the world, taking root first among the Greeks, who modified some characters into written vowels. The Latin alphabet of the Romans evolved from the Greek around the sixth century B.C. By the ninth century A.D., Japan had developed strong phonetic components in its written language; Korea by the 15th. Indeed, of the several hundred written languages in the world today, only Chinese still relies on a writing system in which individual characters represent individual words. These characters often mean one thing when used alone, but something else when combined. The Chinese character for "sincerity," for example, shows the character for "man" alongside the one for "word," literally a man standing by his word.

Wei drew characters in his head, taking pride in this mental calligraphy. One morning, more than two years after he was placed in solitary confinement, his food tray included a ballpoint pen—another prisoner or a sympathetic guard had smuggled it to him.

Wei began to write letters to his family on the rough sheets he had for toilet paper. Guards found these letters and demanded to know where he had hidden the pen. Wei refused to say. After guards failed to find the ballpoint, which Wei had tied to a string and lowered inside the hollow metal rods of his bed, the warden ordered him to another cell. Wei sneaked the pen with him.

NORSE RUNES
"leaf"

Since writing's invention, people have used it to combat loneliness and establish a sense of self. In the fourth century B.C., Aristotle saw writing as a way to express "affections of the soul." Recent studies have documented that writing about feelings can alleviate depression, boost the immune system, and lower blood pressure.

How, then, do people in societies without writing express themselves? Of the more than 10,000 languages ever spoken, most had no written form. "We talk to each other, listen, visit, and trust the spoken word," says Guujaaw, a leader of the Haida Nation. "Expressing yourself without writing is natural."

The Haida have lived on the Queen Charlotte Islands off the coast of British Columbia for more than 10,000 years. Guujaaw and I are walking on Sgan Gwaii, a small island in the south that has some of the world's last temperate rain forest. Mosses and ferns cushion our steps. In the ocean, sea lions and puffins dive for fish.

"Like most other cultures in the Western Hemisphere, you never developed writing until outsiders brought it in," I say. "Do you think that's because you had no need for writing?"

"Are you suggesting that writing is better than speaking?" Guujaaw asks in response to my question.

The answer seems obvious, I say. Things get distorted when people repeat them to one another, especially over long periods of time.

"Things get distorted in writing as well," he says. "Oral histories from our people go back thousands of years. They are a living history. They provide a link between storyteller and
continued on page 36

Dedicated to the Egyptian god Amun, the mortuary temple of Ramses III, Madinet Habu, towers on the west bank of the Nile. Its elaborate hieroglyphs describe battles with Libyans and invaders called Sea Peoples. To ancient Egyptians writing was a divine gift from Thoth—scribe of the gods, magical healer, lord of wisdom, and patron of scholars.

Complexities of Japanese confront second graders in Kyoto, where students write some of the 200-plus characters for the sound "shou." The language commonly uses 15,000 kanji characters, which are borrowed from Chinese.

continued from page 33

listeners that written stories cannot. In fact, human intimacy and community can best come through oral communication."

Guujaaw leans on a rock. "I'll tell you a Haida story," he says. "Don't write it down. Listen. If you are busy writing, you will miss half the story. A story includes the telling and the listening."

Hearing his story about how animals warn humans not to spoil the water stimulates my senses. Guujaaw's voice, the breeze, the ocean, and the trees around us all flow through me. If I were reading the story, I would be alone in another world—and much less aware of my surroundings.

Plato would have said, "I told you so." Living at a time when writing began to challenge Greece's oral-based culture, he warned that writing would make people "trust to the external written characters and not remember of themselves.... They will be hearers of many things and will have learned nothing."

But Plato lived in the fifth century B.C, when reading was physically difficult. Books were papyrus scrolls often more than 60 feet long; the idea of pages, sparked in large part by the availability of parchment, emerged in Europe in the second century A.D. Space between words

ARABIC
"eye"

National Geographic

did not become standard in Western society until the seventh century. Long after Plato's time, writing served mostly as an aid to memory, something to stimulate the spoken word. People read aloud, a practice that died slowly. St. Augustine, one of the world's leading scholars in the fourth century A.D., was shocked to come upon his mentor St. Ambrose reading silently.

This transition from the spoken to the written word occurred because writing meets certain needs so much more effectively. Writing permits analysis, precision, and communication with future generations in a way not possible via the spoken word. The only way I know about St. Augustine's experience is that he mentions it in a book.

Still, Plato was right—people in an oral culture need strong memories. I have forgotten most of Guujaaw's story by the time we enter Ninstints, an old Haida village.

Ninstints was home to hundreds of Haida families in the mid-19th century, before white people landed. Now all that remains are the foundations of a few houses and some rotting totem poles. Today there are only about 4,000 Haida compared with 40,000 in the 19th century.

Despite such decline, Guujaaw insists that the Haida have not been defeated by people with writing. "We've been here on this land for thousands of years, and we're still here," he says. "Writing is not essential to living. People with writing are a brief chapter in our history."

But Native American oral culture worked best when people went on long hunting or fishing trips and gathered around campfires every evening. Now modern devices like television discourage the sharing of oral traditions.

Days later I share this thought with Pansy Collison, a Haida who teaches high school in Prince Rupert, British Columbia. "Don't forget that oral history is an essential part of our students' identity," she says.

No other invention— perhaps only the wheel comes close—has had a longer and greater impact.

Collison uses storytelling in the classroom to help her students learn their history and build pride in who they are. As part of this, her students write out the oral traditions of their family or clan—she relies on writing to preserve oral history.

As Collison shows me how these written lessons help invigorate oral traditions, I realize I am seeing another example of writing's extraordinary flexibility. Most Native Americans lost ground to outsiders who had weapons and machinery that developed only in societies with writing. But now writing is vital to the Haida's rejuvenation.

In the winter of 1981, after holding Wei in solitary confinement for more than two years, authorities realized they could not keep him from writing. They gave him a new ballpoint pen and better paper and authorized one monthly letter to his two sisters and brother.

In these letters Wei discussed art and offered advice on romance. He was forbidden to write about being beaten or deprived of sleep. He also could not mention his malnutrition, headaches, heart pain, diarrhea, and rotting teeth.

Wei never knew if his letters were delivered. He told his fiancée to find someone else, not knowing that she had already married.

Authorities also told Wei to write to government officials explaining his crime: trying to break up China. He did write to officials but told them they threatened national cohesion by suppressing freedom.

Joseph Stalin, who ruled the Soviet Union from 1928 to 1953, was a master of using writing to control people. Russia and Persia had divided Azerbaijan in the early 1800s. Shortly after taking power, Stalin feared the Azerbaijanis' loyalty to their countrymen in neighboring Iran, formerly Persia. Hoping to divide the two groups, he encouraged the Soviet Azerbaijanis to emulate nearby Turkey and switch from the Arabic alphabet to the Latin alphabet.

continued on page 40

At Ireland's Skellig Michael monastery, Wolinsky's computer displays a website page from the Book of Kells. Kept at Trinity College, Dublin, the illuminated manuscript was housed at Kells, one of the Irish monasteries that preserved classical Greek and Roman writings by copying manuscripts during the Dark Ages.

CHINESE
"can"

National Geographic

CUNEIFORM SIGN
"reed"

National Geographic

continued from page 37

By the 1930s Stalin, concerned about growing ties between Turkey and Azerbaijan, forced the Azerbaijanis to adopt Cyrillic, a script used for writing Russian and other Slavic languages. It had evolved from a script created by missionaries of the Orthodox Church in the ninth century A.D.

This alphabetic clash seems alive as I walk through Baku, Azerbaijan's capital. Newspapers are in Cyrillic, labels on canned food are in the Western Latin alphabet or in the Turkish-style Latin with its umlauts and cedillas, and street signs are in freshly painted Azerbaijani Latin, which has "X," "Ə," and "Q," letters not found in the Turkish alphabet. There is no sign of Arabic letters.

"We chose Latin letters largely because they will help us be modern and will link us to the rest of the world," Oruj Musayev, professor of English at the Azerbaijan State Institute of Languages, tells me. Musayev has just finished compiling the first Azerbaijani—English dictionary using Latin letters. "Our alphabet choice reflects geopolitics. Dropping Cyrillic meant moving away from Russia. Although we're Muslim, we're nonsectarian, so we didn't want to use the Arabic alphabet, which would link us to the mullahs in Iran."

The stakes are high. Azerbaijan has promising oil reserves and is courting Western buyers.

That the West relies on the Latin alphabet is a remnant of the Roman Empire. Latin letters have endured because they serve Western languages well—and using Latin letters has become associated with being "modern."

Azerbaijan is a newly independent country with tremendous problems. Development of oil resources is still a dream, and the country's annual per capita income is about $500, making it one of the world's poorest nations. To have its own alphabet seems a strange indulgence.

"There's nothing new about what's happening in Azerbaijan," Anar says. "An alphabet is a symbol of a country just like a flag. Why do you think different alphabets have appeared in the first place?"

Pride in his nation's writing system helped give Wei his Chinese identity. That most Chinese written characters have remained essentially unchanged for more than 2,000 years provides an emotional and a practical tie to the past.

Many of his letters were to China's leaders, whom he criticized. As punishment, authorities sometimes took away the pen they had given him, but other prisoners took apart pens, often stolen from guards, and smuggled them to Wei.

"Why write?" the guards asked. "No one will ever see your letters."

In late 1993 authorities told Wei he would be released. They were trying to win international support for acting as host of the year 2000 Olympic Games. Wei, who had been in jail for nearly 14 years, refused to leave his cell without copies of his letters. "They've been lost," he was told.

"You can find them," he replied. Twelve hours later, the warden returned with his letters.

Six months later, after the Olympic Committee rejected China, Wei was re-arrested. State security seized his papers but failed to find the computer disks onto which his letters had been transcribed.

continued on page 42

Proud author Carmen Craig holds a story she wrote for her Brookline, Massachusetts, kindergarten class, which is just learning to read. With today's endless audiovisual onslaught, it may be easy to overlook this recurrent miracle: a child's first act of writing—putting thoughts and emotions on paper.

continued from page 40

Tong Yi, the young woman who transcribed Wei's letters onto computer disks, had extraordinary courage. She also had to master the Latin-alphabet keyboard, which requires up to five keystrokes for one Chinese character.

The extra work needed to enter Chinese into a computer raises an important issue. China may become the wealthiest country in the world; it already is a major factor in the international economy. As this economy relies more on computers, does the Chinese writing system put it at a disadvantage?

Usama Fayyad, a senior researcher at Microsoft Corporation, whose job is to think about the long-term future of computers and data storage, says technology will eventually offer efficient and economical ways to bypass keyboards. Voice and handwriting recognition, he tells me, could make it irrelevant which writing system is used. We're in an office on Microsoft's 260-acre campus near Seattle. A painting of clouds floating through a blue sky covers one wall.

Fayyad also says that the distinction between an alphabet and Chinese characters does not matter in terms of how a computer operates. He explains that when you hit a letter on the keyboard, the computer enters that action into its memory as a number. Each letter is a different number, and a sentence inside the computer is a string of numbers. It's up to the computer program to interpret the string of numbers as instructions.

After Wei's re-arrest in 1994 he was placed back in solitary confinement. Two walls of his new cell were glass, so constant monitoring could ensure he did not write. For more than six months not even his family knew

MAYA GLYPH
"plate"

National Geographic

EGYPTIAN
HIEROGLYPHS
"toe"

National Geographic

whether he was dead or alive. In 1997 a book of Wei's letters, The Courage to Stand Alone, *was published in the United States. Tong Yi, who transcribed his letters, had been sentenced to two and a half years in a labor camp. After serving this time, during which she was sometimes beaten, she was allowed to leave China.*

In the summer of 1997 I read *The Courage to Stand Alone* and follow news accounts of Wei's treatment. He is frequently beaten and denied adequate health care. I fear he will die soon.

Then in November 1997 the Chinese government releases Wei, largely in response to international pressure, and puts him on an airplane to the United States. A few weeks later I meet him at his office in the Center for the Study of Human Rights at Columbia University.

I am startled by Wei's smile and how well he looks. He explains that he can eat only soft food until his teeth are fixed, and sips tea as we talk.

"Writing," he says, "kept me alive. I sometimes thought about a letter for a week before writing anything. It's something that you must do even if you do not have the leisure of being in prison. To write, you must work methodically, forming your thoughts and prompting other people to think as they read. Writing requires work at both ends. That's what makes it special."

Wei plans to write a book about the experiences, feelings, and ideas he could not put in his letters, which he knew would be read by prison officials.

"I wish I could read it in Chinese," I say.

Wei laughs. "You can learn," he says, writing

"It means 'friendship,'" Wei says.

Critical Responses

1. What powers of writing are highlighted in this article? What other powers does writing have?

2. As the story of Wei Jingsheng unfolds, how does it illuminate the theme of the article? How is Wei's story related to the discussion of particular types of writing and functions of writing over time?

3. What is gained through oral story-telling? What can be lost? In what ways can writing threaten oral cultures? In what ways can it sustain them?

4. "Writing requires work at both ends," says Wei. What does he mean by this? What is the nature of this work in academic settings? What about in personal, professional, political, and other contexts? Are there significant differences? Important similarities?

Writing Topics

1. You've probably heard the expression, "The medium is the message," coined by Marshall McLuhan. You're also probably proficient in communicating through many different kinds of media, especially those that allow you to text, email, post, and so on. Examine a contemporary electronic medium and consider how it affects the message you write.

2. Looking at the question from a complementary point of view, consider how the medium affects the reception of the message. What are some differences between electronic texts and paper ones? Do you read certain kinds of writing in certain distinct ways?

3. Censorship is a powerful force. What are some of its aims? Are there instances in which censorship is legitimate or acceptable? How does censorship itself affirm the powers that writing can have?

4. "Writing is not essential to living," says one of the Haida people whom Swerdlow interviews. Write a paper in which you argue for or against this position, and take into account the other side.

Further Explorations

1. How is writing related to identity, according to Swerdlow? How is it related to yours? Consider the many different kinds of writing you do and discuss its significance to who you are.

2. Writers have always had a lot to say about writing, and there are many websites that collect such observations. Whether individually or in groups, browse through some sites and select several quotations; examine their implications and consider their applicability to the kinds of writing you do in school.

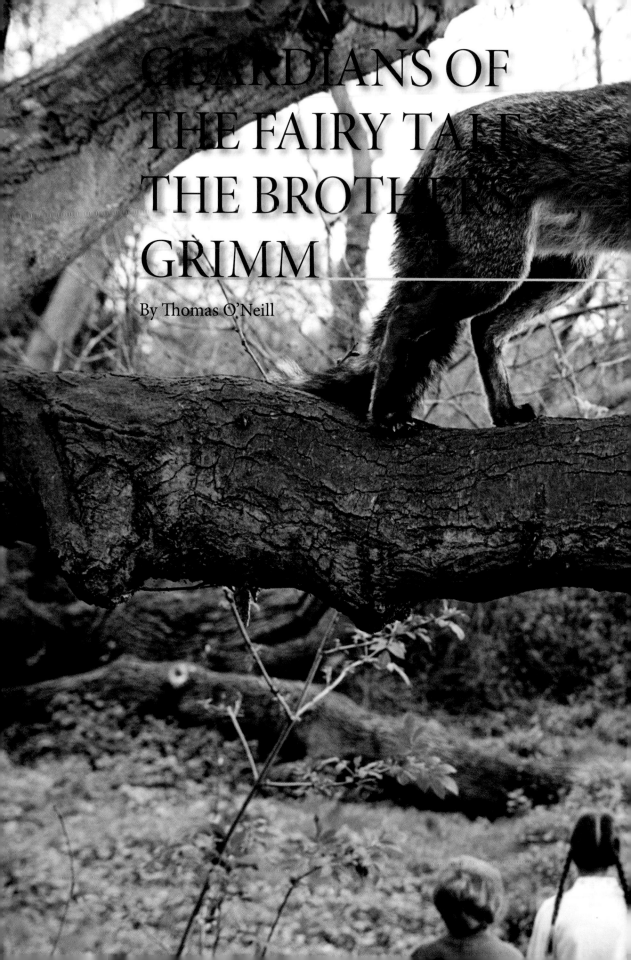

GUARDIANS OF THE FAIRY TALE: THE BROTHERS GRIMM

By Thomas O'Neill

GUARDIANS OF THE FAIRY TALE: THE BROTHERS GRIMM

Is a fairy tale just a tall tale? How is it also quite real? What does our speaking of Cinderella stories, Peter Pan syndromes, or fairy tale endings suggest? How have fairy tales filtered into our lives and contributed to the way we understand ourselves and our world? These are just some of the questions raised and addressed in the following article, which explores the work and the legacy of the Brothers Grimm.

A fox watches two children entering the woods, emulating the story of Hansel and Gretel.
Image Source/Getty Images

An original woodcut produced in 1879 of Jacob (standing) and Wilhelm. They produced seven editions of Children's and Household Tales, the first in 1812.

ZU_09/iStockphoto.com

IN THE EARLY 1800s BROTHERS JACOB AND WILHELM GRIMM PUBLISHED A BOOK OF FAIRY TALES, LARGELY GATHERED FROM STORYTELLERS IN CENTRAL GERMANY.

ECHOES OF THE WORLD-FAMOUS TALES STILL RESOUND,

FROM CASTLES TO DEEP, DARK FORESTS.

Once upon a time there lived in Germany two brothers who loved a good story—one with magic and danger, royalty and rogues. As boys they played and studied together, tight as a knot, savoring their childhood in a small town. But their father died unexpectedly, and the family grew poor. One brother became sickly; the other, serious beyond his years. At school they met a wise man who led them to a treasure—a library of old books with tales more seductive than any they had ever heard. Inspired, the brothers began collecting their own stories, folktales told to them mostly by women, young and old. Soon the brothers brought forth their own treasure—a book of fairy tales that would enchant millions in faraway places for generations to come.

The Brothers Grimm, Jacob and Wilhelm, named their story collection *Children's and Household Tales* and published the first of its seven editions in Germany in 1812. The table of contents reads like an A-list of fairy tale

Soon the brothers brought forth their own treasure—a book of fairy tales that would enchant millions in faraway places for generations to come.

celebrities: Cinderella, Sleeping Beauty, Snow White, Little Red Riding Hood, Rapunzel, Rumpelstiltskin, Hansel and Gretel, the Frog King. Dozens of other characters—a carousel of witches, servant girls, soldiers, stepmothers, dwarfs, giants, wolves, devils—spin through the pages. Drawn mostly from oral narratives, the 210 stories in the Grimms' collection represent an anthology of fairy tales, animal fables, rustic farces, and religious allegories that remains unrivaled to this day.

Such lasting fame would have shocked the humble Grimms. During their lifetimes the collection sold modestly in Germany, at first only a few hundred copies

continued on page 50

Adapted from "Guardians of the Fairy Tale: The Brothers Grimm" by Thomas O'Neill: National Geographic Magazine, December 1999.

The first and second edition of Children's and Household Tales displayed at the renovated Brothers Grimm Museum in 2012.

continued from page 47

a year. The early editions were not even aimed at children. The brothers initially refused to consider illustrations, and scholarly footnotes took up almost as much space as the tales themselves.

Jacob and Wilhelm viewed themselves as patriotic folklorists, not as entertainers of children. They began their work at a time when Germany, a messy patchwork of fiefdoms and principalities, had been overrun by the French under Napoleon. The new rulers were intent on suppressing local culture. As young, workaholic scholars, single and sharing a cramped flat, the Brothers Grimm undertook the fairy tale collection with the goal of saving the endangered oral tradition of Germany.

For much of the 19th century teachers, parents, and religious figures, particularly in the United States, deplored the Grimms' collection for its raw, uncivilized content. An American educator in 1885 railed: "The folktales mirror all too loyally the entire medieval worldview and culture with all its stark prejudice, its crudeness and barbarities." Offended adults objected to the gruesome punishments inflicted on the stories' villains. In the original "Snow White" the evil stepmother is forced to dance in red-hot iron shoes until she falls down dead. In "The Goose Maid" a treacherous servant is stripped, thrown into a barrel studded with sharp nails, and dragged through the streets.

Even today some protective parents shy from the Grimms' tales because of their reputation for violence.

Despite its sometimes rocky reception, *Children's and Household Tales* gradually took root with the public. The brothers had not foreseen that the appearance of their work would coincide with a great flowering of children's literature in Europe. English publishers led the way, issuing high-quality picture books such as *Jack and the Beanstalk* and handsome folktale collections, all to satisfy a newly literate audience seeking virtuous material for the nursery. Once the Brothers Grimm sighted

Inevitably the boy and girl fall in love and live happily ever after.

this new public, they set about refining and softening their tales, which had originated centuries earlier as earthy peasant fare. In the Grimms' hands, cruel mothers became nasty stepmothers, unmarried lovers were made chaste, and the incestuous father was recast as the devil.

In the 20th century the Grimms' fairy tales have come to rule the bookshelves of children's bedrooms. And why not? The stories read like dreams come true: Handsome lads and beautiful damsels, armed with magic, triumph over giants and witches and wild beasts. They outwit mean, selfish adults. Inevitably the boy and girl fall in love and live happily ever after. *Read me another one, please.*

And parents keep reading because they approve of the finger-wagging lessons inserted into the stories: Keep your promises, don't talk to strangers, work hard, obey your parents. According to the Grimms, the collection served as "a manual of manners."

The Grimms' texts have undergone so many adaptations and translations, often with the intent of censoring objectionable material such as the violence meted out to villains or of making the themes more relevant to contemporary tastes, that most of us know them only in their sanitized versions. The dust-jacket copy of a recent translation plaintively wonders if all the retellings don't "greatly reduce the tales' power to touch our emotions and intrigue our imaginations."

In a fourth-grade classroom in Steinau, Germany, the town where the Grimms spent part of their childhood, I listened as the storyteller Elfriede Kleinhans, an opponent of prim retellings, asked the boys and girls how the princess managed to turn a frog into a prince at the climax of the "The Frog King," the first tale in the Grimms' collection. "She kissed it," the children sang out. "No," said Kleinhans. "She threw the ugly frog at the wall as hard as she could, and it awoke as a prince. That's

Little Red Riding Hood is one of the most popular and famous fairy tales. The Brothers Grimm supposedly adapted it from a 14th century Italian tale.

Roberto A Sanchez/Getty Images

what the real story says." The children looked as if they didn't believe her.

Scholars and psychiatrists have thrown a camouflaging net over the stories with their relentless, albeit fascinating, question of "What does it mean?" Did the tossing of the frog symbolize the princess's sexual awakening, as Freudian psychologist Bruno Bettelheim asserted, or does the princess provide a feminist role model, as Lutz Röhrich, a German folklorist, wondered, by defying the patriarchal authority of her father, the king? Or—maybe—a frog is just a frog.

Enthralled since childhood by the geography of the Grimms' tales—the ominous forests, the brooding castles, the firelit cottages and clamorous village streets—I traveled to Germany to see if I could trace the contours of my imaginary map and possibly discover who these Brothers Grimm really were and how they became the preeminent cartographers of make-believe. My plan was to visit towns in Hesse where the brothers lived and worked to find out who told them the stories and how much the Grimms doctored what they heard. And I would roam the back roads to see if landscapes evoked by the fairy tales still lingered in the Hessian countryside.

Snow streaked the ground in brushstrokes as I drove east from Frankfurt and its glass skyscrapers into Grimm country. Except for their final years in Berlin, Jacob and Wilhelm spent most of their lives in the small towns and provincial cities of today's state of Hesse in the German midsection, close to what—once upon a time—was the border with East Germany. Except for the autobahn's ribbon of concrete and roadside clusters of metal silos, the Hessian countryside today might look remarkably familiar to the Grimms. Red-roofed villages nestle in the folds of hills and along river valleys. Stone castles rise from nearby heights, sprouting towers and battlements. Fields that will later ripen with corn and beets roll toward thick forests that frame the horizon like the borders of a woodcut.

The oldest of six children, Jacob and Wilhelm were born a year apart in the mid-1780s in Hanau, a market town less than a day's carriage ride from Frankfurt. Their father, Philipp, the son of a clergyman, was educated in law and served as Hanau's town clerk, a solid middle-class vocation. Father Grimm preached a life of faith, zealous work, and family loyalty. Their mother, Dorothea, gave the boys freedom to wander the countryside where, as Wilhelm later noted, their "collector's spirit" was born as they chased down butterflies and bugs.

By 1791 the family had moved northeast to Steinau, another small trade center, where the father took the position of district magistrate. The Grimms lived well in a large turreted stone house that doubled as the local courthouse. It survives today as a museum of Grimm manuscripts and memorabilia, with revolving exhibits of contemporary fairy tale illustrators.

At the center of Steinau stands a gaunt 16th-century castle ringed by a grassy moat. Wandering one night through the tiny town, the kind of quiet, uneventful town "where the fox and hare say good night to each other," as the Germans say, I entered the moon-shadowed courtyard of the castle and listened to my boots ringing on the cobblestones. In so many of the Grimms' tales an aspiring commoner is ushered into just such a royal space, challenged to make a princess laugh or to bring back three golden hairs from the devil's head. Success meant riches and a royal bride. When the Grimms wrote of castles in their tales, perhaps they remembered this boyhood place.

The Steinau years marked the end of ease and innocence for Jacob and Wilhelm. In 1796 their father died at the age of 44. Dorothea was forced to move her family of six children out of the government residence.

With financial help from Dorothea's sister, a lady-in-waiting for a Hessian princess, Jacob and Wilhelm, at 13 and 12, were sent north to the city of Kassel to attend the Lyzeum, an upper-crust high school. Sharing the same room and bed, the boys coped with loneliness and social slights by studying for ten hours a day. They proved themselves brilliant students, graduating at the top of their classes. The physical effort took its toll on Wilhelm, however. Already of delicate health, he suffered a serious asthma attack at school. Weak lungs and recurring illnesses would vex him the rest of his life.

Like fairy tale heroes, the Grimm brothers were tested with hard luck and formidable obstacles before it was time for them to meet the wise man who would lead them out of the dark. The meeting took place in the university city of Marburg where Jacob in 1802 and Wilhelm a year later pursued degrees in law.

It was here that a young aristocratic law professor, Friedrich Carl von Savigny, impressed by Jacob's appetite for learning, opened his private library to the older Grimm brother. That changed Jacob's life. He spent hours poring over Savigny's collection of rare manuscripts of medieval epics and hero's tales. The experience awoke in Jacob a passion for deciphering and saving ancient German literature and folktales, a cause that his younger brother would also embrace.

Jacob did not look and act the part of a fiery activist. Short and sturdy, he was by temperament an introvert, his whole being dedicated to bookish research. At Marburg he would decline invitations to stroll the countryside, saying he preferred "a walk in literature." Fellow students called him "the old one." Wilhelm, a determined scholar like his brother, was more outgoing. "Wilhelm had an eye for women, and women had an eye for him," Heinz Rölleke, a Grimm scholar at the University of Wuppertal, told me. Fervent letters passed between Wilhelm and Jenny von Droste-Hülshoff, a wealthy young woman whom he met in a storytelling circle.

Class differences foiled any chance of marriage. Wilhelm at the age of 39 would marry a childhood friend, Dortchen Wild, daughter of a pharmacist and herself a prominent source of fairy tales for the collection. Jacob, a lifelong bachelor, was by far the dominant partner intellectually, initiating most of their projects. Yet the brothers worked well together, signing their joint undertakings simply "Brothers Grimm."

Children's and household tales, their great collaboration, began in an almost offhand fashion. Immersed in editing and translating medieval manuscripts, the brothers started to gather fairy tales as a favor for a friend planning a collection of German folk literature. After several years the Grimms had assembled 49 tales, taking a few from old books, the rest from acquaintances in Kassel. But when the friend failed to produce the collection, the brothers decided to expand their efforts and publish their own volume.

Collecting fairy tales must have provided Jacob and Wilhelm a welcome distraction from their living circumstances. Their mother had died in 1808. Money grew scarcer. Employed as a librarian for the detested resident French ruler, Jacob could barely support his five siblings. Wilhelm was sick from asthma and a weak heart and was unable to work. In 1812, the year the fairy tales were first published, the Grimms were surviving on a single meal a day—a hardship that could explain why so many of the characters in their book suffer from hunger.

Though new editions of the fairy tales continued to appear until 1857, two years before Wilhelm's death, collection of almost all the oral tales took place when the brothers were in their impressionable 20s.

Altogether some 40 persons delivered tales to the Grimms. Many of the storytellers came to the Grimms' house in Kassel. The brothers particularly welcomed the visits of Dorothea Viehmann, a widow who walked to town to sell produce from her garden. An innkeeper's daughter, Viehmann had grown up listening to stories from travelers on the road to Frankfurt. Among her treasures was "Aschenputtel"—Cinderella.

With the exception of Viehmann, the brothers rarely identified their correspondents. Their names and the tales credited to them were learned in most cases only after careful study of the margin notes in the brothers' personal copies of the *Tales*.

Given that the origins of many of the Grimm fairy tales reach throughout Europe and into the Middle East and Orient, the question must be asked: How German are the Grimm tales? Very, says scholar Heinz Rölleke. Love of the underdog, rustic simplicity, sexual modesty—these are Teutonic traits.

The coarse texture of life during medieval times in Germany, when many of the tales entered the oral tradition, also colored the narratives. Throughout Europe children were often neglected and abandoned, like Hansel and Gretel. Accused witches were burned at the stake, like the evil mother-in-law in "The Six Swans." "The cruelty in the stories was not the Grimms' fantasy," Rölleke points out. "It reflected the law-and-order system of the old times."

Possibly the most German touch of all is the omnipresence of the forest, the place where fairy tale heroes confront their enemies and triumph over fear and injustice. Rural German society traditionally depended on the *Wald*. The forest was where farmers grazed their pigs on acorns, royals hunted deer, and woodcutters selected logs for the massive beams still seen in the halftimbered barns and houses of Hessian towns.

Storytellers knew that to place characters in a dark trackless woods would stir up associations of danger and suspense. "The forest was not seen as a safe place. Townspeople would avoid it," forester Hermann-Josef Rapp told me as we drove wet logging roads through the Reinhardswald, a large forest in the hills of northern Hesse. "There were outlaws and illegal hunters. And Germans have always been afraid of wolves."

Nowadays the Reinhardswald is thick with beech and introduced spruce, serving local sawmills. But to behold those mighty oaks that

continued on page 56

People often avoided forests due to wolves, outlaws, or bandits. Thus, a dark, omnipresent forest was an ideal setting for many of the Grimm's stories.

continued from page 53

were the preferred species in most Grimm fairy tales, one has to visit a remnant forest near Sababurg Castle. Rapp, a trunk of a man in a green oilskin jacket, led me into that forest one day in a pouring rain. Here massive, arthritic-looking oaks, some of them 400 years old or more, loomed like Gothic ruins. I spooked myself staring at the thick, grasping limbs, the wild hairlike mosses, the knobby eyes, the holes that gaped like mouths. How could Little Red Riding Hood's mother ever have let that sweet little girl go into such woods as these?

The editorial fingerprints left by the Grimms betray the specific values of 19th-century Christian, bourgeois German society. But that has not stopped the tales from being embraced by almost every culture and nationality in the world. What accounts for this widespread, enduring popularity? Bernhard Lauer points to the "universal style" of the writing. "You have no concrete descriptions of the land, or the clothes, or the forest, or the castles. It makes the stories timeless and placeless."

The tales allow us to express "our utopian longings," says Jack Zipes of the University of Minnesota, whose 1987 translation of the complete fairy tales captures the rustic vigor of the original text. "They show a striving for happiness that none of us knows but that we sense is possible. We can identify with the heroes of the tales and become in our mind the masters and mistresses of our own destinies."

Fairy tales provide a workout for the unconscious, psychoanalysts maintain. Bruno Bettelheim famously promoted the therapeutic value of the Grimms' stories, calling fairy tales the "great comforters." By confronting fears and phobias, symbolized by witches, heartless stepmothers, and hungry wolves, children find they can master their anxieties. Bettelheim's theory continues to be hotly debated. But most young readers aren't interested in exercising their unconscious. My 11-year-old daughter,

The tales allow us to express "our utopian longings."

Lucy, thinks it's cool that witches cast spells and that heroines always seem to get their man. Boys I know go for stuff like the cloak that makes a hero invisible and a rifle that never misses.

The Grimm tales in fact please in an infinite number of ways. Something about them seems to mirror whatever moods or interests we bring to our reading of them. This flexibility of interpretation suits them for almost any time and any culture.

Jacob and Wilhelm moved on from their jobs as librarians in Kassel to teach at universities in Göttingen and Berlin. Between them they published more than 35 books. The brothers also made a name for themselves as patriots, risking their livelihoods by speaking out in favor of democratic reform. But in their last years they retreated from politics and teaching to concentrate on writing the *German Dictionary,* one of the most ambitious scholarly projects of 19th-century Europe.

The brothers did not live to finish the dictionary or to see the fulfillment of their abiding dream: the founding in 1871 of the German nation. Wilhelm died of an infection in 1859 at the age of 73. Jacob in his eulogy bestowed upon his beloved Wilhelm the name *Märchenbruder,* the "fairy tale brother." Jacob died four years later. He had just finished writing the dictionary definition for *Frucht,* or fruit, a fitting end to a fertile life.

The Brothers Grimm, for the final fairy tale in their collection, chose a short, parable-like tale called "The Golden Key." A poor boy goes out into a wintry forest to collect wood on a sled. In the snow he finds a tiny key and near it an iron box. The boy inserts the key. He turns it. He lifts the lid.

That is where the story ends. For once the brothers avoid a tidy ending. Instead, they have issued a golden invitation, since accepted by countless readers, to open the brothers' books with the key of the imagination. Only then can readers discover what wonderful things await them.

Critical Responses

1. What makes a story a fairy tale? What makes a fairy tale powerful?

2. On the one hand, the tales recorded by the Grimms came from a particular time and place. On the other, they are said by some to be "universal." How does O'Neill navigate these two perspectives? How do you?

3. Why were original versions of Grimms' tales sanitized in some instances? In what ways have some of these sanitized versions become objectionable themselves?

4. How does O'Neill's approach to his subject relate to the Grimms' approach to theirs? As you address this question, focus on the structure and style of the article, as well as on O'Neill's quest.

Writing Topics

1. "Writing has an almost magical power," observes Joel Swerdlow in "The Power of Writing," another article featured in this reader. How is this observation applicable to this article on fairy tales? How does the Grimm Brothers' work illuminate this power?

2. Write a plot summary of a familiar fairy tale. Then look up the tale in its original version. As you compare similarities and differences, consider their significance from a broader cultural point of view.

3. What are the characteristics of fairies? How do ideas about fairies relate to stories that we call fairy tales but that have no fairies in them?

4. In what ways do fairy tales continue to serve as a "manual of manners" for children? Are lessons they teach appropriate or inappropriate, or some combination of both, in your view? Taking the question further, do you think it's appropriate for fairy tales to have such a role at all?

Further Explorations

1. What stories were you drawn to as a child, and what drew you to them? Do they continue to resonate in your life today? If so, how? If not, why not?

2. Look at a popular adaptation of a fairy tale, such as a Disney version, and analyze the adaptation from a specific frame of reference, such as gender or race or any other that is appropriate to the context. Discuss your views with classmates. Is there a consensus in your evaluations and interpretations?

A SKETCH IN TIME: BRINGING THE CIVIL WAR TO LIFE

By Harry Katz

A SKETCH IN TIME: BRINGING THE CIVIL WAR TO LIFE

While the American Civil War was the first war to be extensively photographed, photographic equipment was too bulky to be carried into combat, and photographic images were too delicate to withstand the conditions as well. Thus, most representations of the actual conflicts were made by artists who sketched what they saw in the heat of battle, on the spot. It was their black and white drawings, published in newspapers, which brought the Civil War to life for contemporaries. Even in our image-saturated world, they may well do the same for us.

Union soldiers bury their comrades and burn their horses after the Battle of Fair Oaks. Alfred Waud, on assignment as a "special artist" for Harper's Weekly, sketched the grim scene.

A column of Confederate troops fording the
Potomac River while Union scouts watch.

THE WORLD CAME TO UNDERSTAND THE CIVIL WAR THROUGH THE EYES OF BATTLEFIELD ARTISTS. LIVING ALONGSIDE THE TROOPS,

COMBAT ILLUSTRATORS RISKED DEATH, INJURY, AND DISEASE TO CONVEY THE BLOW-BY-BLOW OF BATTLE WITH PENCIL AND PEN, CHARCOAL, AND CRAYON.

THEIR WORK, SKETCHED IN THE DIREST OF CIRCUMSTANCES, SHOWS TERRIBLE VIOLENCE BUT ALSO MOMENTS OF SURPRISING GRACE.

The fierce shock, the heaving tumult, the smoky sway of battle from side to side, the line, the assault, the victory— they were a part of all, and their faithful fingers, depicting the scene, have made us a part also.

At the time of the civil war, camera shutters were too slow to record movement sharply. Celebrated photographers such as Mathew Brady and Timothy O'Sullivan, encumbered by large glass negatives and bulky horse-drawn processing wagons, could neither maneuver the rough terrain nor record images in the midst of battle. So newspaper publishers hired amateur and professional illustrators to sketch the action for readers at home and abroad. Embedded with troops on both sides of the conflict, these "special artists," or "specials," were America's first pictorial war correspondents. They were young men (none were women) from diverse backgrounds—soldiers, engineers, lithographers and engravers, fine artists, and a few veteran illustrators—seeking income, experience, and adventure.

It was a cruel adventure. One special, James R. O'Neill, was killed while being held prisoner by Quantrill's Raiders, a band of Rebel guerrillas. Two other specials, C. E. F. Hillen and Theodore Davis, were wounded. Frank Vizetelly was nearly killed at Fredericksburg, Virginia, in December 1862, when a "South Carolinian had a portion of his head carried away, within four yards of myself, by a shell." Alfred Waud, while documenting the exploits of the Union Army in the summer of 1862, wrote to a friend: "No amount of money can pay a man for going through what we have had to suffer lately."

Adapted from "A Sketch in Time: Bringing the Civil War to Life" by Harry Katz: National Geographic Magazine, May 2012.

Near Bull Run, Union Gen. John Pope's Army of Virginia plods through a pummeling summer rainstorm in search of Rebel forces.
© 2012 LIBRARY OF CONGRESS/National Geographic Image Collection

The English-born Waud and Theodore Davis were the only specials who remained on assignment without respite, covering the war from the opening salvos in April 1861 through the fall of the Confederacy four years later. Davis later described what it took to be a war artist: "Total disregard for personal safety and comfort; an owl-like propensity to sit up all night and a hawky style of vigilance during the day; capacity for going on short food; willingness to ride any number of miles horseback for just one sketch, which might have to be finished at night by no better light than that of a fire."

In spite of the remarkable courage these men displayed and the events they witnessed, their stories have gone unnoticed: Virginia native son and Union supporter D.H. Strother's terrifying assignment sketching the Confederate Army encampments outside Washington, D.C., which got him arrested as a spy; Theodore Davis's dangerously ill-conceived sojourn into Dixie in the summer of 1861 (he was detained and accused of spying); W.T. Crane's heroic coverage of Charleston, South Carolina, from within the Rebel city; Alfred Waud's detention by a company of Virginia cavalry (after he sketched a group portrait, they let him go); Frank Vizetelly's eyewitness chronicle of Jefferson Davis's final flight into exile.

Special artists worked fast, identifying a war scene's focal point, blocking out the composition in minutes, and fleshing it out later in

camp. They took great pride in making their renderings as faithful as possible. Writing from the front lines in northern Virginia in the spring of 1862, Edwin Forbes noted that his sketches had been made "at considerable risk for the country is overrun with small gangs of sneaking Secessionists, who are as bloodthirsty as [Confederate Gen.] Albert Pike. For one day I got an escort of ten men and made some sketches in comparative safety… All who have seen them say they are very accurate. I need hardly assure you that I do my best to make them so, as fidelity to fact is, in my opinion, the first thing to be aimed at."

The artists dispatched their sketches from the battlefield by horse courier, train, or ship to the publisher's office, where a home artist copied the image onto blocks of wood. Engravers then carved different sections of the drawing, the most experienced of them working on detailed figures and complex compositions, and the apprentices taking on the simpler background tasks. Once the engraving was completed, it was electrotyped—copied onto metal plates in preparation for printing. The engravings could also be copied and sent overseas to foreign publishers for added revenue. Usually it took two to three weeks for the drawn image to appear in print, although important events or battles could be rushed into print in a matter of days.

continued on page 66

Confederates set Samuel Mumma's farm ablaze to keep it from Union hands. By the time Alfred Waud made this sketch, using Chinese white pigment to depict flames, Union troops were in control of the area.

Union hospital attendants collect the wounded after a skirmish in the ten-month campaign for Petersburg.

continued from page 63

Two pictorial weeklies dominated the national scene in 1861, both published in New York City: *Frank Leslie's Illustrated Newspaper* and *Harper's Weekly*. Before immigrating to America, veteran English pressman Henry Carter—known by his pen name, Frank Leslie—had managed the engraving department at the *Illustrated London News*, the world's first and most prestigious pictorial weekly. Even before the war began, *Leslie's*, which debuted in 1855, routinely boasted print runs above 100,000, and special editions could top three times that number.

The journal claimed to be strictly neutral, and within months of President Lincoln's election in November 1860, Leslie sent William Waud, Alfred's younger brother, to Charleston to document the growing secessionist sentiment. Also English-born, William could claim neutral status and reasonably represent his publisher's desire "to produce a paper which shall be so entirely free from objectionable opinions or partizan views of national policy, that it can be circulated in every section of the Union and be received in every family as a truthful exponent of facts as they occur." William Waud's sketches predate the attack on Fort Sumter and offer a glimpse into the last days of the prewar South. He was sketching among the crowds watching from the seawall as Confederate guns fired on Fort Sumter.

In contrast to Frank Leslie, Fletcher Harper—publisher of *Harper's Weekly* and a scion of the renowned Harper Brothers literary publishing house—stood firmly with the Republican Party, President Lincoln, the abolitionists, and the Union. His views, his reporters, and his pictorial weekly, which had started in 1857, were decidedly not welcome in Secessia. Initially *Harper's* was more literary than journalistic, befitting the journal's erudite heritage. The war changed all that. By the beginning of the second year, Harper had hired top talent—including Alfred Waud, Winslow Homer, and Thomas Nast—giving the artists the resources to fill the journal's pages with compelling and persuasive war images.

Alfred Waud, the most prolific special, created many of the most memorable sketches of critical moments at Antietam and Gettysburg, where he was the first artist to arrive on the field. On July 21, 1861, he traveled to the Bull Run battlefield in the photographic wagon owned and driven by his friend Mathew Brady. Already known as a boon companion and crack artist, at Bull Run Waud took up arms against the Confederates. The next day, returning from the field, he pulled his pistol on a Union soldier attempting to commandeer his horse. Gen. George Meade often favored Waud with requests to sketch Rebel defenses, offering him special access. Waud enjoyed close relationships with numerous officers but also reveled in his life with the common soldier.

As the war progressed, no artist portrayed life in camp more intimately than *Leslie's* Edwin Forbes, who often focused on human-interest and figure study. His sketches of soldiers relaxing, cooking, cleaning, reading, shaving, and engaging in sports and other daily activities record their shared existence and collective humanity.

Winslow Homer, born in Boston, Massachusetts, and destined for artistic stardom, created some of his most celebrated paintings from sketches he made as an illustrator at the front. During the Peninsular Campaign in Virginia—Gen. George B. McClellan's initial, unsuccessful assault on Richmond in the

> **The artists had no control over their work after it left the field.**

summer of 1862—Homer brought remarkable verve to his work but chafed at the restrictions of military life. In addition, according to his mother, he "suffered much, was without food 3 days at a time & all in camp either died or were carried away with typhoid fever... He came home so changed that his best friends did not know him."

Homer's Bavarian-born colleague, Thomas Nast, became America's most influential editorial cartoonist. Supporting the Lincoln Administration and Republican Party, he demonized the Rebels and advocated for emancipation, heaping derision on those in the North who opposed the war effort and sought negotiated peace with the Confederacy. By 1864, coverage of the Union victories by the special artists, along with Nast's acerbic illustrations, helped consolidate public support for the war effort and win Lincoln a second term. Senior officers on both sides came to value the military knowledge of the specials, offering them commissions and employing their skills as scouts to sketch fortifications.

The artists had no control over their work after it left the field. At the December 1862 Battle of Fredericksburg, Arthur Lumley, a Dublin-born Irishman working for the *New-York Illustrated News,* sketched Union troops pillaging the town. Incensed, he wrote on the back of the drawing: "Friday Night in Fredericksburg. This night the city was in the wildest confusion sacked by the union troops=houses burned down furniture scattered in the streets=men pillaging in all directions=a fit scene for the French revolution and a discrace [*sic*] to the Union Arms." The journal never published the inflammatory image.

Both Harper and Leslie did their part to shape public opinion, censoring images considered too negative or graphic and altering drawings to make them more stirring or upbeat. *Harper's* editors, for instance, made Alfred Waud's drawing of a leg amputation at an Antietam field hospital look less gory to accommodate squeamish readers. Engravers freshened another Waud sketch of exhausted horses dragging artillery carts, giving them lifted heads and spirited tails and making them kick up clods of mud—an animated portrait of teamsters racing ammunition to the front.

Nonetheless, by depicting scenes as realistically as they could, Waud, Lumley, Henri Lovie, and others undermined the popular myth of the war as a romantic adventure. As citizens grew accustomed to the violent imagery, censorship eased.

Although the confederacy had virtually no pictorial press, specials operating in southern theaters created hundreds of images. One outlet was the *Illustrated London News*. With Lincoln's election, the British took a keen interest in American affairs, and after the war started, debate over whether to recognize the Confederacy consumed politicians and the public. In May 1861 the veteran British war artist Frank Vizetelly arrived in America fresh from covering Giuseppe Garibaldi's campaign to liberate the Italian peninsula from Austrian rule. Vizetelly's initial impressions of the Union Army were favorable, and he reported back to London of patriotic fervor, high morale, and camp camaraderie.

That changed on July 21 at the Battle of Bull Run, a Union debacle. A week later Vizetelly contributed an unflattering sketch, "The Stampede From Bull Run," along with this blunt description: "At half-past five the Federal troops were in full retreat, pursued at different points by the black horse cavalry of Virginia. Retreat is a weak term to use when speaking of this disgraceful rout… The terror-stricken soldiers threw away their arms and

accoutrements, herding along like a panic-stricken flock of sheep, with no order whatever in their flight… Wounded men were crushed under the wheels of the heavy, lumbering chariots that dashed down the road at full speed. Light buggies, containing members of Congress, were overturned or dashed to pieces in the horrible confusion of the panic."

Vizetelly, now banned from the Union lines, was determined to get to the Richmond front, and the following summer he simply assigned himself to the Confederate States Army. With the help of Confederate sympathizers and a freed slave, he crossed the Potomac below the capital and joined Lee's army along the Rapidan River. Taking up the Rebel cause, he wrote: "Surrounded as I am by the Southern people… I emphatically assert that the South can never be subjugated." Vizetelly loved the officers, the soldiers, the people, the land, and the cause of the Confederacy. For the first time in the war, the South had its own special artist, although he worked for a newspaper published in London.

Some northern artists advocated openly for black emancipation. In May 1866, a year after hostilities ended, Alfred Waud created an emotional and symbolic coda to the war with his portrayal of black troops mustering out in Little Rock, Arkansas. Many specials turned to sketching the American scene as soldiers dispersed and people returned to peaceful living.

Within a generation sketch artists were eclipsed by photographers using Kodaks. But even today, artists are still going to battle-fronts—in Afghanistan, for instance—sent by the military and the media to interpret warfare in ways cameras cannot, capturing for the record the inner life of the soldier caught up in a larger drama.

Critical Responses

1. The title of the article, "A Sketch in Time," can be read in several ways. What are they, and in what ways are they related? How does the title of the article thereby capture its subject?

2. Katz mentions that many illustrations were censored for being too graphic or negative and that images were altered to appear more positive or poignant. How does this compare to images from today's wars?

3. What makes an illustration appear "realistic"? Can photographs be said to be more realistic than drawings? What about the reverse?

4. Thinking about this question in a slightly different way, consider what makes a representation credible or believable—or not.

Writing Topics

1. Objectivity and timeliness are two crucial standards of photojournalism; images are also judged by their relevance to a story, as well as by their own narrative qualities. Apply these criteria to one of the Civil-War era drawings in the article and evaluate it accordingly.

2. How is the process of drawing itself visible in some of these sketches?

How does this contribute to bringing the Civil War to life?

3. Civil War reenactments are another way of bringing the Civil War to life. Why do you think people perform reenactments? What effect do these reenactments have on your view of history?

4. Looking at one of the sketches and a photograph of a reenactment, compare not only the story each one tells, but also the way each one tells it, and discuss the significance of similarities and differences you find.

Further Explorations

1. While photographs of actual Civil War battles are rare, many photographs of soldiers, camps, and so on were in fact taken and can be seen online, collected on reputable sites such as the National Archive and the Library of Congress. Examine several images and consider what they say about the war, bearing in mind that photos could be staged as well as done on the spot.

2. Many other articles about war appear in *National Geographic* Magazine, with many accompanying photos as well. Select several images of a recent or contemporary conflict and describe their apparent aims and effects.

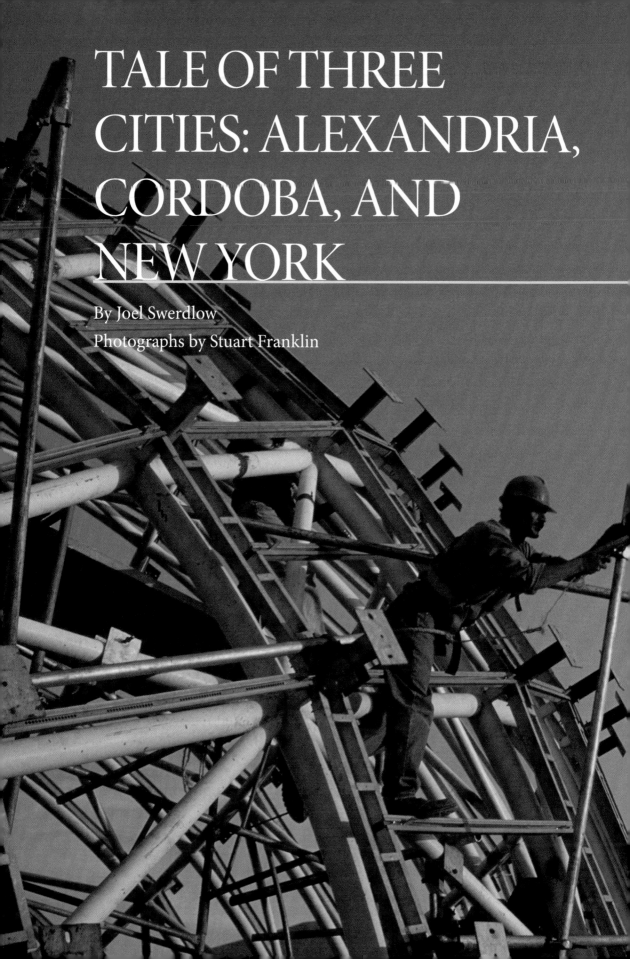

TALE OF THREE CITIES: ALEXANDRIA, CORDOBA, AND NEW YORK

By Joel Swerdlow

Photographs by Stuart Franklin

TALE OF THREE CITIES: ALEXANDRIA, CORDOBA, AND NEW YORK

Both urban decay and urban renewal are familiar concepts today. But what is it that makes cities rise or decline, deteriorate or flourish? Taking ancient Alexandria, medieval Cordoba, and modern New York as test cases, this article's tales of these three cities suggest answers that have persisted over three millennia; whether they remain exemplary in the future is another question. As you read these urban histories, you may wish to speculate on what future cities might be like.

Celestial in shape and ambition, a planetarium rises over the dusty soils of Alexandria, Egypt. It is part of a new library meant to emulate the famed Ptolemaic library and museum that made Alexandria a cultural beacon before the first century A.D. Alexandria in ancient times, Cordoba, Spain, in the tenth century, and New York City today—each helped shape the culture of an age. Marked by both glory and strife, these cities hold lessons for the urban stars of the next millennium.

Far below the bustling streets of modern Alexandria, the catacombs of Kom el-Shoqafa unfold like a scroll revealing the city's hybrid past. Jackal-headed figures of Anubis, the Egyptian god of death, guard the main tomb armed as Roman soldiers. The wealthy family that built this vault around A.D. 100 filled it with Greek, Egyptian, and Roman motifs—as if hedging their bets with the gods.

CIVILIZATION WILL ENDURE,
BRICK UPON BRICK,
BUILDING CITY AFTER CITY,
FOR CENTURIES TO COME.

Nearly half the world's population lives in cities.

Smoke and the fragrance of roasting quail float up from long charcoal grills lining the perimeter of Suq el-Attarine, the Market of Scents, in Alexandria, Egypt. It is October, the season when quail fly south from Europe, tire over the Mediterranean Sea, land on beaches, and are easily trapped. Along sidewalks men sit on benches and puff apple-cured tobacco through water pipes called *sheesha*. Some play dominoes. Above us hang the purple flowers of jacaranda trees.

The tranquil scene recalls earlier times in the city that Alexander the Great founded more than 2,300 years ago. But as I stroll from the marketplace toward the harbor, I am clearly in a modern city. Apartment buildings, home to most of Alexandria's nearly three and a half million people, surround me. Traffic jams the streets. Supermarkets, cell phones, motorcycles, and teenagers in baseball caps are everywhere.

Nearly half the world's population lives in cities. The number of megacities—those with populations of more than ten million—will exceed two dozen by 2015, up from fourteen in 1995.

All cities share certain characteristics. They are places to buy and sell, to worship, to share companionship. They are where new ideas trigger changes in science and art, where cultures meet and evolve. But why and where do cities, these centers of trade and knowledge, grow? What causes some to flourish and others to fade? I am in Alexandria at the beginning of my journey to three great cities to seek the answers.

I have begun here because in A.D. I this was one of the few international cities. Part of Africa, close to Arabia, and home to Europeans from Greece and Rome, Alexandria was a crossroads for trade that ranged from China to Britain. Strabo, a geographer in the first century A.D., called Alexandria "the greatest emporium in the inhabited world." After Alexandria I will visit Córdoba, Spain, western Europe's largest city in A.D. 1000, now a modest town supported mainly by agriculture. In its prime Córdoba was, in the words of one

continued on page 76

Adapted from "Tale of Three Cities: Alexandria, Córdoba, and New York" by Joel Swerdlow: National Geographic Magazine, August 1999.

At historic Plaza del Potro an octagonal fountain evokes
Islamic style—a stone oasis for weary souls.

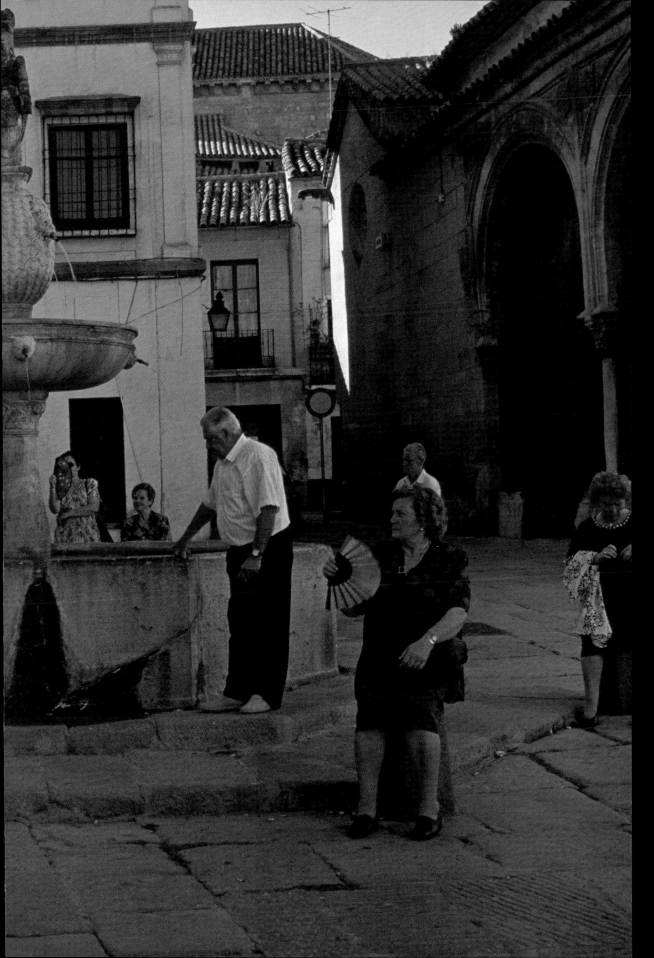

continued from page 73

observer, "the mother of towns; the abode of the good and godly, the homeland of wisdom." My travels will end in New York City, a modern epicenter of finance and culture. New York, writes Joan Didion, is "an infinitely romantic notion, the mysterious nexus of all love and money and power."

Dodging cars speeding along El-Horreyah Avenue, Alexandria's busiest street, I arrive at the waterfront. I see small fishing boats at anchor, young boys jumping off rocks into the water, and, beyond, the natural harbor that Alexander the Great saw in 331 B.C.

Alexander's engineers realized that Mediterranean currents running west to east would keep the harbor navigable and free of Nile River silt. They also knew that the Island of Pharos, if joined to the mainland by the construction of a pier, would offer an effective wave breaker.

The city grew steadily as a center for trade. About four decades after Alexander's death in 323 B.C. Ptolemy II built a lighthouse, known as one of the seven wonders of the ancient world. It rivaled the Pyramids in height at about 400 feet and had as many as 300 rooms. Fires, reflected in mirrors on top of the lighthouse, could be seen for some 35 miles, alerting ships to Egypt's reefs and shifting coastline.

In the 14th century it collapsed during an earthquake, and the Egyptians built a fortress here using, some accounts say, stones from the lighthouse. From my waterside café table I can see the fortress, where team members from the Alexandria-based Centre d'études Alexandrines are easing into wet suits. They will dive down 20 feet, where they are cataloging statues, columns, and other architectural elements near the lighthouse site.

The past—and the answers it might hold—feels impossibly distant as I wander up the coast near where Cleopatra's palace once stood. Somewhere in this area, perhaps beneath my feet, lies the sarcophagus holding

The city grew, made wealthy by agriculture and mining in surrounding regions.

Alexander the Great. It disappeared from recorded history in the third century A.D. Also buried here in a site yet to be located is the famous Alexandria library, founded early in the third century B.C. as part of the Mouseion, the great research center of its day.

The idea of a library was not new. Egyptian papyrus libraries existed in 3200 B.C., and Athens had a library in the fourth century B.C. But Alexandria's library was on a scale new to the Mediterranean world, and the city was notorious for its aggressive pursuit of texts.

The United Nations and other international agencies are cooperating with the Egyptian government to finance a new 200-million-dollar Alexandria Library near a possible site of the old one. Cranes swing steel beams overhead, and workers scamper up the scaffolding surrounding the building's circular framework.

Mohsen Zahran, the library's project manager, talks about reviving "the lighthouse of knowledge." The new library, he says, "will encourage peace and the exchange of ideas throughout the region and provide a place for scholars of diverse backgrounds to meet."

Little is known about how the ancient Mouseion operated because so few written records have been found. But we do know that it was a place for scholars to meet. From throughout their known world Alexandria's rulers invited nearly a hundred learned men to the Mouseion, where they lived in a communal residence and ate together in a dining hall. From these scholars came Euclidian geometry, the first scientific dissections of human bodies, a translation of the Hebrew Bible into Greek, and a compilation of Homer's epic poems.

Scholarly pursuits had immediate commercial applications. Translations helped Alexandrians to better understand their trading partners, and new maps enabled traders to calculate distances more accurately.

Enticing as a bridal blush, the grounds at Córdoba's Fortress of the Christian Monarchs owe their enchantment to the Arabs. Using waterwheels and canals, these people of the desert turned Córdoba into a garden scented by citrus, jasmine, and other fragrant plants they introduced.

Alexandria had hit upon a winning formula: Trade produces wealth, wealth pays for knowledge, and knowledge stimulates more trade.

From where I stand, I can see freighters in Alexandria's harbor. That harbor, which now handles about 75 percent of the freight entering and leaving Egypt, has proved resilient. In the middle of the third century A.D. the city was torn by riots and religious conflicts: "Every street was polluted with blood, every building of strength converted into a citadel," wrote Edward Gibbon in *The Decline and Fall of the Roman Empire*. Earthquakes struck around A.D. 365. A plague wiped out much of the population in the late sixth century, and in

the seventh century Muslims, less reliant than their predecessors on sea trade, conquered Egypt. Yet in A.D. 1000, more than 1,300 years after its founding, Alexandria was still an emporium of the world.

In A.D. 1 Alexandria's chief trading partner was Rome. By 1000 Rome had declined from the seat of a worldwide empire to a city of 35,000, and Alexandria was trading heavily with another power: Cordoban-controlled Spain.

Córdoba, in the south-central Iberian Peninsula, had been a provincial capital under the Romans and was controlled by the Phoenicians before that. By A.D. 715 the Umayyads, a Muslim dynasty ruling from Damascus, had

continued on page 80

"Taxi!" Hailed as icons of New York, yellow cabs haul a million people a day in this city of 7.5 million. "What New York did ... with congestion was to make an art of it," wrote architecture historian Douglas Haskell. The first U.S. city with an elevated railway and an under-river tunnel for cars, New York became a theater for the art of urban movement.

WIRED AND RESTLESS *Stars in a steel constellation, the towers of midtown Manhattan burn with a relentless energy that typifies New Yorkers themselves. Audacity began early on this island, the smallest of New York's five boroughs. In 1626 Dutch official Peter Minuit "bought" Manhattan from resident Lenape Indians for the equivalent of $24. At that time it was an Eden of fertile hills. Transformed by money and engineering, it became one of the most densely populated places on Earth—the crown jewel of capitalism.*

continued from page 77

annexed most of the peninsula. Around mid-century a revolution destroyed the family and a surviving prince fled to Córdoba, where he proclaimed himself emir. The city grew, made wealthy by agriculture and mining in surrounding regions.

By the middle of the ninth century the city had running water, sewers, hospitals, paved and lit streets, promenades, gardens, and fountains. Contemporary observers described Córdoba's population as enjoying some 80,000 shops, 60,000 mansions, 1,600 mosques, 900 public baths, and 70 libraries. The craftsmen of Córdoba carved rock crystal and manufactured leather, paper, linen, and silk.

In the tenth century Córdoba's caliphs welcomed ambassadors from much of Europe and the Middle East. Scholars invented new surgical techniques and instruments, advanced understanding of medicinal herbs, accurately observed and measured celestial phenomena, and refined methods of irrigation, plant grafting, and crop rotation. Córdoba's merchant and naval fleet, based at the Mediterranean port of Almería, was among the largest in the world.

I walk through Medina Azahara, site of one of the world's great palaces in the year 1000. Built five miles from the city by a caliph of Córdoba, the palace and grounds held more than 4,000 marble columns and, reportedly, mechanical birds and lions and shimmering pools of mercury. Hundreds of buildings sprawled over some 275 hillside acres.

A mob from Córdoba accompanied by Berber mercenaries demolished the palace around 1010, and soon Medina Azahara was abandoned. Stone floors, broken walls, and crumbling arches now stretch for hundreds of yards in all directions; more ruins lie buried under the green fields beyond. Pilfered pieces of marble columns and chunks of carved stone from the palace today adorn Córdoba's shops, restaurants, bank lobbies, and the patios of private homes.

Córdoba's decline as a major city was swift. Yet Córdoba endures.

At the Cubillas River on my way to the city, I crossed the Pinos Puente stone bridge. More than a thousand years ago caravans carrying leather and silk goods from Córdoba crossed the river at this exact spot. From local farmers I purchased olive oil; some of the trees that produce this oil, they told me, grew from cuttings taken from trees standing when the Muslims ruled Córdoba. Indeed, olive oil has always been a major export here. The Spanish call it *aceite*, derived from *zayt*, Arabic for olive oil.

Black pony, large moon,
and olives in my saddlebag.
Although I know the roads,
I will never reach Córdoba.

Federico García Lorca, a Spanish poet, sensing that past glory had made Córdoba an unattainable ideal, wrote these words in the early 20th century. Yet Córdoba *is* reachable—not the city once called "the mother of towns" but a thriving, and timeless, agricultural city of about 320,000 people. Fields of olive trees end where downtown department stores and office buildings begin. In cobblestone streets a millennium old, young couples walk arm in arm past sidewalk cafés.

Córdoba: once a powerhouse, undermined by its geographic location and political instability, now a small Spanish city supported by agriculture and steeped in romance.

As my plane floats over New York City, I look down at the empty berths of its harbor and wonder whether future generations will ever stroll around ruins in New York the way I strolled around the ruins of Medina Azahara.

Like Alexandria, New York was born beside a natural harbor. In 1950 the waterfront handled almost 20 percent of the nation's sea cargo, measured by weight. Today it handles less than 6 percent.

People, however, have always been New York's greatest import. Since 1860 between 20 and 50 percent of all New Yorkers have been foreign-born.

Easy-access jobs attract many immigrants to New York. So does the opportunity to make money. "The New York City economy is porous," says Mitchell Moss, director of New York University's Taub Urban Research Center. "There are many ways to enter. You wash dishes, then you own your own restaurant, then you manage the building." A large share of New York's immigrants, says Moss, are skilled and well educated. "No other city attracts the kinds of people who come here," he says. More than 700,000 of these new arrivals make Queens one of the most ethnically and racially diverse counties in the United States. Its public library, the country's busiest, loans material in 50 languages.

I'm standing on the sidewalk outside the Flushing branch of the Queens Library at 9:30 A.M., a half hour before the doors open. More than a dozen people are here, waiting to go in. By 10:30 the library resembles a busy supermarket, with clerks shouting "Next, please" to people lined up to check out books.

An English conversation group is meeting on the lower level, and I sit in for a while. Some of the students describe New York as a school, where they learn about survival in America. "If I can make it there, I'll make it anywhere," says one, quoting a 1977 show tune.

Most of the people in the group are immersed in the city. One describes a matinee performance of Bizet's *Carmen;* another recounts a recent visit to Rockefeller Center. The daughter of a third has just completed a recital at the Juilliard School.

I join an English language class in another room, where I sit between an opera singer from Shanghai and a botanist from Uzbekistan.

Yuzef Murdakhayev, the botanist, invites me home for lunch. His wife, Margarita, brings out apricots, almonds, pistachios, chickpeas, and dumplings. Yuzef, who speaks Russian, Persian, and Turkish, has written three books and about 300 scholarly articles. Books fill one wall of his living room. "Why bring clothes?" Yuzef says. "I brought books."

Unable to find work as a botanist because he does not yet speak English well, Yuzef helps his two sons with their jewelry manufacturing business. Two of his grandchildren, born in New York, are American citizens, and the rest of the family expects to gain citizenship soon.

If I can make it there, I can make it anywhere.

After lunch Yuzef walks me to the subway. Emerging 40 minutes later from Grand Central Terminal, I am immediately struck by the energy, the anything-is-possible attitude, that makes Manhattan unique. It comes from the concentration of people, the sky-scraping architecture, and from money, Manhattan's main import. Trillions of dollars move through the city each day.

Billions of dollars pass annually over the desk of Dan Stern, a 37-year-old investment banker. He has lived in New York since graduating from business school in the late 1980s. Stern's corner office on the 43rd floor of a midtown office building has a view of Central Park. In addition to a desk and credenza, it has an easy chair and sofa for visitors, a small tree, and a table holding an orchid in full bloom. A chalkboard covers an entire wall—Stern uses it for financial calculations.

Most of the day Stern stands in front of his computer screen, talking on the telephone about deals and potential deals, including the purchase and sale of hotels, factories, and publishing ventures. He occasionally checks e-mail or an online stock quotation or *asks his* assistant to send documents via fax or overnight delivery.

Despite the money involved—30 million dollars for a "small" deal—Stern is relaxed and soft-spoken. "Putting together a profitable venture is like making a movie," he tells me. "You have to balance ideas, capital, and talent. Your judgment about people has to be good."

Dan Stern's world is electro-personal. With telephone, e-mail, fax, and computer, he can communicate all over the globe. But at every step a personal relationship or face-to-face contact is crucial.

This electronic dealing characterizes knowledge-based industries, like finance, corporate management, and advertising, which now produce almost a third of the private-sector jobs in New York City.

DoubleClick, an Internet advertising company, was started in Atlanta in 1995 and moved to New York the next year. The company places 200 million website advertisements a day, reaching 40 million people each month.

"We could be anywhere," says Kevin O'Connor, the co-founder and chief executive officer. "We're in New York because a Madison Avenue address gives us instant credibility, especially overseas."

DoubleClick is hiring people at the rate of one a day and will soon have a thousand employees. It's a "24-7" company—open all the time.

At 2 A.M. I chat with the four DoubleClick employees on duty. Two are from China, one is from Ukraine, and one has a father from Hong Kong and a mother from Burma.

Victor Ng is 21 years old and studies computer science full-time at a local college. "Do you do schoolwork during slow periods between phone calls and e-mails?" I ask.

"I don't have time," he says, pointing toward five books on network operations and problem solving. "I read those. I have to keep up with practical applications."

Victor doesn't have time to study for school because he is studying for work. He seems to be a living manifestation of the winning formula I'd discovered in Alexandria, Egypt: Trade produces wealth, wealth pays for knowledge, and knowledge stimulates more trade. What Victor learns produces more business for DoubleClick. With increased profits DoubleClick pays for more knowledgeable employees. Knowledgeable employees bring more business.

The next morning I wander south from DoubleClick toward the Union Square area, which was full of small factories at the beginning of the 20th century—when

manufacturing was the single most important source of jobs in New York. The buildings, many of which housed artists' studios in the 1960s, are now stores, offices, and restaurants.

School buses wrapped around the block in front of a former glove-and-belt factory prompt me to go inside. Ballet Tech now occupies the top two floors. Under exposed pipe and pressed-tin ceilings are classrooms and mirrored dance studios.

Twenty years ago Eliot Feld, who had danced with the New York City Ballet at age 11 and in 1969 formed his own dance company, was wondering where to find young dancers. Watching public schoolchildren on a subway, he realized they were an untapped pool of talent, and Ballet Tech was born.

More than 800 young students, selected from the 30,000 who audition each year, arrive by bus several times a week from throughout the city. After the fifth grade another selection process narrows the student body to 60, who attend middle and high school full-time at Ballet Tech. Of these, fewer than a dozen eventually join Feld's professional company.

"Dance training should not be wed to our notion of classic ballet, which is essentially a 19th-century idea of what ballet should be," Feld tells me. "Dance should capture what you feel when you walk the streets of New York. It should challenge accepted wisdom, weave in the new, allow change and growth. Art is always an argument with the past."

Watching Feld, I realize I'm witnessing the essence of the three cities—and the two millennia—that I've visited: human interaction fueling challenges to the known and a desire to create something better.

Ballet slippers are still slapping the hardwood floor as I leave. Subway sounds drift in a window. Joining the crowds rushing along the sidewalk, I keep hearing Feld. "You can't only do what's possible," he told his young dancers. "You *change* what's possible."

Critical Responses

1. What was the "winning formula" of Alexandria? How is it manifested elsewhere today?

2. Why have libraries been so significant to cities? What is the specific role of libraries in each of the cities described?

3. How would you characterize the persona of the author? How are these characteristics relevant to the subject of the article? How do they contribute to illustrating urban life?

4. In what ways have cities been crucibles for knowledge-based industries? In what ways might the electronic technologies on which knowledge-based industries rely in the 21st century affect cities in the future?

Writing Topics

1. What does it mean to be "cosmopolitan"? In defining the term, consider its applicability to one of the cities represented here—and, conversely, how that city may have contributed to the meaning of "cosmopolitan."

2. The opposite of cosmopolitan, "provincial" is often cast as a negative quality. What is its literal meaning, though? What makes its connotations negative, and from what perspective? Use examples of your own to illustrate provincialism.

3. What are some of the advantages of virtual libraries? What about the advantages of traditional libraries? How might the functions of virtual libraries complement those of traditional ones—and vice versa?

4. Compare the depiction of New York in this article with that of either London or Dubai as depicted in other articles in this reader. Each may be said to be at the cutting edge—but of what?

Further Explorations

1. If you could choose any city in the world to explore, what would that city be, and what makes you choose that one specifically? What aspects of the city would you want to investigate, and how would you go about doing so?

2. Identifying yourself according to origins—urban, suburban, rural—form classroom groups around each category, discuss and define the main characteristics of each, and then compare your findings with other groups in the class.

© 2006 STEVE WINTER/National Geographic Image Collection

Studying the Image

1. Describe what the children are doing in the picture. Why do you think they have come to the river to play? How do you think their experiences on the river will help connect them to the natural world?

2. The children appear to be playing by the river without any restrictions from adults. How could this scene be considered a metaphorical contrast to the government's rule over the people of Myanmar? Do you think that one reason for the people's connection to the river is the sense of freedom it provides?

Writing Assignment

The author of "Myanmar's River of Spirits" notes that the Irrawaddy River is polluted. Do research to determine whether the government has made any efforts to clean it up. Then write a letter to a government official arguing for the river's restoration, and suggest the best ways to accomplish this task.

© JOSEPH THOMAS NORIEGA/National Geographic Image Collection

Studying the Image

1. How would you describe the expression on the older child's face? Why do you think the photographer took a photo that partially obscured the children? Does this technique create a metaphorical relationship between the children and their environment?

2. In the article "John Dau: A Survivor's Story," the author notes that after most of the adults were slaughtered, the children helped each other survive. What do you think the psychological effects would be of this tremendous responsibility?

Writing Assignment

Dau states that the Lost Boys of Sudan had a strong will to survive the horrors of their experiences. Interview people who have served in wars and compare their survival instincts with that of the boys in the article.

© 1945 W. LANGDON KIHN/National Geographic Image Collection

Studying the Image

1. Why do you think Native Americans chose the totem as a form of communication? How do you think the environment dictates a particular form?

2. Many people today use emoticons such as a smiley face to help convey their feelings. Why do you think emoticons have become such a popular form of expression? Do you see any similarities between emoticons and the figures on the totems in the picture?

Writing Assignment

Research the meaning of the symbols on the totems in the picture. What symbols did Native Americans typically carve and paint on totems? Write an essay arguing that pictographic communication, such as the figures on a totem pole, is an effective form of communication.

Studying the Image

1. The author of "Guardians of the Fairy Tale: The Brothers Grimm" explains that the Grimm brothers collected "folk tales told to them mostly by women young and old." Why do you think women rather than men told these stories? Do you think these stories appeal more to women than to men?

2. Describe the relationship between the adult and child in the picture, noting their body language. Why do you think children like having stories read to them instead of reading them on their own?

Writing Assignment

How would you describe the look on the child's face? What is the dominant emotion being expressed? Decide which one of Grimm's tales could evoke that emotion and write a summary of the story from the child's point of view.

© LIBRARY OF CONGRESS/National Geographic Image Collection

Studying the Image

1. How does the artist evoke the viewer's sympathy toward the boy in the picture? Note technique as well as visual details in your response.

2. How would you describe the mule? Why do you think the artist included it in the picture? What is the relationship between the mule and the boy? Could this relationship be considered symbolic of the moment in history that it depicts?

Writing Assignment

Imagine that you are a politician in the first decades of the 19th century. Write a speech arguing for the abolition of slavery, using the picture as a method of expressing your position on this issue.

© 1984 B. ANTHONY STEWART/National Geographic Image Collection

Studying the Image

1. The article "Tale of Three Cities: Alexandria, Cordoba, and New York" determines that immigration and cultural diversity has made New York City flourish. The Statue of Liberty is a symbol of America's acceptance of people from other countries. Choose one ethnic group that has settled in New York and note the contributions it has made to the vitality of the city.

2. What are some of the problems that residents encounter in New York City? How has the city tried to resolve these problems and how successful have they been? Do you think the city will continue to enjoy its status as one of the most exciting and desirable places to live?

Writing Assignment

Research the current debate on immigration policies in the United States. After thinking about where you stand on the issue, write an argumentative essay outlining the policy our country should adopt.

PART 2
Living with *National Geographic*

The selections in the following three sections address universal themes from both specific local points of view and broad global ones. "Food, Scarcity, Sustainability" provides the point of entry, with connections between particular foods and ways of life being one emphasis ("Rice: The Essential Harvest," "Olive Oil: Elixir of the Gods," "Caffeine"), and agricultural and fishing practices that can both cause food crises and resolve them being another ("Seafood Crisis," "The End of Plenty," "Our Good Earth").

In "Work, Play, Love," the investigations of "21st-Century Slaves" and "The Price of Gold" shed light on some of the most dire conditions of labor in our world today. Play as an antidote to work ("County Fairs") and as a means for making connections round the world ("The Beautiful Game: Why Soccer Rules the World") follows. Then, the "Enigma of Beauty" is studied scientifically as is the chemistry of attraction in "This Thing Called Love."

The final section considers relationships between people, places, and ways of life, "People and Places." While "Into the Amazon" recounts efforts to create a safe haven for aboriginal peoples, "Last Days of the Rickshaw" reveals collisions between class and caste. New ways of adapting old ways of life also figure here ("Celt Appeal"), and whereas in "London on a Roll," trend setting turns out to be an on-going tradition. In "Dubai: Sudden City," everything is so new that it's hard to pin down what it is. But this isn't the case for the numbers of people who populate the world. The path-breaking article with which this reader closes, "Population Seven Billion," surveys all us living in the world today.

SECTION A
Food, Scarcity, Sustainability

ARTICLES IN THIS SECTION:

"Rice: The Essential Harvest"

"Olive Oil: Elixir of the Gods"

"Caffeine"

"Seafood Crisis: Time for a Sea Change"

"The End of Plenty: The Global Food Crisis"

"Our Good Earth: Soil"

A visual literacy section will appear at the end of the chapter.

Fresh fruit on display at an open air market.
© 2006 PAUL CHESLEY/National Geographic Image Collection

RICE: THE ESSENTIAL HARVEST

By Peter T. White

RICE: THE ESSENTIAL HARVEST

Adaptable to a great variety of growing conditions, rice is a vital crop in nearly one hundred countries. Cultivated for thousands of years, it continues to nurture body and spirit in many cultures. But as the population grows exponentially, can enough rice be coaxed out of the land to feed the billions of people for whom it is the most basic staple? What does science suggest? What does tradition? These are among the essential questions asked by Peter T. White, who, as a *National Geographic* writer and editor, traveled from Malaysian rice paddies to the California rice bowl in search of answers.

A farmer harvests fair trade rice in Haryana, India.

Rice terraces in the Ifugao Province of the Philippines.
© Vanni Noble/The Image Bank/Getty Images

WILL THERE BE ENOUGH OF THE
WORLD'S MOST VITAL CROP
TO FEED THE FUTURE,
OR WILL IT WISK AWAY IN THE WIND?

What is she doing, this bewitching young woman of Bali? Moistening her forehead with holy water, then her temples and her chest just below the throat. Now she sticks on a dozen luminously white kernels of uncooked rice. On her copper-colored skin they gleam like jewels.

What's the idea? She smiles. *"Mula keto,"* she says–that is what is done. A priest in the Hindu temple at Sukawati, where I just saw scores of other women, and men and children also, doing the same, tells me why: "Rice is the embodiment of Dewi Sri, the rice mother, goddess of life and fertility. This is a symbolic way for our bodies to absorb the life force she gives us. Without it we would be dead things."

In a sense this can be said not only of the three million Balinese but of much of humankind. Rice is the world's number one food crop. And to me the most intriguing.

Here are some facts that surprised me:

The grass species *Oryza sativa*—sown, or cultivated, rice—is thought to exist in 120,000 varieties. Some are red, some black. The "wild rice" prized by gourmets looks like rice but isn't; it's a grass of a different genus.

Rice is the world's number one food crop.

A tenth of the seven million tons of rice grown in the U.S. each year goes into beer. Ground up and boiled, it's put into mash tanks along with barley malt, before hops are added and fermentation begins. Why rice? "For lighter color and more refreshing taste," says an Anheuser-Busch brewmaster. "It's a significant element in what makes Budweiser Budweiser."

And as I was to learn in globe-girdling travel to get a grip on rice, so to speak, its cultivation has been influential in ways I hadn't envisioned. Fostering a courtship pattern in Italy. Shoring up family ties in West Africa. Benefiting ducks and geese in California. ...

I start out in the Philippines, at IRRI, the International Rice Research Institute, near Manila, where dramatic rice history was made. Financed by the Ford and Rockefeller Foundations, it opened in 1962 amid fear that because Asia's population growth was outstripping its food production, there would be

Adapted from "Rice: The Essential Harvest" by Peter T. White: National Geographic Magazine, May 1994.

At harvest, a combine equipped with a stripper header, which plucks grains but leaves stalks standing, can haul in as much as 250 tons of rice in one day.

© Juan Silva/The Image Bank/Getty Images

widespread famine. To avert such a calamity, IRRI did something of farreaching consequence. It transformed the rice plant. Its principal plant breeder, Gurdev S. Khush, tells me how: Height reduced from about five feet to three, so that when more fertilizer makes for heavier panicles, or clusters of rice grains, the stalks won't fall over. Growing period reduced from about 160 days to 110, so that in warm climates, if irrigation is available to supplement seasonal rainfall, there can be two or three crops a year instead of one. "We also bred in resistance to disease and insects—to blast and bacterial blight, to plant hoppers and stem borers."

IRRI's new dwarf varieties were so productive, and so widely adapted, that in the 25 years from 1967 to 1992 the world rice harvest doubled. "The outstanding case is Indonesia," says Dr. Khush. "From 15 million tons to 48, more than triple!" This, along with a similar upturn in wheat, has been called the green revolution.

But now, he adds, the rice plant must be redesigned once more. To keep pace with Asia's still rising population, rice production will have to increase another 60 percent by the year 2020. The current dwarf varieties have 20 to 25 stalks, but only 15 or so produce panicles, with about a hundred grains, or seeds, each; the rest are sterile. "We are aiming for what we call an ideotype—one with fewer stalks but thicker, stronger ones, each bearing a panicle with twice as many grains."

The building blocks for this science-directed evolution are the seeds in cold storage at IRRI's Genetic Resources Center—some 80,000 rice samples. Thousands are crossbred each year. Most of the resulting plants will be discarded, and only a few with the most desirable qualities kept to be grown again until, after six generations, they'll "breed true"—having become new varieties. Seeds of the most promising will be sent to some of the 89 major rice-growing countries for testing under local conditions and possible breeding with local varieties.

In the central luzon plain north of Manila, where paddies stretch for miles along both sides of the National Highway, I get impressions of labor-intensive rice cultivation in the lowland tropics—it's mud, sweat, and more mud.

A young man plows with his water buffalo, sometimes ankle-deep in gooey black mire, sometimes knee-deep. Couldn't he wear rubber boots? No, they'd slip or get stuck. He's 28, he says, and his wife works as a housemaid in Hong Kong; every two years she's back for a month. "She'll do it two more years; then we'll have enough money saved to buy a tractor, and she'll stay home and we'll have three children."

There's reliable irrigation here; it's always warm, and so, with cultivation going all year-round, different stages of the rice cycle occur simultaneously. Atop narrow dikes bordering the fields, I walk—carefully—to where young people transplant seedlings brought from a seedbed. Like this: Hold a bundle of foot-long seedlings in the left hand, bend forward 45 degrees, legs kept straight, and with the right thumb and index and middle fingers push in a couple of seed-lings at a time—into the mud, in neat rows.

It's done rapidly, and it's hard on the back. I clock one young man: 98 insertions in 72 seconds, before he straightens up to get the next bundle. Oops, his right leg abruptly sank a foot deep.

Why this laborious transplanting? So the rice will have a head start over the weeds. If

> **W**e are aiming for what we call an ideotype—one with fewer stalks but thicker, stronger ones, each bearing a panicle with twice as many grains.

seed were sown directly, you'd need much more seed and have bigger weed problems, requiring increased herbicide use. Where labor is cheap and chemicals are expensive, transplanting is in.

I see rice standing emerald green and three feet high—the immature grains are filling with milky fluid. In other places they're already golden beige and full of starch, ready for harvest in fields now drained. I see stalks cut with sickles and brought to a portable threshing machine. The bagged rough rice goes to mills in the villages and towns along the National Highway; part of the road is covered with it, spread out in the sun to dry a bit before milling.

Now I'm on a hill in Bali, looking down on a valley with terraced rice fields rising one above the other—a mosaic in shades of green, a sunny panorama of bucolic peace. But it's more than that; it's a manifestation of human beings striving to stay in harmony with nature, with the supernatural, and with one another. And rice is never far from their minds.

Water from higher up, from 3,300-foot-high Lake Batur, feeds springs and streams and then flows down through networks of dams, tunnels, and pipes to narrow channels and tiny weirs, so that each field can get a share. To make sure of that, hundreds of farmers' irrigation associations apportion who'll get how much and when. Each association, or *subak*, maintains a temple at its water source; there are smaller temples at outlets down the line and little shrines in individual fields. All these are for rituals at every stage of the rice cycle—plowing, transplanting, harvesting.

"Such rituals are the main characteristic of Balinese agriculture," I'm told by Nyoman Sutawan, a professor of agricultural economics at Bali's Udayana University. "Praying and making offerings unite the farmers so they'll cooperate, which is essential."

continued on page 102

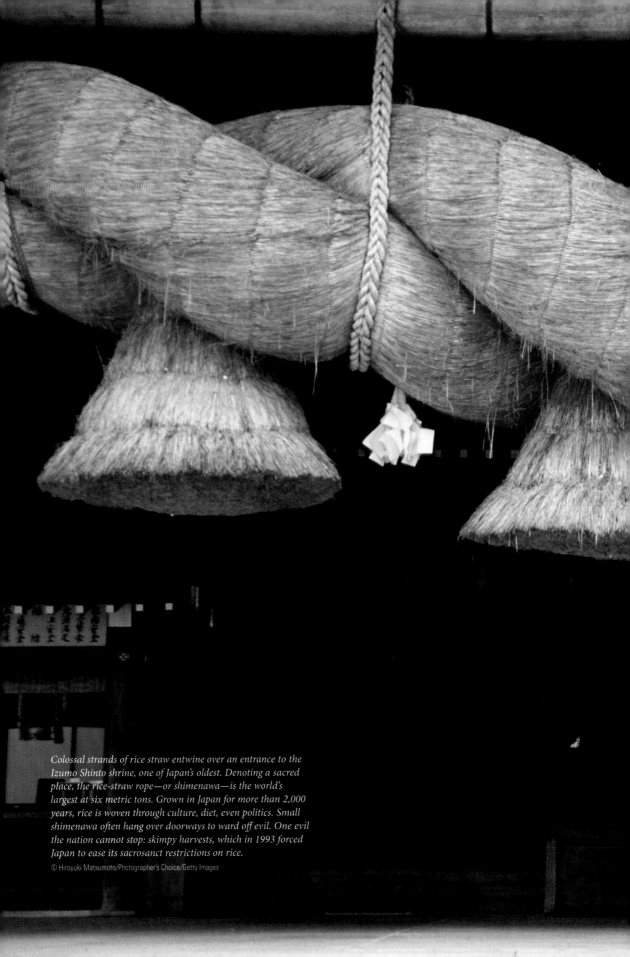

Colossal strands of rice straw entwine over an entrance to the Izumo Shinto shrine, one of Japan's oldest. Denoting a sacred place, the rice-straw rope—or shimenawa—is the world's largest at six metric tons. Grown in Japan for more than 2,000 years, rice is woven through culture, diet, even politics. Small shimenawa often hang over doorways to ward off evil. One evil the nation cannot stop: skimpy harvests, which in 1993 forced Japan to ease its sacrosanct restrictions on rice.

continued from page 99

The making of offerings in Bali never stops—at shrines in the family compound, at clan temples, subak temples, and hundreds of village temples, at full moon, at new moon, on auspicious days, on every 15th day when possibly harmful spirits are especially prevalent. And rice is invariably involved.

Every morning, after cooking the daily rice, housewives put some on small pieces of banana leaf and set these down where spirits are likely to be. On the kitchen stove, in the courtyard. In Guang village I follow a young woman as she leaves more offerings at the compound entrance and on the road outside. A little white dog traipses after her and gobbles up the rice. "The spirits must be fed so they'll be happy and not bother us," she tells me. But didn't the dog do the eating? That doesn't matter, she says, the spirit had already enjoyed the essence of the offering.

To temple anniversary festivals women walk with elaborate offerings balanced on their heads—round constructions three to six feet high, made up of fruit, flowers, incense sticks, and a variety of rice cakes dyed brown, yellow, green, pink. I see the women put their offerings down to pray, then carry them home again; they've been blessed by the gods, and now the family will enjoy eating all that's edible in them.

For a big wedding, or a tooth-filing ceremony, or purification after a cremation, Balinese may order huge offerings fashioned from dyed rice-flour paste molded into panels with a profusion of geometric designs or figures of animals, humans, or gods. A lady says it takes her and half a dozen helpers three days to make one that's eight feet high, with 33 colors. The biggest she's seen, a temple offering, measured 15 feet.

How much rice do the Balinese eat? An average of a pound a day each—and that's before it becomes heavier as it takes on water in the cooking. In Myanmar it's a bit more than a pound; in Thailand and Vietnam about three-quarters; and in Japan a little more than

The spirits must be fed so they'll be happy and not bother us.

a third. Americans, by contrast, consume an average of 22 pounds *a year.*

Cultivated rice, so scientists theorize, originated in more than one place along a broad arc from northeastern India to Myanmar, Thailand, Laos, and Vietnam to China. Solid evidence in the form of rice grains 4,000 or more years old has been unearthed from 31 sites in China. The most significant of these is in the lower Yangtze River plain at the village of Hemudu in Zhejiang Province, because it also yielded sophisticated tools of animal bone and wood—signs of a highly developed Neolithic civilization of 7,000 years ago.

Farmers digging a flood-control ditch in 1973 came upon pieces of pottery and called an archaeologist. Lin Hua-dong of the Zhejiang Academy of Social Science remembers his amazement at what he found 12 feet down. "A mass of rice grains looking fresh and yellow," he tells me. "But in a couple of minutes, on contact with the air, they turned dark brown, and soon they were black." A museum at Hemudu displays dozens of those slender black grains. They look as if they'd been burned.

Outside the museum with this ancient rice, farmers raise rice of the newest sort—rice with hybrid vigor, a remarkable Chinese achievement. Fifty-five percent of the country's rice land is planted in such rice, with a considerable increase in yield. These lands turn out two-thirds of all the rice in China. Researchers at IRRI and in India, Japan, and the U.S. are still trying to catch up.

In Changsha, I hear that the Hunan Institute of Cultural Relics and Archaeology has evidence of 8,000-year-old rice. That would be the oldest ever found! I rush to see Pei An-ping, who excavated at Pengtoushan, near Lixian, 120 miles northeast of Changsha. He shows me a pottery fragment with the impression of a rice husk—the grain disappeared in the firing, leaving only the impression. Carbon dating put its age at between 7,800 and 8,200 years.

Scientists from Japan, the U.S., and Britain have seen this, says Dr. Pei, and they couldn't decide whether it's from a wild or cultivated variety. Dr. Pei believes it is the latter.

Back in Zhejiang Province, I'm in time for something big at CNRRI, the Chinese National Rice Research Institute, near the capital, Hangzhou. It's a three-day rice evaluation tasting, supervised by Professor Shen Zongtan. "We have 150 samples from 15 provinces," he says. "Some may look good but do not have very good eating quality."

Four dozen evaluators from all over China sit at four tables and pass around small aluminum boxes, each with a number, to rate their contents on tally sheets for smell, appearance, and taste, from five for the best down to one. Occasionally they sip a little water and spit it into a basin.

At first I don't detect many differences, and so I get a little bit of coaching. White and bright is good, a little yellow not good. When you chew it, is it springy? Good. Or does it stick to your mouth? Not so good. After chewing does it dissolve smoothly—it should. Or does it stay a little lumpy?

Soon I sniff and taste, sip and spit, and evaluate. "Very soft, doughy, a two. Soft but with character, slightly sweet fragrance, a four. ..."

Once the results are tabulated, says Professor Shen, "we'll take the ten best, consider yield, pest and disease resistance, and growth duration, and choose which to popularize." As for me, whenever eating rice since then, I've been silently giving it a number. Any fives? Just one, in Washington, D.C.: Firm, springy, fragrance of butter and chives—Uncle Ben's brand, cooked by my wife.

Next stop, Japan. At the Grand Shrines of Ise, 190 miles southwest of Tokyo, the most revered precinct of Japan's Shinto religion, white-robed priests cook rice twice daily and present it to the sun goddess, Amaterasu, who, they say, is the ancestor of the imperial family.

"The goddess brought a handful of rice from the heavens," a senior priest tells me, "so that we may grow it and prosper." He adds that in the first ceremony performed by each new emperor, he steps behind a screen to meet the goddess and emerges as the embodiment of Ninigi no Mikoto, the god of the ripened rice plant. Then every autumn the emperor sends to Ise the first stalks harvested from the rice field he himself has planted on the imperial palace grounds. All Japanese, says the priest, owe their *kokoro*—their spiritual essence, their Japaneseness—to the goddess, "and they maintain it by eating rice, rice grown in Japan."

Japanese law, in fact, long restricted the importation of rice. "Rice is a very special case," explained Koji Futada, then parliamentary vice minister for agriculture, forestry, and fisheries. "It is our staple food, and so we must have a reliable supply as a matter of national security. That is why we politicians favor self-sufficiency, the domestic growing of all the rice we eat."

Also because the farmers exert disproportionate influence in elections?

"Yes," he said, "that is also true."

Europe first heard about rice from writers who'd been to India with Alexander the Great. Later, Greek authors of medical texts influential in imperial Rome, and in the West and the Arab world through the Middle Ages, prescribed rice for gastrointestinal complaints, citing its cooling and astringent effects. Doctors today endorse this notion of rice's effects and recommend giving rice powder mixed with water and salt to children suffering from diarrhea in nations such as Bangladesh and Pakistan, and in the Middle East. It helps the patient retain body fluids.

Today Europe's biggest producer is Italy, notably in the Piedmont region, in the province of Vercelli. Here a great plain, once marshy, but drained since Renaissance times, inclines gently from the foothills of the Alps southward to the Po River, crisscrossed by a gigantic irrigation network. When the fields are flooded in spring, I'm told, villages appear as islands afloat on shimmering mirrors.

Now in September the fields are beige. Among them here and there rise tile-roofed quadrangles, each once the center of a rice property with stables for oxen and horses, dormitories for workers, a church. Young women from all over Italy came to work here from April to October—it was a respectable way to earn a dowry. They were called *mondine*, cleaners, because they did a lot of weeding. Also transplanting and harvesting. Quite a few married local young men. All that ended as mechanization spread in the 1960s.

At a quadrangle that once housed 300 women and 50 men I hear that the landowner in Genoa rents out his 1,200 acres—now seven people take care of it all. And I meet a mondina who came from the south—Maria Manfrenato, 60, squat and lively, with curly black hair piled high. Yes, it was hard work, she says—long hours with your feet in mud and water, constantly bent over. "But we sang while working. If you didn't sing, your back would hurt more. When I tell young people, they say I was crazy, but I enjoyed it—we had a lot of fun." And yes, she married a man from Vercelli.

In contrast to Italy time seems to have stood still in Senegal, on the southern bank of the wide Casamance River, where I find the Esudadu Jola people, remarkable for their thousand-year-old way with rice.

When brackish water from the mangrove swamps seeps through their dikes, they flush it out with rainwater piped from field to field through conduits made from hollowed-out trunks of the *Borassus* palm. To cultivate during the rainy season, they use no plows, no animals. Our cattle, they say, are not for work, only for sacrifices at ceremonies. Their tool is the *kajando*, or fulcrum shovel, an elongated wooden spade with a metal edge and a six-foot handle. You slice into the wet clay soil and lift sizable chunks by levering against your left leg just above the knee. Then you turn the chunks over as you drop them to the right and left, building up ridges. The dug-out space becomes a furrow.

At the village of Samatit, I see a dozen men slice, lift, and turn, and in a few minutes they've transformed a diked field overgrown with rice stubble and foot-high weeds into neat ridges and furrows. Soon it'll all be flooded, and women will start transplanting.

The fastest man with a kajando is Kuñarigei—age 36, six feet tall, barefoot and wearing only a loincloth, his skin glistening in the humid 93° heat. He is a science teacher in a secondary school in the faraway capital, Dakar. For the three months of the school vacation—from July to October, coinciding with the rainy season—he returns to the village to help his father, Suti, the 65-year-old village chief, who works in the fields from dawn to dusk.

Nowadays most of the older boys go away to city schools, but they also come back to help, says Kuñarigei, and so do most of the girls who work as domestics in Dakar. "They do a lot of transplanting with their mothers. Some have had to quit their jobs and now will have to find new ones."

The Jola and other West Africans skilled in rice growing, shipped as slaves to colonial America, were instrumental in building a prosperous southern riceplanting society, notably in tidewater South Carolina. It flourished in the 18th and 19th centuries and began fading after the Civil War. Today U.S. production is concentrated in Arkansas, Louisiana, Texas, Mississippi—and California, one of the most efficiently mechanized rice producers in the world and for a long time the most controversial.

"Our yield is wonderful, 8,500 pounds per acre," says Bob Herkert of the California Rice Industries Association. "That's among the highest anywhere. As we drive in the Sacramento Valley, between the Coast Ranges and the Sierra Nevada, Bob makes appointments for me over his mobile phone and ticks off some pluses of this great American rice bowl.

Poorly drained clay soil, for one thing. That's ideal for rice because it holds in the precious irrigation water from the Shasta and Oroville Dams. Precision leveling of the fields with laser-controlled earthmovers. That eliminates high and low spots, so less water will be needed; all

continued on page 106

A market trader preparing rice for sale at a market in Mocuba, Mozambique, Africa.

© Aminart/Photolibrary/Getty Images

continued from page 104

in all, water use is down 30 percent.* "We seed by airplane, and depth of water is critical—say, five and a half inches," he adds. An inch lower and weeds will outgrow the rice. An inch too much and the seed won't get well enough established.

"Environmentalists hated us," Bob goes on, "but no more." When the fields were drained, a lot of herbicide went into the river, and the city of Sacramento had to treat its drinking water heavily. To some it tasted awful. "We thought we had to drain after seven days or the chemicals would hurt the crop. But we found that if we keep the water moving, with pumps, we can hold it for 28 days and the chemicals break down naturally." Now the herbicide discharge is down by 99 percent.

Not that the California rice growers have no critics any more. One big complaint: Why put rice into a semiarid valley and use 1.5 million acre-feet of water a year—that's nearly half of what 16 million people use from metropolitan Los Angeles all the way to San Diego! Replies Marc Reisner, an environmentalist author who criticized the rice growers but recently changed his mind: "Rice uses much less water than does cotton in the San Joaquin Valley farther south, and that provides no environmental benefit. But rice can."

How so? The California rice bowl, I learn from Jack Payne, a biologist from Ducks Unlimited, can be a boon to waterfowl migrating from Alaska and Canada along the Pacific flyway. Now there's a pilot project: With practically all of California's natural wetlands gone, some rice farmers in the Sacramento Valley, where fields lie fallow from October to February, let them flood early, so mallards, pintails, widgeons, snow geese, and tundra swans will come and winter here. . . .

At Williams, I visit an energy plant fueled by rice hulls. They're piled up outside in beige mountains, partly covered with black plastic.

"Electricity for 30,000 homes," says a manager. Yes, it's the biggest operation of its kind.

As I drive off again, I notice a big gray cloud on the October horizon—smoke from burning rice stubble. That also used to upset environmentalists; it made smog that sat on the valley like a lid. Now such burning must be approved by a county pollution-control officer. Today it's OK; there's no temperature inversion, so the smoke will disperse quickly. A new law requires that burning be reduced each year until nearly all is stopped by 2000. That's where those migrating birds should be of help. In the rice fields they'll feed on waste grains, aquatic insects, snails—and at the same time stamp down the rice straw, helping decompose it. "They're our partners," says Steve Dennis, who farms at Maxwell. "They leave little deposits of fertilizer." A great swoop of white-fronted geese has just set down nearby and is starting to feed, stamp, and fertilize.

At the end of my rice travels I remember what I was told by Klaus Lampe, the director general of IRRI. He said that because population expansion is not yet under control, research will have to find ways to grow more rice on less land and with less water in view of increasing urbanization. And with fewer inputs of chemical fertilizers, insecticides, and herbicides, for environmental reasons.

Also with less labor, because, in the poorer areas of Asia, many of the next generation may not be willing to walk 50 miles in the mud behind a water buffalo just to prepare two acres for planting—they'll move to the cities.

"So we have to make rice production more attractive work—with mechanization and with pay comparable to a factory job, for example. And to make the economics of rice such that a farmer can produce so much at so low a cost that it will be affordable for both the rural and the urban poor." Dr. Lampe thinks it can be done.

And I want to believe that it will be.

Critical Responses

1. "Rice is the world's number one food crop," writes White. "And to me the most intriguing." What is the nature of his fascination with rice and how does he convey it through his word choice, sentence structure, and other elements of writing style?

2. In what ways is rice sacred in the examples given in this article? What do the rituals described suggest about the cultures in which they are significant?

3. Continuing with this theme, compare rice to olive oil, which is also featured in one of this reader's food articles. What are some similarities and differences in their economic, social, and religious importance?

4. What additional perspectives do other articles on the global food supply in this reader, including the "The End of Plenty: The Global Food Crisis" and "Our Good Earth: Soil," contribute to "Rice: The Essential Harvest"?

Writing Topics

1. What is the geographical route that White takes in his research? How is this related to the histories of rice that he relates here?

2. While rice is an essential staple in much of the world, in some contexts it is also treated as a gourmet item. What makes some types of rice gourmet? What are contexts in which rice is attributed with gourmet qualities? Is gourmet rice necessarily distinct from rice that is a staple?

3. What staple is essential to the diet on which you grew up? Is it typical of the place where you did? What does this staple say about your cultural identity in itself and in relation to the broader culture of the country?

4. As White notes in passing, what is commonly called "wild rice" belongs to another genus than cultivated rice. Research this "wild rice," and write a paper discussing its role in specific Native American cultures.

Further Explorations

1. Describe your favorite food in an essay in which you illustrate what makes it so appetizing to you and do so in such a way as to make it appetizing for your reader.

2. Form two research groups—one for corn, and the other for potatoes—and report on their histories and their roles as staples in diet and culture, by themselves and in comparison to rice.

OLIVE OIL: ELIXIR OF THE GODS

By Erla Zwingle

Photographs by Ira Block

OLIVE OIL:
ELIXIR OF THE GODS

A freelance journalist for over thirty years, Erla Zwingle has written over two dozen features for *National Geographic* Magazine on places ranging from the Alps to Australia; on women in general as child bearers and as singular great monarchs; on broad topics such as global warming and on specific concerns such as preserving Italy's artistic heritage. Bringing her eclectic perspectives to bear on olive, Zwingle writes eloquently about the virtues and values of this essential staple for which Mediterranean peoples have had manifold uses for thousands of years, and suggests why this "elixir of the gods" is becoming more widely popular among us mortals.

Century-old ceramic urns store Italian olive oil, made at this Tuscan estate for nearly 1,200 years. Valued through the ages for food, fuel, salve, and sacrament, the olive's liquid gold remains unsurpassed among oils.

In uniform splendor legions of young olive trees swarm the hills of Andalusia in Spain, world leader in olive production. Thriving on heat and sun, gray-green olive groves have long inspired artistic souls. Wrote Renoir: "… the sky that plays across them is enough to drive you mad."

FOR 4,000 YEARS IT HAS SERVED THE MEDITERRANEAN CULTURE AS EVERYTHING FROM MONEY TO MEDICINE. NOW THE REST OF THE WORLD IS DISCOVERING

THE MOST VERSATILE FRUIT JUICE EVER SQUEEZED.

You can burn it, wash with it, lubricate squeaky hinges with it. Cosmetics are based on it, diamonds polished with it. Kings, babies, and the dying are anointed with it. It's loaded with vitamin E. It has no cholesterol. It's an amazing preservative, keeping fish, cheese, and even wine good for years. Boiled, it's one of the more ingenious weapons of war and torture. And, of course, you can eat it. For 4,000 years it has served the Mediterranean cultures as everything from money to medicine. Now the rest of the world is discovering olive oil, the most versatile fruit juice ever squeezed.

Until recently, for people beyond the Mediterranean olive oil retained an aura of the exotic; it was something eaten in odd ethnic dishes or lost on the specialty shelf in the grocery store somewhere between the kumquats and the saffron. Olive oil was usually first encountered in restaurants, where it unjustly acquired a reputation for being heavy, as it was often low quality and sometimes adulterated with anything from animal fat to glycerine.

But olive oil began gaining new respect after a study published in 1970 revealed that

Until recently, for people beyond the Mediterranean olive oil retained an aura of the exotic.

Mediterranean peoples have the lowest rate of heart disease among Western nations, a condition partly attributed to their liberal use of olive oil (it is rich in monounsaturated fat—the "good" fat—and also in antioxidants, which help prevent plaque buildup in the arteries). By the end of the eighties, olive oil had experienced an unprecedented boom in Western countries. This was apparently the result of a convergence of happy circumstances: Consumers were more interested in nutrition, more eager to choose natural products, and more willing to pay a higher price for a high-quality product. And as people discovered the appeal of numerous foreign foods, from shiitake mushrooms to Sumatran coffee, olive oil was bound to benefit. For the 1982-83 season the U.S. imported nearly ten million gallons of olive oil. In the 1997-98 season it imported almost five times that amount.

One frosty November morning I was balanced atop a ladder leaning against an olive

Adapted from "Olive Oil: Elixir of the Gods" by Erla Zwingle: National Geographic Magazine, September 1999.

tree in the Italian region of Tuscany. Sunlight slanted over the steep grassy hillside and folded itself among the olive trees and Chianti grapevines, gradually melting the shards of frost. A cloth was spread on the ground beneath me, and I was clawing at the branches with a yellow rakelike tool with seven curved tines. Olives were flying everywhere. Giuseppe Giotti, an olive farmer with ruddy cheeks and a massive black mustache, hovered anxiously below.

How you harvest olives depends on many factors—including the number of trees, the amount of money and time available, and the type of olive. Although the techniques vary, they're almost all strenuous, from stripping the olives by hand to beating the branches with long sticks. Giuseppe, like many olive farmers, doesn't own enough property to make it profitable to buy machinery (he has only 600 trees), and he doesn't make enough money from the oil to pay extra workers. His two sons have jobs, so the only people helping him today were Maria, his 73-year-old mother, and, temporarily, me. I was starting to sweat. The branches were springy and loaded with leaves, and the hard purple-green olives all seemed to be clustered inside. Behind every bottle of olive oil, I soon learned, is a troupe of tired people in old clothes.

After about 45 minutes I had removed all the olives I could find, plus a few that only Giuseppe could see. I climbed down the ladder, and we slowly gathered up the drop cloth, bouncing all the olives toward the center. We poured them clumsily into a large bucket. Olives fell into the grass and stuck to the soles of Giuseppe's boots.

Giuseppe's farm has been in the family for at least a hundred years. "I was in the Navy for 30 years," he said, "but when my father died, I came back." Now the future of the farm depends entirely on him.

With about half the harvest already done, he hoped to finish in another month or so. "If the rains don't start," he said. "The important thing is that it doesn't rain." Wet olives ferment faster inside their hundred-pound bags, and fermentation can ruin the oil's flavor. But he's looking forward to a substantial harvest. This year he'll pick more than two tons of olives, which should give him about a hundred gallons of oil.

Crowning a hillside 40 miles to the south is the abbey of the aptly named Monte Oliveto Maggiore, Mount of the Olive Grove. Here Don Celso Bidin, one of 37 Benedictine brothers, oversees the monastery's olive mill, one of the few in Tuscany that still use traditional methods. Though milling techniques have been modernized, the simple process remains the same everywhere: Crush the whole olive, pit and all, separate the liquid from the solids, then separate the water from the oil.

Don Celso was a trim, robust figure in blue coveralls, with serious eyes but a cheerful expression. He showed me around the mill. Olives tumbled into a huge basin under two ponderous grindstones. (Animals once provided the power; now it's motors.) A roar filled the room as the stones crushed the olives, drowning the crooning of the doves in the cypresses outside. Workers spread the resulting dark brown paste on round, woven nylon mats and stacked them on a spindle. A metal plate was added, then the whole column of mats was squeezed by a hydraulic press at 400 atmospheres—the famous "pressing" of the oil. Water and oil slowly dripped from the mats and passed into a settling tank, where the oil rose to the top. Every week Don Celso bottled it by hand.

The Mediterranean world has regarded the olive as sacred for thousands of years. The ancient Egyptians credited the goddess Isis with teaching mankind its cultivation and uses. The Greeks believed that Athena, goddess of wisdom, bestowed the olive on mankind, thereby winning a contest among the gods for presenting the most useful gift. The Bible is brimming with references to olive oil, from the parable of the wise and foolish virgins (oil as lamp fuel) to the story of the Good Samaritan (oil as unguent) to the Prophet Elisha's rescue of the destitute widow (oil as item of trade).

Farmers on the eastern shores of the Mediterranean domesticated the wild olive tree some 6,000 years ago and began extracting its oil about 2,000 years later. Phoenician voyagers spread olive cultivation to Greece and Spain, and the Greeks took it to Italy. Today 74 percent of the world's supply of olive oil comes from those three nations.

The Tuscan olive groves are romantic, woven into scenery from a Renaissance tapestry: velvety green hills clad with vines and topped by castles, all softened by a golden haze. The landscape lacks only a knight on horseback and a desperate damsel. But in Spain, particularly the southernmost region of Andalusia, oil is big business. Andalusia alone produces 192 million gallons a year, nearly 90 percent of Spain's output. In two years, one expert predicts, Spain will produce half the world total of olive oil, and you can see why: Sturdy, squat trees march off to the horizon, endless ranks of silvery-green plants corrugating the soil. Although most landowners have relatively small holdings because of the subdivision of property over the generations, the aggregate tracts are vast. It doesn't come as a complete surprise that the International Olive Oil Council is based in Madrid.

Once again there was the roar of machinery, but now it was from the production lines at Aceites del Sur outside Seville, one of Spain's foremost oil bottlers. Juan Ramón Guillén, the president, was giving me a tour of his empire. Every day tanker trucks filled with olive oil roll up to the huge storage tanks outside; inside, bottles and cans of all sizes race down conveyor belts. Graying and dapper, Guillén has a metabolism calibrated to the rate of production—we fairly galloped through the plant, bounding from topic to topic.

In one room Guillén showed me shelves full of the company's products, in all brands, sizes, colors, and scripts. Aceites del Sur exports to

The Mediterranean world has regarded the olive as sacred for thousands of years.

60 countries, blending and marketing the oils according to cultural preferences. The can of La Española for Spain showed a young lady seated demurely in a bucolic olive grove; on the can of La Española destined for the United Arab Emirates, the young lady had been tactfully removed. Al-Amir oil was in a simple, small green tin. "The king of Saudi Arabia gives this as a traditional gift to pilgrims to Mecca," Guillén explained. "In the Arab countries they eat oil and also use it as a hair tonic. In India they put it on their hair but don't eat it."

Into a small laboratory reeking of solvents. "This is where we analyze the oil," he said. "Everyone thinks that all olive oil is the same. But some is sweet, some is bitter." Oil is analyzed not only to establish acidity but also for blending purposes. "In America they like an oil very, very light that doesn't taste of anything," Guillén said. "In Mexico they like darker and spicier. In the Arab countries they want oil that's green and sweet. They eat a lot of bread, and they like to 'paint' the bread."

He offered me a series of small glasses of oil to taste. I took about a teaspoon's worth of each into my mouth and gave a quick series of short, sharp slurps; not very attractive, but this way the flavors suffuse the nose and palate. A professional taster can distinguish a hundred different flavors, from straw to apple, artichoke to wood, almond to flowers. I could only manage one or two. The Manzanilla was fruity and smooth. The Moroccan Picholine was soft and sweet. I wanted to try the Picual, but Guillén quickly said it was "only for blending a little bit for the Arabs." He kept trying to dissuade me from sampling it. I insisted. And I liked it—it was strong and a little bitter, with a powerful aroma of olive.

The best olive oil is extra virgin. To merit the term, which conveys that it has not been altered, the oil must result only from mechanical extraction without being

continued on page 116

"Greek olives and olive oil are the best," says Konstantinos Kokkalis of Athens, whose unabashed bias typifies rival growers in the Mediterranean. Since its fabled birth as a gift from Athena, the olive tree has been revered by Greeks, who have the world's highest per capita use of olive oil. "The olive," says Kokkalis, "is blessed by God."

continued from page 113

heated, have less than one percent acidity, and meet a series of exacting standards for flavor and aroma—a judgment rendered by panels of professional tasters. The oils that fall short in either category are acceptable, though less interesting and slightly less nutritious than extra-virgin oil. They are marketed in several ways. There is "virgin olive oil," "refined olive oil," or simply "olive oil." These are essentially bland oils that may have been refined by a chemical process, with some amount of extra-virgin oil added to enhance the flavor and color.

Most big olive oil brands achieve a standard flavor that their customers like, then have to replicate it every year. The customer keen on extra-virgin oil knows there could be variations. But the typical shopper isn't looking for surprises. The only way the large companies can consistently produce an oil that matches their customers' expectations is to blend various oils according to their own recipe. However, not every country produces enough to satisfy both local and export demand—Italy foremost of all. Therefore that bottle of Italian oil may very well contain Greek or Spanish olive oil too, though recent changes in international trade standards now require exact labeling of the contents.

Still, the Greeks and Spanish are not entirely happy with this situation. Their oil deserves to be better known, they believe, but it is hidden in the shadow of the image of Italian oil. The Italians were first to capture the foreign market—73 percent of the European olive oil the U.S. imports comes from Italy—and they continue to dominate at least with their reputation for high-quality oil. The others chafe. "You know what we say?" a Greek asked me. "Italian oil is like water." Said a Spaniard, "They import our oil to make theirs better." An Italian snorted, "The Spanish know nothing about olive oil."

Until recently Spain was content to sell in bulk to foreign blenders. But in Greece, which is awash in first-class oil, the many small producers accuse the Greek bureaucracy and a sort of mafia of middlemen of preventing them from bottling and marketing their oil as their own.

"So," one Greek farmer asked me, a little aggressively, "where do you think the best oil comes from?" I knew what I was supposed to answer, but I couldn't do it. "That's easy," I replied. "The best oil comes from the country with the most beautiful women."

But that was just a dodge. By that point I'd become a sort of olive oil junkie. Any oil I was eating was suddenly the best I'd ever had. I loved the peppery jolt of Italian oil from the Leccino or Correggiolo olives (great for frying foods). In Spain the Picual, Arbequina, or Hojiblanca varieties were full of character, yet also delicately aromatic (perfect on grilled fish). In Greece, the ubiquitous Koroneiki rendered an oil that was fruity and full of body (celestial on salad). I poured olive oil on everything: meat, vegetables, even cheese.

And I never tired of hearing what wonders olive oil could work. I read a study that demonstrated that foods fried in olive oil retain more nutritional value than those fried in other kinds of oil. Another study showed that women who eat olive oil more than once a day have a 45 percent reduced risk of developing breast cancer. It may have therapeutic effects on peptic ulcers and prevent the formation of gallstones. A Greek housewife said it makes the perfect hair conditioner (equal parts vinegar and oil) as well as the ideal burn treatment (mixed with lime and water). "My wife suffered from back pain," said a Cretan farmer. "Somebody told her to take two tablespoons of olive oil every morning on an empty stomach. She did this for ten days, and she was cured."

In the greek city of Kalamata—best known for its briny black table olives but home to delectable extra-virgin oil too—Panayiotis Sardelas consumes his oil in another form. He is founder, manager, and, I suspect, also foreman, truck driver, and accountant of

To your health! At Casa Benigna in Madrid, Rafael and Maria Alcalá make liberal use of olive oil. Its monounsaturated fats and antioxidants benefit the body—a welcome but secondary perk for Maria. "A meal without olive oil," she says, "would be a bore."

one of the few soap factories in the Peloponnese using olive oil. His workshop and warehouse are in a big cluttered shed on the airport road.

"I started 40 years ago," he said. "I had an olive mill, and people asked me to make soap, so I took the risk. There was an old woman working for me, and she taught me how to make it. I started with a hundred pounds, and after three or four years it was four tons."

He buys the sediment that settles from new oil and mixes it with caustic soda and soapstone. He boils it all for 12 hours in a tank with a conical bottom. When it begins to solidify, he removes the caustic soda, which has sunk to the bottom, and washes the mixture with salt water to remove any remaining traces.

"The old people know that this soap is better than chemical ones," he said. "It lasts longer than other soaps, and you can use it for everything. Cut it in chips and put it in your washing machine. Some doctors prefer this soap for washing their hands."

I took a small but heavy chunk of the muddy beige soap. It had a mulchy, sensible-shoes sort of odor. I asked if he ever thought of adding perfume. "No, no." He looked perplexed. "If you want something pure, you wouldn't mix something in it." That night I tried it. It didn't lather much, but afterward my skin felt startlingly smooth.

The soap factory was an OSHA nightmare, full of detritus and bits of things held together by other things. The rusty three-ton tank was empty; Sardelas had already made his batch. But atop the cluttered work-table a clear, bright little flame was burning. A plain glass full of olive oil. A floating wick. He noticed my glance. "Oh," he said simply. "We pray here every morning for a good day."

Beyond the city, the stony, austere hills stretched to the sea. Small splotches of color—a flowering pink almond tree, a golden mimosa—softened the land's bony outlines. Dark clouds were spreading veils of rain across the mountains; no harvest tomorrow. The evening moved slowly up the hillsides. The darkness rose, filling the hollows. But the olive trees held out to the end. They tossed eagerly in the wind, full of brightness, full of oil, full of life.

Critical Responses

1. What kind of aura surrounds olive oil? How does Zwingle account for its allure?

2. Pursuing this question from another angle, consider her style of writing. What is the nature of her engagement in her subject? How does it affect your response?

3. Furthermore, what do the photographs contribute? What is the dominant mood of each one? How do they complement and supplement the text?

4. What are the health benefits of olive oil? To what extent do these account for its growing popularity? To what extent are they also part of its mystique? How, more generally, do the physical and the symbolic dimensions of olive oil mingle? And is this mingling unique to this substance or does it apply to other foods and beverages as well?

Writing Topics

1. What distinguishes each of the three main olive oil producing countries described here? What unites them? Which seems more significant, the differences or the similarities? Why? What are the implications?

2. How does olive oil as described by Zwingle compare with rice as described by Peter White in another article in this reader? In looking at both, focus on what makes each not only a food staple, but also a cultural staple.

3. As a noun, a verb, or a base for an adjective, the word "taste" has a number of distinct but related definitions. What are they and what kinds of "taste" do you find exemplified in this essay on olive oil? How is olive oil a matter of "taste" in its various denotations and connotations?

4. "Culture" and "cultivation" are also critical concepts. After working out their various definitions, show how olive oil illustrates them, separately and together.

Further Explorations

1. Examine an advertisement for imported olive oil online or in a magazine. How is it represented? What aspects (e.g., historical, medicinal, artisanal, and so on) are highlighted? Who is the targeted audience? Do the same for domestic olive oil, and compare your findings.

2. Divide into three or four groups and have each group identify a food or beverage that has both nutritional and symbolic value and create a profile of its attributes. Compare these with olive oil and with other selections made by your class groups. Does a broader profile emerge from your collective research?

CAFFEINE

By T.R. REID

CAFFEINE

At any given moment, how many people do you see drinking coffee or tea or soda or some other energy drink on your school campus? Are you one of the seemingly ever-growing number of caffeine junkies? What makes this stimulant so popular and so pleasurable, so essential and so addicting? Undertaking an exhausting journey to study the culture and the cults of caffeine in many countries, award-winning journalist T. R. Reid consumed a great deal himself in search of the answers to such questions.

Coffee beans with a sack and scoop.
© Vladimir Shulevsky/StockFood Creative/Getty Images

A worker picks red coffee beans at an
Indonesian coffee plantation. These beans are
used to make coffee called Kopi Luwak which is
one of the most expensive coffees in the world. It
can cost between $100 to $600.
© Ulet Ifansasti/Stringer/Getty Images

IT IS THE

WORLD'S MOST WIDELY CONSUMED PSYCHOACTIVE DRUG,

AND IS BOTH LEGAL AND UNREGULATED IN NEARLY ALL PARTS OF THE WORLD. THE MORE WE HAVE THE MORE WE NEED TO SURVIVE.

"It's like putting your whole system on fast-forward," Lee Murphy shouts above the din as he glides across the floor with four-inch-high soles on his dancing shoes, a gold ring in his chin, and a slender silver and blue can of Red Bull energy drink in each hand. "By four or five in the morning you're totally blotto," the 29-year-old London nurse explains. "That's where the Red Bull comes in. I drink these two tins, it's like drinking a pint of speed." For Lee Murphy and other habitués of the all-night club scene around the world—not to mention a legion of marathon runners, mountain bikers, fighter pilots, college crammers, and late-night truckers hoping to cover another hundred miles before turning in—the canned concoctions marketed as energy drinks represent a fizzy new manifestation of one of mankind's oldest stimulants: caffeine. The active ingredient in the hugely successful Austrian product Red Bull is a solid jolt of caffeine, blended with a handful of other ingredients. One 8.3-ounce can has two to three times the amount of caffeine as a 12-ounce can of soda.

It is the only habit-forming psychoactive drug we serve to our children (in all those sodas and chocolate bars).

"The kids in the clubs, they think they've happened upon this great new invention," says Neil Stanley, director of sleep research at the Human Psychopharmacology Research Unit at Britain's University of Surrey. "But we've known for centuries that caffeinated drinks work. They get you out of an energy slump and make you more alert. Really all they've found is a new kind of caffeine delivery system."

The dual power to counter physical fatigue and increase alertness is part of the reason caffeine ranks as the world's most popular mood-altering drug, eclipsing the likes of nicotine and alcohol. The drug is encountered not just at the soda fountain or the espresso bar but also in diet pills and pain relievers. It is the only habit-forming psychoactive drug we routinely serve to our children (in all those sodas and chocolate bars). In fact, most babies in the developed world enter the universe with traces of caffeine in their bodies, a transfer

Adapted from "Caffeine" by T. R. Reid: National Geographic Magazine, January 2005.

through the umbilical cord from the mother's latte or Snapple.

Caffeine's pervasiveness is a cause for concern among some scientists and public health advocates, but that hasn't dampened its popularity. Sales of Red Bull and copycat energy drinks with names like Red Devil, Roaring Lion, RockStar, SoBe Adrenaline Rush, Go Fast, and Whoop Ass are booming. Meanwhile new coffee shops are opening so fast all over the world that even the most dedicated devotee of the triple-shot, no-foam, double-caramel, skinny macchiato can't keep track. Every working day, Starbucks opens four new outlets somewhere on the planet and hires 200 new employees. There's a joke in many cities that Starbucks is going to open a new store in the parking lot of the local Starbucks, but this is not true. Yet.

It was less than 200 years ago that people first figured out that the buzz they got from coffee and tea was the same buzz, produced by the same chemical agent. An alkaloid that occurs naturally in the leaves, seeds, and fruit of tea, coffee, cacao, kola trees, and more than 60 other plants, this ancient wonder drug had been prescribed for human use as far back as the sixth century B.C., when the great spiritual leader Lao-tzu is said to have recommended

> **In a sense, caffeine is the drug that made the modern world possible.**

tea as an elixir for disciples of his new religion, Taoism.

But it wasn't until 1820, after coffee shops had proliferated in western Europe, that a new breed of scientist began to wonder what it was that made this drink so popular. The German chemist Friedlieb Ferdinand Runge first isolated the drug in the coffee bean. The newly discovered substance was dubbed "caffeine," meaning something found in coffee. Then, in 1838 chemists discerned that the effective ingredient in tea was the same substance as Runge's caffeine. Before the end of the century the same drug would be found in kola nuts and cacao.

It's hardly a coincidence that coffee and tea caught on in Europe just as the first factories were ushering in the industrial revolution. The widespread use of caffeinated drinks—replacing the ubiquitous beer—facilitated the great transformation of human economic endeavor from the farm to the factory. Boiling water to make coffee or tea helped decrease the incidence of disease among workers in crowded cities. And the caffeine in their systems kept them from falling asleep over the machinery. In a sense, caffeine is the drug that made the modern world possible. And the more modern our world gets, the more we seem to need it. Without that useful jolt of coffee—or Diet Coke or Red Bull—to get us out of bed and back to work, the 24-hour society of the developed world couldn't exist.

"For most of human existence, your pattern of sleeping and wakefulness was basically a matter of the sun and the season," explains Charles Czeisler, a neuroscientist and sleep expert at Harvard Medical School. "When the nature of work changed from a schedule built around the sun to an indoor job timed by a clock, humans had to adapt. The widespread use of caffeinated food and drink—in combination with the invention of electric light—allowed people to cope with a work schedule set by the clock, not by daylight or the natural sleep cycle."

HOW BIG IS YOUR BUZZ?

Drugmakers have to label the amount of caffeine in their offerings, but food and beverage companies don't. A sample of familiar products shows how fast your dose can add up.

Hershey's milk chocolate almond bar, 6 oz	25 mg
Espresso, 1-oz shot	40 mg
Brewed tea, 8-oz cup	50 mg
Coca-Cola, 20-oz bottle	57 mg
Red Bull energy drink, 8.3-oz can	80 mg
Excedrin pain reliever, 2 tablets	130 mg
Brewed coffee, 12-oz cup	200 mg
Mountain Dew, 64-oz Double Big Gulp	294 mg

A coffee taste tester tests the flavor of freshly ground coffee in Varginha, Brazil. Tasters limit their caffeine intake by spitting out most of what they test.

© Benjamin Lowy/Getty Images News/Getty Images

Czeisler, who rarely consumes any caffeine, is a bundle of wide-awake energy in his white lab coat, racing around his lab at Boston's Brigham and Women's Hospital, grabbing journal articles from the shelves and digging through charts to find the key data points. "Caffeine is what's called a wake-promoting therapeutic," he says.

"Caffeine helps people try to wrest control away from the human circadian rhythm that is hardwired in all of us," says Czeisler. But then a shadow crosses the doctor's sunny face, and his tone changes sharply. "On the other hand," he says solemnly, "there is a heavy, heavy price that has been paid for all this extra wakefulness." Without adequate sleep—the conventional eight hours out of each 24 is about right—the human body will not function at its best, physically, mentally, or emotionally, the doctor says. "As a society, we are tremendously sleep deprived."

In fact, the professor goes on, there is a sort of catch-22 at the heart of the modern craving for caffeine. "The principal reason that caffeine is used around the world is to promote wakefulness," Czeisler says. "But the principal reason that people need that crutch is inadequate sleep. Think about that: We use caffeine to make up for a sleep deficit that is largely the result of using caffeine."

Dietrich Mateschitz isn't losing sleep over how much caffeine he consumes. A big, friendly man with a big, friendly smile that beams out from his stubble of white beard, the Austrian marketing whiz describes himself as "comfortable with risk," whether he's climbing a rocky cliff, helicopter skiing, mountain biking an impossibly steep trail in the Alps—or doing business. Mateschitz ought to be comfortable with risk, because the biggest chance he ever took paid off in spectacular fashion, placing a whole new

continued on page 128

Freshly ground organic coffee from a farm near Salento, Colombia, also known as Colombia's "Coffee District".

Workers pick ripe coffee beans in Buon Ma Thuot, Vietnam. The bright red color signals that coffee "cherries" are ripe—ready to pick and spread in the sun to dry so the beans inside can be removed. With more than a million acres of coffee under cultivation, Vietnam ranks among the world's top bean producers.

Workers rake drying coffee cherries into baskets. These beans will be roasted and used to make instant coffee.
© Bloomberg/Getty Images

continued from page 125

product on supermarket shelves, spawning hundreds of competitors, and making himself a billionaire, all within 15 years.

In the 1980s Mateschitz was working for Blendax, a German cosmetics company, marketing skin care products and toothpaste in East Asia. His regular overnight flights from Frankfurt to Tokyo and Beijing inevitably resulted in jet lag, which Mateschitz came to despise. He was a salesman, after all; he needed to be at the peak of energy to do his job right. But the long flights left him drained and worn. He began to notice that taxi drivers in most Asian cities were regularly sipping from small bottles of tonic. After one exhausting flight to Bangkok, he asked the cab driver to share the drink.

Eureka! "Jet lag was gone," he recalls. "Suddenly, I felt so awake." Relating the story nearly two decades later, Mateschitz still remembers the sheer excitement of that moment of discovery. "I found these drinks all over Asia, and there were huge markets for them. I started thinking: Why doesn't the West have this product?"

The West, of course, already had the key ingredient of those Asian mixtures: caffeine. The drink that worked so well for Dietrich Mateschitz, a Thai tonic named Krating Daeng (that is, Red Bull), was a blend of caffeine, an amino acid called taurine, and a carbohydrate, glucuronolactone. The Austrian quit his toothpaste-selling job and invested his life savings in a license to sell Krating Daeng in the West.

After tinkering somewhat with the flavoring and the packaging—and adding carbonation—he launched the beverage in Europe in the late 1980s.

I guess we all have to get our stimulants one way or another.

At first, stores didn't know what to do with an energy drink. There was no such product, and thus no market for it. Mateschitz solved that problem with a brilliant marketing campaign. "You don't drink Red Bull. You use it," the ads proclaimed. "You've got better things to do than sleep." "Red Bull gives you wings."

The idea of giving a soft drink a "function" by adding in hefty doses of a habit-forming drug makes some people more than a little nervous. France and Denmark have banned energy drinks like Red Bull altogether, citing health concerns about the elevated caffeine level, as well as the addition of other supplements. Initially, even cans of Red Bull sold in its home country, Austria, carried the warning *Nicht mit Alkohol mischen*—Don't mix with alcohol.

Alarms were raised in Ireland after an 18-year-old basketball player drank several cans of Red Bull before a game—and then collapsed and died on the court. A coroner's inquest was inconclusive about whether Red Bull had contributed to this sudden death. But the unexplained collapse of an athletic young man prompted the government in Dublin to establish a Stimulant Drinks Committee to study the impact of energy drinks on Ireland's public health.

"The first thing I noticed, when the committee was meeting, was how much coffee they drank," says Martin Higgins, the energetic chief executive of Ireland's food safety promotion board, which supervised the study. "I guess we all have to get our stimulants one way or another." Although the committee looked at all the ingredients of Red Bull and similar products, it concluded that caffeine was the major attraction. "It wasn't so much energy or physical strength that people were buying," Higgins says. "It was that caffeine buzz, particularly in the nightclub setting. And it was the caffeine that prompted the most concern from the committee."

In the end, the Stimulant Drinks Committee found no serious risk from consumption of caffeinated energy drinks—at moderate levels. The group recommended warning labels saying the drinks are unsuitable for children, pregnant women, and people sensitive to caffeine, as well as public health reminders that caffeinated energy drinks should not be consumed for rehydrating purposes during sports or exercise.

Caffeine is still a drug, though, which may explain why it makes people worry. Over the years population studies have shown that people who consume caffeine have higher rates of kidney and bladder cancer, fibrocystic breast disease, pancreatic cancer, and osteoporosis. Yet such findings cannot prove that caffeine caused the disease. All that can be studied are short-term effects.

Like other drugs, caffeine does have a definite impact on mental and physical functions. Repeated studies have shown that caffeine is analeptic (it stimulates the central nervous system) and ergogenic (it improves physical performance). It is also a diuretic, though recent studies show that it is not dehydrating in moderate amounts, even in athletes, as has been widely believed. Caffeinated drinks do increase urine output, but only about the same as water. Caffeine boosts blood pressure, too, but this effect is temporary. And while some studies have shown that caffeine increases calcium loss, any effect is so small that it could be eliminated with as little as two tablespoons of milk a day.

Indeed much of the research suggests that caffeine may have benefits for human health. Studies have shown it can help relieve pain, thwart migraine headaches, reduce asthma symptoms, and elevate mood. As a mental stimulant, it increases alertness, cognition, and reaction speed; because it combats fatigue, it improves performance on vigilance tasks like driving, flying, solving simple math problems, and data entry.

And despite its nearly universal use, caffeine has rarely been abused. "With caffeine, overuse tends to stop itself," says Jack Bergman, a behavioral pharmacologist in the department of psychiatry at Harvard Medical School. "You get jittery and uncomfortable, and you don't want to continue." The point at which an individual reaches that jittery stage varies greatly. Some people seem to be genetically more susceptible to caffeine's effects and may have increased anxiety after consuming even small amounts. In a minority of people, doses of 300 milligrams or more may prompt an increase in tension, anxiety, even panic attacks, which may account for why studies show that nervous people generally have lower caffeine consumption.

After decades of testing, caffeine remains on the FDA's list of food additives "generally recognized as safe." "Looking at all the studies of caffeine, it is very hard to argue that moderate consumption is bad for you," says Bergman. "The behavioral effects are real, but mild. It undoubtedly produces some physical dependence. I get up in the morning and usually have a couple cups of coffee. But when I don't, the withdrawal symptoms aren't severe."

Some caffeine users might argue with Bergman: A day or so without caffeine can cause headaches, irritability, a lack of energy, and, of course, sleepiness. But compared with giving up cocaine or heroin, getting over caffeine is short and easy. Withdrawal symptoms tend to disappear in two to four days, though they can last up to a week or more. Still, the desire to avoid withdrawal pangs may explain why billions of humans so eagerly consume caffeine every day. The person who says, "I'm a monster until that first

Looking at all the studies of caffeine, it is very hard to argue that moderate consumption is bad for you.

cup of coffee in the morning," is describing a mild form of addiction.

In fact, Jack James contends that the widespread physical dependence on caffeine may have skewed research findings, exaggerating caffeine's mood-boosting effects. If scientists compare two groups of subjects—some who have been given caffeine and others who have not—any improvement in mood or performance in the caffeinated group could be simply a relief from withdrawal symptoms. "It may be that we are all on one of those endless cycles," agrees Derk-Jan Dijk, a physiologist at the University of Surrey's sleep research center. "You take caffeine, and you are more alert. Then the next morning, the effect has worn off and you need more of the drug to restore the alertness. But maybe we could step off the cycle. For those of us who work during the day, we might do just as well without caffeine."

On the other hand, that coffee ritual in the morning, maybe with your doughnut, is a normal part of life that we enjoy. It's calming. It helps order the day. And all that can be useful for anybody. Over the centuries humans have created countless rituals to accompany consumption of their favorite drug. Often, the ritual has grown to transcend the beverage. In Japan's austerely elegant *chanoyu,* or tea ceremony, the simple surroundings of the tearoom, the soft rustle of kimono across tatami floor, the spare beauty of a hand-molded brown cup, matter as much as the tea itself.

The British have turned their afternoon ritual into a pageant of pomp and luxury. In the glittering splendor of London's Fortnum & Mason food emporium, afternoon tea is served amid green marble pillars and huge floral sprays, in fine china cups of gold and green. Obsequious waiters serve finger sandwiches, scones with clotted cream, and tropical fruit tarts with the Earl Grey or Lapsang

Deftly poured steamed milk tops a cappuccino.
© librarymook/Flickr/Getty Images

Souchong. A pianist in the center of the room plays "On the Sunny Side of the Street"—just right, because you do indeed feel rich as Rockefeller, at least until the teapot runs dry and the check arrives.

Americans, true to form, have engineered a rather more casual set of caffeinated rituals: a cruller and coffee at the local Dunkin' Donuts, or instant with powdered creamer and Sweet'n Low at the desk. In the past decade or so, however, America's morning rite of caffeine consumption has moved decidedly upscale. A flood of new coffee shops has turned the 75-cent cup of perked joe, refills free, into a six-dollar extravaganza brewed and blended expressly for each customer by a personal barista.

"We have built a whole new ritual of coffee in this country," says Howard Schultz, the man who invented Starbucks. In two decades Schultz turned a single espresso bar in a coffee shop at the corner of Fourth and Spring in Seattle into a Fortune 500 company, building a global icon so familiar that *Playboy* has done a feature on the "Women of Starbucks." A five-cup-a-day coffee drinker himself, the

51-year-old Schultz is a picture of intensity as he prowls his office and recalls how it all began.

Schultz was a coffee bean salesman for a Seattle coffee bean store named Starbucks—after the first mate in Melville's *Moby Dick*—when he visited Milan in 1983 and fell in love with the ambience of that great Italian institution, the espresso bar. "It was about excellent coffee, but it was more than that," he says in passionate tones. "It was about conversation. About community. About human connection. And fine coffee was the link. I thought, You know, we could do this in Seattle."

On a drizzly (what else?) Seattle morning in April 1984, Schultz set up a tiny espresso bar in the rear corner of the coffee bean store, offering mysterious beverages like caffe latte that the likes of Dunkin' Donuts had never dreamed of.

Within days there were long lines on the sidewalk outside, and Howard Schultz never looked back. He soon left the company and opened his own espresso bar, called Il Giornale, or The Daily. Two years later he bought out his former employer, and now there are more than 8,500 Starbucks around the world, with another 1,500 scheduled to open this year.

Schultz doesn't like to emphasize the role caffeine may play in his company's success: "I don't think it's the caffeine. I think the ritual, the romance of the thing, is really more important."

Look, mate, I know it's a drug, but I need that buzz.

But the caffeine is there. A few miles down the interstate from Schultz's office, at the Starbucks roasting plant in Kent, Washington, supervisor Tom Walters knows that firsthand. "I've been asked not to make the connection between coffee and caffeine," Walters says as he strolls past mountains of 70-kilogram burlap sacks holding fresh-picked beans from Colombia, Costa Rica, Nicaragua, Indonesia. "But we see a hell of a lot of caffeine around here. When you roast the beans, the caffeine forms a kind of fuzz on the roaster. So when we're too busy to get a coffee break, some people just run a finger down the casing of the roaster and lick it, and get their jolt that way."

Getting that jolt, of course, is why many of the most popular beverages on Earth—coffee, cola, tea—just happen to contain caffeine. Whether it's a graduate student downing mocha in the lab or a monk sipping green tea while chanting in the temple, mankind's favorite stimulant is at work every day, all over the world.

And every night as well. Back amid the flashing lights and cascading noise of London's Egg, Lee Murphy is dancing now to the driving electronic beat of "Give It What You've Got!" He takes a long swig from one of his two cans of Red Bull. "Look, mate, I know it's a drug," he shouts over the din. "But I need that buzz."

Critical Responses

1. What are positive effects of caffeine according to this article? What are negative ones? Does the author seem to give a balanced picture?

2. "In a sense, caffeine is the drug that made the modern world possible," observes Reid. "And the more modern our world gets, the more we seem to need it." How does he illustrate these interrelated developments? Can you provide further illustrations?

3. While the main focus of the article is on caffeine consumption, what are some critical issues related to the production of caffeinated beverages and foods? Do you think they should have been included?

4. How is the burgeoning of Starbucks and Dunkin' Donuts a response to demand? How does the supply and the variety of caffeinated beverages offer fuel demand? And how do you see this cycle from an economic perspective, a health perspective, and a broader cultural perspective?

Writing Topics

1. "We use caffeine to make up for a sleep deficit that is largely the result of using caffeine," observes one of the researchers interviewed in this article. What factors contribute to this predicament? What possible ways are there to get out of it?

2. Considering how volatile the effect of mixing alcohol and caffeine can be, should the sale and purchase of caffeinated beverages be regulated in some way comparable to that of alcoholic ones?

3. What is the difference between a habit and a ritual? What about a habit and an addiction?

4. How might caffeine addiction and computer addiction complement one another? To what extent might each reinforce or exacerbate the other?

Further Explorations

1. What is your caffeinated beverage of choice, if any? Are you a Starbucks type, a Dunkin' fan, or neither? Write a demographic profile of yourself based on your preferences.

2. Research the "fair trade" movement in coffee, tea, and cocoa. What are the problems this movement seeks to improve? How? Is the movement proving effective?

SEAFOOD CRISIS: TIME FOR A SEA CHANGE

Are world fisheries on the verge of collapse? Can imbalances in the world catch be corrected? Is it possible for the countries that are responsible for the majority of over-fishing to cooperate to address the crisis? What about the countries that consume more fish than others? And what does eating a tuna fish sandwich for lunch have to do with such huge questions? The article below will give some answers, as well as suggest where you yourself fit in the global food chain.

SEAFOOD CRISIS: TIME FOR A SEA CHANGE

By Paul Greenberg

A worker pushes salmon down the butchering
line at a fish cannery in Astoria, Oregon.

JUST BEFORE DAWN A SEAFOOD SUMMIT CONVENES NEAR HONOLULU HARBOR. AS TWO DOZEN OR SO BUYERS ENTER THE UNITED FISHING AGENCY WAREHOUSE, THEY DON WINTER PARKAS OVER THEIR ALOHA SHIRTS TO BLUNT THE CHILL OF THE REFRIGERATION.

THEY FLIP OPEN THEIR CELL PHONES, DIAL THEIR CLIENTS IN TOKYO, LOS ANGELES, HONOLULU— WHEREVER EXPENSIVE FISH ARE EATEN—AND WAIT.

Soon the big freight doors on the seaward side of the warehouse slide open, and a parade of marine carcasses on pallets begins. Tuna as big around as wagon wheels. Spearfish and swordfish, their bills sawed off, their bodies lined up like dull gray I beams. Thick-lipped opah with eyes the size of hockey pucks rimmed with gold. They all take their places in the hall.

Auctioneers drill core samples from the fish and lay the ribbons of flesh on the lifeless white bellies. Buyers finger these samples, trying to divine quality from color, clarity, texture, and fat content. As instructions come in over cell phones, bids are conveyed to the auctioneer through mysterious hand gestures. Little sheets of paper with indecipherable

One by one fish are auctioned and sold to the highest bidder.

scribbling are slapped on a fish's flank when a sale is finalized. One by one fish are auctioned and sold to the highest bidder. In this way the marine wealth of the north-central Pacific is divided up among some of the world's most affluent purchasers.

Every year more than 170 billion pounds (77.9 million metric tons) of wild fish and shellfish are caught in the oceans— roughly three times the weight of every man, woman, and child in the United States. Fisheries managers call this overwhelming

continued on page 140

Adapted from "Seafood Crisis: Time for a Sea Change" by Paul Greenberg: National Geographic Magazine, October 2010.

The Ocean Food Chain

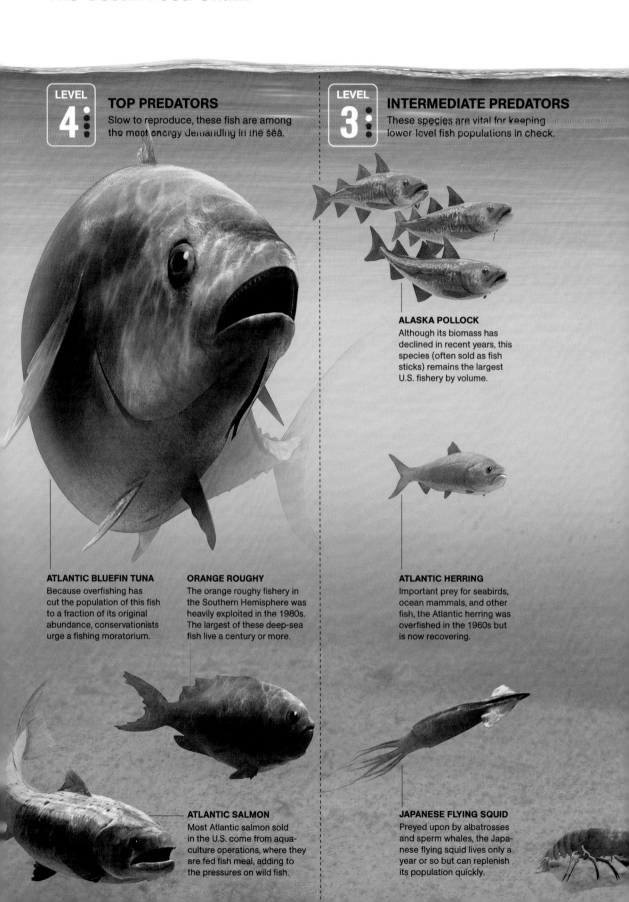

LEVEL 4

TOP PREDATORS
Slow to reproduce, these fish are among the most energy demanding in the sea.

LEVEL 3

INTERMEDIATE PREDATORS
These species are vital for keeping lower-level fish populations in check.

ALASKA POLLOCK
Although its biomass has declined in recent years, this species (often sold as fish sticks) remains the largest U.S. fishery by volume.

ATLANTIC BLUEFIN TUNA
Because overfishing has cut the population of this fish to a fraction of its original abundance, conservationists urge a fishing moratorium.

ORANGE ROUGHY
The orange roughy fishery in the Southern Hemisphere was heavily exploited in the 1980s. The largest of these deep-sea fish live a century or more.

ATLANTIC HERRING
Important prey for seabirds, ocean mammals, and other fish, the Atlantic herring was overfished in the 1960s but is now recovering.

ATLANTIC SALMON
Most Atlantic salmon sold in the U.S. come from aquaculture operations, where they are fed fish meal, adding to the pressures on wild fish.

JAPANESE FLYING SQUID
Preyed upon by albatrosses and sperm whales, the Japanese flying squid lives only a year or so but can replenish its population quickly.

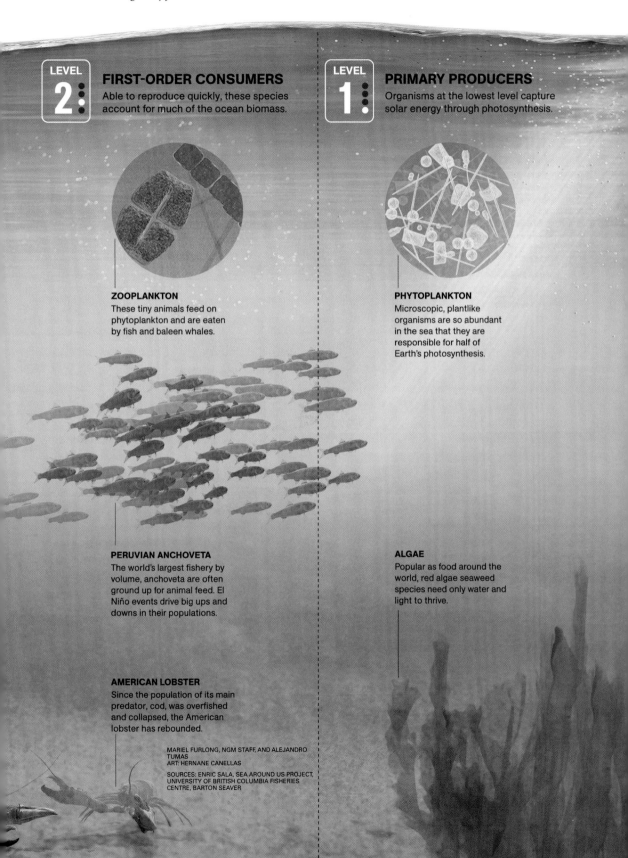

Phytoplankton and algae drive ocean ecosytems. They capture solar energy through photosynthesis and, when eaten by zooplankton, transfer that energy up the food chain. Small fish eat zooplankton and in turn are eaten by big fish, which are targeted by fishermen.

LEVEL 2:

FIRST-ORDER CONSUMERS
Able to reproduce quickly, these species account for much of the ocean biomass.

LEVEL 1:

PRIMARY PRODUCERS
Organisms at the lowest level capture solar energy through photosynthesis.

ZOOPLANKTON
These tiny animals feed on phytoplankton and are eaten by fish and baleen whales.

PHYTOPLANKTON
Microscopic, plantlike organisms are so abundant in the sea that they are responsible for half of Earth's photosynthesis.

PERUVIAN ANCHOVETA
The world's largest fishery by volume, anchoveta are often ground up for animal feed. El Niño events drive big ups and downs in their populations.

ALGAE
Popular as food around the world, red algae seaweed species need only water and light to thrive.

AMERICAN LOBSTER
Since the population of its main predator, cod, was overfished and collapsed, the American lobster has rebounded.

MARIEL FURLONG, NGM STAFF, AND ALEJANDRO TUMAS
ART: HERNANE CANELLAS

SOURCES: ENRIC SALA, SEA AROUND US PROJECT, UNIVERSITY OF BRITISH COLUMBIA FISHERIES CENTRE, BARTON SEAVER

continued from page 137

quantity of mass-hunted wildlife the world catch, and many maintain that this harvest has been relatively stable over the past decade. But an ongoing study conducted by Daniel Pauly, a fisheries scientist at the University of British Columbia, in conjunction with Enric Sala, a National Geographic fellow, suggests that the world catch is neither stable nor fairly divided among the nations of the world. In the study, called SeafoodPrint and supported by the Pew Charitable Trusts and National Geographic, the researchers point the way to what they believe must be done to save the seas.

They hope the study will start by correcting a common misperception. The public imagines a nation's impact on the sea in terms of the raw tonnage of fish it catches. But that turns out to give a skewed picture of its real impact, or seafood print, on marine life. "The problem is, every fish is different," says Pauly. "A pound of tuna represents roughly a hundred times the footprint of a pound of sardines."

The reason for this discrepancy is that tuna are apex predators, meaning that they feed at the very top of the food chain. The largest tuna eat enormous amounts of fish, including intermediate-level predators like mackerel, which in turn feed on fish like anchovies, which prey on microscopic copepods. A large tuna must eat the equivalent of its body weight every ten days to stay alive, so a single thousand-pound tuna might need to eat as many as 15,000 smaller fish in a year. Such food chains are present throughout the world's ocean ecosystems, each with its own apex animal. Any large fish—a Pacific swordfish, an Atlantic mako shark, an Alaska king salmon, a Chilean sea bass—is likely to depend on several levels of a food chain.

To gain an accurate picture of how different nations have been using the resources of the sea, the SeafoodPrint researchers needed a way to compare all types of fish caught. They decided to do this by measuring the amount of "primary production"—those microscopic organisms at the bottom of the marine food web—required to make a pound of a given type of fish. They found that a pound of bluefin tuna, for example, might require a thousand pounds or more of primary production.

In assessing the true impact that nations have on the seas, the team needed to look not just at what a given nation caught but also at what the citizens of that nation ate. "A country can acquire primary production by fishing, or it can acquire it by trade," Pauly says. "It is the sheer power of wealthy nations to acquire primary production that is important."

Nations with money tend to buy a lot of fish, and a lot of the fish they buy are large apex predators like tuna. Japan catches less than five million metric tons of fish a year, a 29 percent drop from 1996 to 2006. But Japan consumes nine million metric tons a year, about 582 million metric tons in primary-production terms. Though the average Chinese consumer generally eats smaller fish than the average Japanese consumer does, China's massive population gives it the world's biggest seafood print, 694 million metric tons of primary production. The U.S., with both a large population and a tendency to eat apex fish, comes in third: 348.5 million metric tons of primary production. And the size of each of these nations' seafood prints is growing. What the study points to, Pauly argues, is that these quantities are not just extremely large but also fundamentally unsustainable.

Exactly how unsustainable can be seen in global analyses of seafood trade compiled by Wilf Swartz, an economist working on Seafood-Print. As the maps show, humanity's consumption of the ocean's primary production changed dramatically from the 1950s to the early 2000s. In the 1950s much less of the ocean was being fished to meet our needs. But as affluent nations increasingly demanded apex predators, they exceeded the primary-production capacities of their exclusive economic zones, which extend up to 200 nautical

> **N**ations with money tend to buy a lot of fish, and a lot of the fish they buy are large apex predators like tuna.

What We Eat Makes a Difference

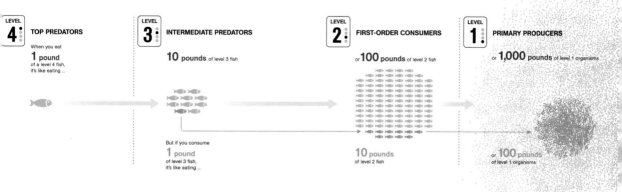

LEVEL 4 — TOP PREDATORS

When you eat **1 pound** of a level 4 fish, it's like eating ...

LEVEL 3 — INTERMEDIATE PREDATORS

10 pounds of level 3 fish

But if you consume **1 pound** of level 3 fish, it's like eating ...

LEVEL 2 — FIRST-ORDER CONSUMERS

or **100 pounds** of level 2 fish

10 pounds of level 2 fish

LEVEL 1 — PRIMARY PRODUCERS

or **1,000 pounds** of level 1 organisms

or **100 pounds** of level 1 organisms

MARIEL FURLONG, NGM STAFF, AND ALEJANDRO TUMAS

SOURCE: SEA AROUND US PROJECT, UNIVERSITY OF BRITISH COLUMBIA FISHERIES CENTRE

A top predator requires exponentially more energy to survive than a fish at a lower level of the food chain. When wealthy nations catch or buy top predators, they increase their impact on the ocean compared with poor nations, which tend to eat smaller fish.

miles from their coasts. As a result, more and more of the world's oceans had to be fished to keep supplies constant or growing.

Areas outside of these zones are known in nautical parlance as the high seas. These vast territories, the last global commons on Earth, are technically owned by nobody and everybody. The catch from high-seas areas has risen to nearly ten times what it was in 1950, from 1.6 million metric tons to around 13 million metric tons. A large part of that catch is high-level, high-value tuna, with its huge seafood print.

The wealthier nations that purchase most of the products of these fisheries are essentially privatizing them. Poorer countries simply cannot afford to bid for high-value species. Citizens in these nations can also lose out if their governments enter into fishing or trade agreements with wealthier nations. In these agreements local fish are sold abroad and denied to local citizens—those who arguably have the greatest need to eat them and the greatest right to claim them.

Although supermarkets in developed nations like the U.S. and Japan still abound with fish flesh, SeafoodPrint suggests that this abundance is largely illusory because it depends on these two troubling phenomena: broader and broader swaths of the high seas transformed from fallow commons into heavily exploited, monopolized fishing grounds;

and poor nations' seafood wealth spirited away by the highest bidder.

Humanity's demand for seafood has now driven fishing fleets into every virgin fishing ground in the world. There are no new grounds left to exploit. But even this isn't enough. An unprecedented buildup of fishing capacity threatens to outstrip seafood supplies in all fishing grounds, old and new. A report by the World Bank and the Food and Agriculture Organization (FAO) of the United Nations recently concluded that the ocean doesn't have nearly enough fish left to support the current onslaught. Indeed, the report suggests that even if we had half as many boats, hooks, and nets as we do now, we would still end up catching too many fish.

Some scientists, looking at the same data, see a different picture than Daniel Pauly does. Ray Hilborn, a fisheries scientist at the University of Washington, doesn't think the situation is so dire. "Daniel is fond of showing a graph that suggests that 60 to 70 percent of the world's fish stocks are overexploited or collapsed," he says. "The FAO's analysis and independent work I have done suggests that the number is more like 30 percent." Increased pressure on seafood shouldn't come as a surprise, he adds, since the goal of the global fishing industry is to fully exploit fish populations, though without damaging their long-term viability.

continued on page 144

Where Fish Are Caught

The opening of new fishing grounds during the past half century has caused a boom in the world catch, as fleets with increased range and capacity have spread out across the open seas. Now the consequences of overfishing are apparent in every ocean.

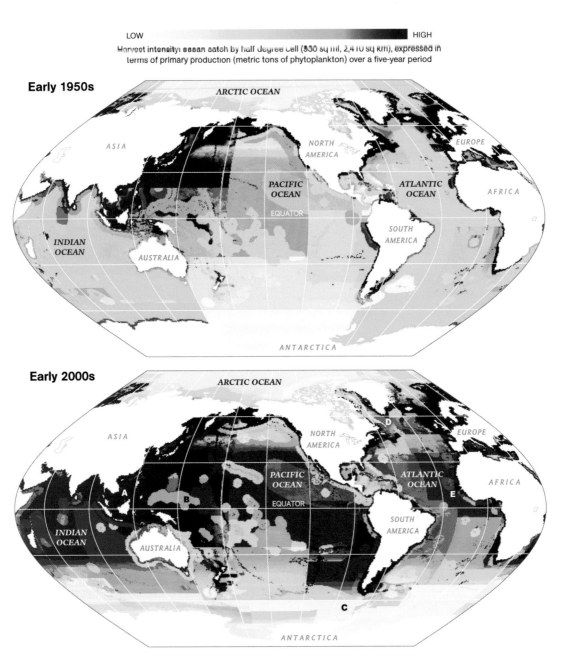

LOW ▬▬▬▬▬▬▬▬▬▬ HIGH

Harvest intensity: ocean catch by half degree cell (930 sq mi, 2,410 sq km), expressed in terms of primary production (metric tons of phytoplankton) over a five-year period

Early 1950s

Early 2000s

HARVESTING PATTERNS

A: Southeast Asia
The popularity of sushi has taken a toll on tuna stocks. Several species are showing signs of decline.

B: Exclusive economic zones Created in 1982, the zones have slowed the growth of fisheries within 200 nautical miles of nations' coasts.

C: Global south
After fleets moved into waters around Antarctica, Chilean sea bass stocks were quickly depleted.

D: North Atlantic
A thousand years of fishing by everyone from Vikings to modern Spaniards has driven cod to near collapse.

E: Eastern Atlantic
European fleets have targeted Africa's coasts. Leaders selling fishing rights may ignore costs to local food supplies.

Who Catches and Who Consumes

Wealthy nations once obtained most of their fish by fishing. Today they're more likely to buy a swordfish than to catch it. Japan purchases more than twice as much fish as it catches, while Peruvians, the number two seafood producers in the world, consume barely any at all.

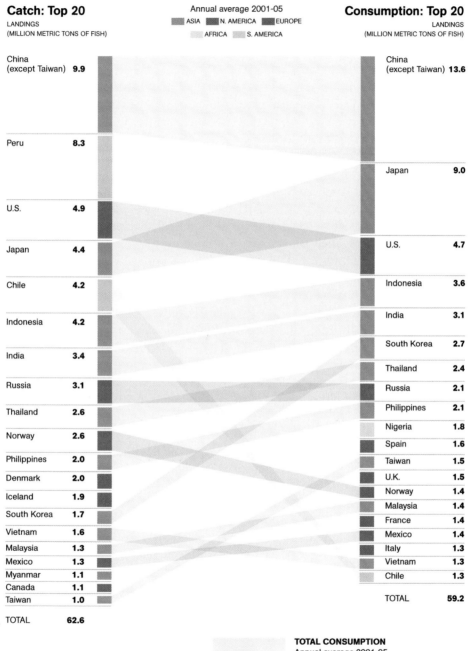

Catch: Top 20
LANDINGS
(MILLION METRIC TONS OF FISH)

Annual average 2001-05
ASIA N. AMERICA EUROPE
AFRICA S. AMERICA

Consumption: Top 20
LANDINGS
(MILLION METRIC TONS OF FISH)

Catch		Consumption	
China (except Taiwan)	9.9	China (except Taiwan)	13.6
Peru	8.3	Japan	9.0
U.S.	4.9	U.S.	4.7
Japan	4.4	Indonesia	3.6
Chile	4.2	India	3.1
Indonesia	4.2	South Korea	2.7
India	3.4	Thailand	2.4
Russia	3.1	Russia	2.1
Thailand	2.6	Philippines	2.1
Norway	2.6	Nigeria	1.8
Philippines	2.0	Spain	1.6
Denmark	2.0	Taiwan	1.5
Iceland	1.9	U.K.	1.5
South Korea	1.7	Norway	1.4
Vietnam	1.6	Malaysia	1.4
Malaysia	1.3	France	1.4
Mexico	1.3	Mexico	1.4
Myanmar	1.1	Italy	1.3
Canada	1.1	Vietnam	1.3
Taiwan	1.0	Chile	1.3
TOTAL	62.6	TOTAL	59.2

Food **67%**

Industrial **33%**

TOTAL CONSUMPTION
Annual average 2001-05

Not all of the fish that are caught are eaten. A third of today's catch is used for industrial purposes, such as the manufacturing of paints and cosmetics or feed for farm-raised salmon, tuna, and even pigs and chickens.

LEFT PAGE, MAPS: MARTIN GAMACHE, NGM STAFF
CHARTS: MARIEL FURLONG, NGM STAFF, AND ALEJANDRO TUMAS
SOURCE: SEA AROUND US PROJECT, UNIVERSITY OF BRITISH COLUMBIA FISHERIES CENTRE

continued from page 141

Many nations, meanwhile, are trying to compensate for the world's growing seafood deficit by farming or ranching high-level predators such as salmon and tuna, which helps maintain the illusion of abundance in the marketplace. But there's a big problem with that approach: Nearly all farmed fish consume meal and oil derived from smaller fish. This is another way that SeafoodPrint might prove useful. If researchers can tabulate the ecological value of wild fish consumed on fish farms, they could eventually show the true impact of aquaculture.

Given such tools, policymakers might be in a better position to establish who is taking what from the sea and whether that is just and sustainable. As a global study, SeafoodPrint makes clear that rich nations have grossly underestimated their impacts. If that doesn't change, the abundance of fish in our markets could drop off quickly. Most likely the wealthy could still enjoy salmon and tuna and swordfish. But middleclass fish-eaters might find their seafood options considerably diminished, if not eliminated altogether.

What then is SeafoodPrint's long-range potential? Could some version of it guide a conservation agreement in which nations are given a global allowance of oceanic primary production and fined or forced to mend their ways if they exceed it?

"That would be nice, wouldn't it?" Pauly says. He points out that we already know several ways to shrink our impact on the seas: reduce the world's fishing fleets by 50 percent, establish large no-catch zones, limit the use of wild fish as feed in fish-farming. Unfortunately, the seafood industry has often blocked the road to reform.

SeafoodPrint could also give consumers a map around that roadblock—a way to plot the course toward healthy, abundant oceans. Today there are dozens of sustainable-seafood campaigns, each of which offers suggestions for eating lower on the marine food chain. These include buying farmed tilapia instead of farmed salmon, because tilapia are largely herbivorous and eat less fish meal when farmed; choosing trap-caught black cod over long-lined Chilean sea bass, because fewer unwanted fish are killed in the process of the harvest; and avoiding eating giant predators like Atlantic bluefin tuna altogether, because their numbers are simply too low to allow any harvest at all.

The problem, say conservationists, is that the oceans have reached a critical point. Simply changing our diets is no longer sufficient if fish are to recover and multiply in the years ahead. What Pauly and other conservation biologists now believe is that suggestions must be transformed into obligations. If treaties can establish seafood-consumption targets for every nation, they argue, citizens could hold their governments responsible for meeting those targets. Comparable strategies have worked to great effect in terrestrial ecosystems, for trade items such as furs or ivory. The ocean deserves a similar effort, they say.

"Barely one percent of the ocean is now protected, compared with 12 percent of the land," Enric Sala adds, "and only a fraction of that is fully protected." That's why National Geographic is partnering with governments, businesses, conservation organizations, and citizens to promote marine reserves and help reduce the impact of fishing around the globe.

In the end, neither Pauly nor Sala nor the rest of the SeafoodPrint team wants to destroy the fishing industry, eliminate aquaculture, or ban fish eating. What they do want to change is business as usual. They want to let people know that today's fishing and fish-farming practices are not sustainable and that the people who advocate maintaining the status quo are failing to consider the ecological and economic ramifications. By accurately measuring the impacts nations have on the sea, SeafoodPrint may lay the groundwork for effective change, making possible the rebuilding of the ocean's dwindling wealth. Such a course, Pauly believes, could give the nations of the world the capability, in the not too distant future, to equitably share a truly bountiful, resurrected ocean, rather than greedily fight over the scraps that remain in the wake of a collapse.

Critical Responses

1. Insofar as numbers and statistics play a significant role in this argument for a "sea change," does the author succeed in making them intelligible? Meaningful? Convincing? How, in other words, does the way that such facts are presented and framed affect an argument?

2. And what is the gist of the argument here? What are the most salient points? What further facts, examples, or explications (or all three) would help to support it?

3. How, according to Greenberg, are the high seas becoming another place where old battles between haves and have not's, rich countries and poor ones, are being played out? What regulations would equalize the playing field? How could they, or should they, be enforced?

4. Would consumer boycotts help to address the current seafood crisis? Why or why not? Would boycotts by certain kinds of consumers be more effective than others? Why and how?

Writing Topics

1. Write an essay that aims to persuade the U.S. seafood industry to support reform of global fishing practices. In the process, consider economic incentives, ecological concerns, and ethical imperatives, and focus on what you think will be most convincing.

2. On the one hand, we've been hearing that a diet that favors fish over meat is a healthier one; on the other, we're reading that overfishing threatens the health of our planet. How can these competing recommendations be placed in reasonable perspectives that can help guide our actions?

3. What role do consumers have in the problems associated with overfishing? What role could consumers play in steps towards solutions? As you consider this question in general, be attuned to differences among consumer groups, and develop your argument accordingly.

4. How have technological advances contributed to the seafood crisis? What does this say about the nature of technological prowess and the connection to ideas of progress?

Further Explorations

1. What goes into a can of tuna fish? What comes out? Taking this article as a starting point, think about all that is involved in producing it, and write an essay detailing what's involved in opening that can.

2. How much fish do you consume on a regular basis and what kind of fish does it tend to be? Using the graphs and measures in this article, determine your "seafood print," individually and as a class. How does the aggregate "seafood print" compare with that of the rest of the country? With that of the rest of the world?

THE END OF PLENTY: THE GLOBAL FOOD CRISIS

By Joel K. Bourne, Jr.

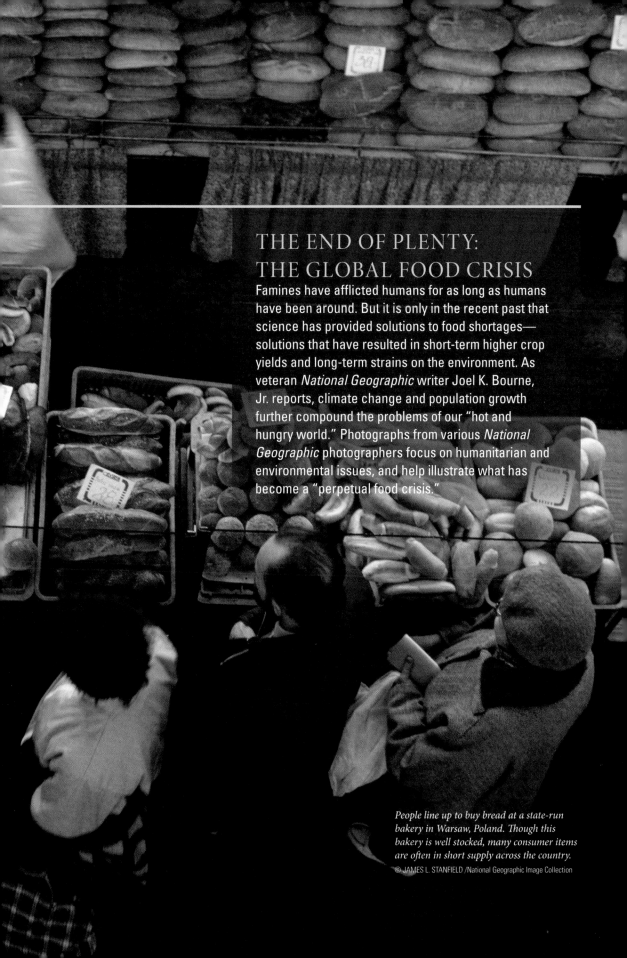

THE END OF PLENTY:
THE GLOBAL FOOD CRISIS

Famines have afflicted humans for as long as humans have been around. But it is only in the recent past that science has provided solutions to food shortages—solutions that have resulted in short-term higher crop yields and long-term strains on the environment. As veteran *National Geographic* writer Joel K. Bourne, Jr. reports, climate change and population growth further compound the problems of our "hot and hungry world." Photographs from various *National Geographic* photographers focus on humanitarian and environmental issues, and help illustrate what has become a "perpetual food crisis."

People line up to buy bread at a state-run bakery in Warsaw, Poland. Though this bakery is well stocked, many consumer items are often in short supply across the country.

© JAMES L. STANFIELD /National Geographic Image Collection

A farmer stands in a muddy marsh in Costa Brava, Spain to cut and tie rice into sheaves. Across the globe, rising demand and flat supplies have rekindled the old debate over whether production can keep up with population.

© 1956 JUSTIN LOCKE/National Geographic Image Collection

WE'VE BEEN
CONSUMING MORE FOOD THAN
FARMERS HAVE BEEN PRODUCING
FOR MOST OF THE PAST DECADE. WHAT WILL IT TAKE
TO GROW MORE?

It is the simplest, most natural of acts, akin to breathing and walking upright. We sit down at the dinner table, pick up a fork, and take a juicy bite, oblivious to the double helping of global ramifications on our plate. Our beef comes from Iowa, fed by Nebraska corn. Our grapes come from Chile, our bananas from Honduras, our olive oil from Sicily, our apple juice—not from Washington State but all the way from China. Modern society has relieved us of the burden of growing, harvesting, even preparing our daily bread, in exchange for the burden of simply paying for it. Only when prices rise do we take notice. And the consequences of our inattention are profound.

Last year the skyrocketing cost of food was a wake-up call for the planet. Between 2005 and the summer of 2008, the price of wheat and corn tripled, and the price of rice climbed five-fold, spurring food riots in nearly two dozen countries and pushing 75 million more people into poverty. But unlike previous shocks driven by short-term food shortages, this price spike came in a year when the world's farmers reaped a record grain crop. This time,

> **Only when prices rise do we take notice. And the consequences of our inattention are profound.**

the high prices were a symptom of a larger problem tugging at the strands of our worldwide food web, one that's not going away anytime soon. Simply put: For most of the past decade, the world has been consuming more food than it has been producing. After years of drawing down stockpiles, in 2007 the world saw global carryover stocks fall to 61 days of global consumption, the second lowest on record.

"Agricultural productivity growth is only one to two percent a year," warned Joachim von Braun, director general of the International Food Policy Research Institute in Washington, D.C., at the height of the crisis. "This is too low to meet population growth and increased demand."

High prices are the ultimate signal that demand is outstripping supply, that there is simply not enough food to go around. Such agflation hits the poorest billion people on the planet the hardest, since they typically spend 50 to 70 percent of their income on food.

Adapted from "The End of Plenty: The Global Food Crisis" by Joel K. Bourne Jr.: National Geographic Magazine, June 2009.

Even though prices have fallen with the imploding world economy, they are still near record highs, and the underlying problems of low stockpiles, rising population, and flattening yield growth remain. Climate change with its hotter growing seasons and increasing water scarcity—is projected to reduce future harvests in much of the world, raising the specter of what some scientists are now calling a perpetual food crisis.

So what is a hot, crowded, and hungry world to do?

That's the question von Braun and his colleagues at the Consultative Group on International Agricultural Research are wrestling with right now. This is the group of world-renowned agricultural research centers that helped more than double the world's average yields of corn, rice, and wheat between the mid-1950s and the mid-1990s, an achievement so staggering it was dubbed the green revolution. Yet with world population spiraling toward nine billion by mid-century, these experts now say we need a repeat performance, doubling current food production by 2030.

In other words, we need another green revolution. And we need it in half the time.

Ever since our ancestors gave up hunting and gathering for plowing and planting some 12,000 years ago, our numbers have marched in lock—step with our agricultural prowess. Each advance—the domestication of animals, irrigation, wet rice production—led to a corresponding jump in human population. Every time food supplies plateaued, population eventually leveled off. Early Arab and Chinese writers noted the relationship between population and food resources, but it wasn't until the end of the 18th century that a British scholar tried to explain the exact mechanism linking the two—and became perhaps the most vilified social scientist in history.

The power of population is indefinitely greater than the power in the earth to produce substance for man.

Thomas Robert Malthus, the namesake of such terms as "Malthusian collapse" and "Malthusian curse," was a mild-mannered mathematician, a clergyman—and, his critics would say, the ultimate glass-half-empty kind of guy. When a few Enlightenment philosophers, giddy from the success of the French Revolution, began predicting the continued unfettered improvement of the human condition, Malthus cut them off at the knees. Human population, he observed, increases at a geometric rate, doubling about every 25 years if unchecked, while agricultural production increases arithmetically—much more slowly. Therein lay a biological trap that humanity could never escape.

"The power of population is indefinitely greater than the power in the earth to produce subsistence for man," he wrote in his *Essay on the Principle of Population* in 1798. "This implies a strong and constantly operating check on population from the difficulty of subsistence." Malthus thought such checks could be voluntary, such as birth control, abstinence, or delayed marriage—or involuntary, through the scourges of war, famine, and disease. He advocated against food relief for all but the poorest of people, since he felt such aid encouraged more children to be born into misery. That tough love earned him a nasty cameo in English literature from none other than Charles Dickens. When Ebenezer Scrooge is asked to give alms for the poor in *A Christmas Carol,* the heartless banker tells the do-gooders that the destitute should head for the workhouses or prisons. And if they'd rather die than go there, "they had better do it, and decrease the surplus population."

The industrial revolution and plowing up of the English commons dramatically increased the amount of food in England, sweeping Malthus into the dustbin of the Victorian era. But it was the green revolution that truly made the reverend the laughingstock of modern economists. From 1950 to today the world has

A farmer harvests corn with his tractor near Bloomington, Illinois. Federal mandates for corn-based ethanol soaked up 30 percent of the 2008 U.S. crop, helping send corn prices over eight dollars a bushel—triple the 2005 price. As long as energy prices remain high, biofuels will compete with food for land and water across the globe.

experienced the largest population growth in human history. After Malthus's time, six billion people were added to the planet's dinner tables. Yet thanks to improved methods of grain production, most of those people were fed. We'd finally shed Malthusian limits for good.

Or so we thought.

At 83, Gurcharan Singh Kalkat has lived long enough to remember one of the worst famines of the 20th century. In 1943 as many as four million people died in the "Malthusian correction" known as the Bengal Famine. For the following two decades, India had to import millions of tons of grain to feed its people.

Then came the green revolution. In the mid-1960s, as India was struggling to feed its people during yet another crippling drought, an American plant breeder named Norman Borlaug was working with Indian researchers to bring his high-yielding wheat varieties to Punjab. The new seeds were a godsend, says Kal-kat, who was deputy director of agriculture for Punjab at the time. By 1970, farmers had nearly tripled their production with the same amount of work. "We had a big problem with what to do with the surplus," says Kalkat. "We closed schools one month early to store the wheat crop in the buildings."

Borlaug was born in Iowa and saw his mission as spreading the high-yield farming methods that had turned the American Midwest into the world's breadbasket to impoverished places throughout the world. His new dwarf wheat varieties, with their short, stocky stems supporting full, fat seed heads, were a startling breakthrough. They could produce grain like no other wheat ever seen—as long as there was plenty of water and synthetic fertilizer and little competition from weeds or insects. To that end, the Indian government subsidized canals, fertilizer, and the drilling of tube wells for irrigation and gave farmers free electricity to pump the water. The new wheat varieties quickly spread throughout Asia, changing the traditional farming practices of millions of farmers, and were soon followed by new strains of "miracle" rice. The new crops matured faster and enabled farmers to grow two crops a year instead of one. Today a double crop of wheat, rice, or cotton is the norm in Punjab, which, with neighboring Haryana, recently supplied more than 90 percent of the wheat needed by grain-deficient states in India.

The green revolution Borlaug started had nothing to do with the eco-friendly green label in vogue today. With its use of synthetic fertilizers and pesticides to nurture vast fields of the same crop, a practice known as monoculture, this new method of industrial farming was the antithesis of today's organic trend. Rather, William S. Gaud, then administrator of the U.S. Agency for International Development, coined the phrase in 1968 to describe an alternative to Russia's red revolution, in which workers, soldiers, and hungry peasants had rebelled violently against the tsarist government. The more pacifying green revolution was such a staggering success that Borlaug won the Nobel Peace Prize in 1970.

Today, though, the miracle of the green revolution is over in Punjab: Yield growth has essentially flattened since the mid-1990s. Overirrigation has led to steep drops in the water table, now tapped by 1.3 million tube wells, while thousands of hectares of productive land have been lost to salinization and waterlogged soils. Forty years of intensive irrigation, fertilization, and pesticides have not been kind to the loamy gray fields of Punjab. Nor, in some cases, to the people themselves.

Researchers have found pesticides in the Punjabi farmers' blood, their water table, their vegetables, even their wives' breast milk. So many people take the train from the Malwa region to the cancer hospital in Bikaner that it's now called the Cancer Express. The government is concerned enough to spend millions on reverse-osmosis water-treatment plants for the worst affected villages.

If that weren't worrisome enough, the high cost of fertilizers and pesticides has plunged many Punjabi farmers into debt. One study found more than 1,400 cases of farmer suicides in 93 villages between 1988 and 2006. Some groups put the total for the state as high as 40,000 to 60,000 suicides over that period. Many drank pesticides or hung themselves in their fields.

"The green revolution has brought us only downfall," says Jarnail Singh, a retired schoolteacher in Jajjal village. "It ruined our soil, our environment, our water table. Used to be we had fairs in villages where people would come together and have fun. Now we gather in medical centers. The government has sacrificed the people of Punjab for grain."

Others, of course, see it differently. Rattan Lal, a noted soil scientist at Ohio State who graduated from Punjab Agricultural University in 1963, believes it was the abuse—not the use—of green revolution technologies that caused most of the problems. That includes the overuse of fertilizers, pesticides, and irrigation and the removal of all crop residues from the fields, essentially strip-mining soil nutrients. "I realize the problems of water quality and water withdrawal," says Lal. "But it saved hundreds of millions of people. We paid a price in water, but the choice was to let people die."

In terms of production, the benefits of the green revolution are hard to deny. India hasn't experienced famine since Borlaug brought his seeds to town, while world grain production has more than doubled. Some scientists credit increased rice yields alone with the existence of 700 million more people on the planet.

Many crop scientists and farmers believe the solution to our current food crisis lies in a second green revolution, based largely on our newfound knowledge of the gene. Plant breeders now know the sequence of nearly all of the 50,000 or so genes in corn and soybean plants and are using that knowledge in ways that were unimaginable only four or five years ago, says Robert Fraley, chief technology officer for the agricultural giant Monsanto. Fraley is convinced that genetic modification, which allows breeders to bolster crops with beneficial traits from other species, will lead to new varie-ties with higher yields, reduced fertilizer needs, and drought tolerance—the holy grail for the past decade. He believes biotech will make it possible to double yields of Monsanto's core crops of corn, cotton, and soybeans by 2030. "We're now poised to see probably the greatest period of fundamental scientific advance in the history of agriculture."

Africa is the continent where *Homo sapiens* was born, and with its worn-out soils, fitful rain, and rising population, it could very well offer a glimpse of our species' future. For numerous reasons—lack of infrastructure, corruption, inaccessible markets—the green revolution never made it here. Agricultural production per capita actually declined in sub-Saharan Africa between 1970 and 2000, while the population soared, leaving an average ten-million-ton annual food deficit. It's now home to more than a quarter of the world's hungriest people.

Tiny, landlocked Malawi, dubbed the "warm heart of Africa" by a hopeful tourism industry, is also in the hungry heart of Africa, a poster child for the continent's agricultural ills. Living in one of the poorest and most densely populated countries in Africa, the majority of Malawians are corn farmers who eke out a living on less than two dollars a day. In 2005 the rains failed once again in Malawi, and more than a third of its population of 13 million required food aid to survive. Malawi's President Bingu wa Mutharika declared he did not get elected to rule a nation of beggars. After initially failing to persuade the World Bank and other donors to help subsidize green revolution inputs, Bingu, as he's known here, decided to spend $58 million from the country's own coffers to get hybrid seeds and fertilizers into the hands of poor farmers. The World Bank eventually got on board and persuaded Bingu

to target the subsidy to the poorest farmers. About 1.3 million farm families received coupons that allowed them to buy three kilograms of hybrid corn seed and two 50-kilogram bags of fertilizer at a third of the market price.

What happened next has been called the Malawi Miracle. Good seed and a little fertilizer—and the return of soil-soaking rains—helped farmers reap bumper crops for the next two years. (Last year's harvests, however, were slightly down.) The 2007 harvest was estimated to be 3.44 million metric tons, a national record. "They went from a 44 percent deficit to an 18 percent surplus, doubling their production," says Pedro Sanchez, the director of the Tropical Agriculture Program at Columbia University who advised the Malawi government on the program. "The next year they had a 53 percent surplus and exported maize to Zimbabwe. It was a dramatic change."

So dramatic, in fact, that it has led to an increasing awareness of the importance of agricultural investment in reducing poverty and hunger in places like Malawi. In October 2007 the World Bank issued a critical report, concluding that the agency, international donors, and African governments had fallen short in helping Africa's poor farmers and had neglected investment in agriculture for the previous 15 years. After decades of discouraging public investment in agriculture and calling for market-based solutions that rarely materialized, institutions like the World Bank have reversed course and pumped funds into agriculture over the past two years.

Malawi's subsidy program is part of a larger movement to bring the green revolution, at long last, to Africa. Since 2006 the Rockefeller Foundation and the Bill and Melinda Gates Foundation have ponied up nearly half a billion dollars to fund the Alliance for a Green Revolution in Africa, focused primarily on bringing plant-breeding programs to African universities and enough fertilizer to farmers' fields. Columbia's Sanchez, along with über-economist and poverty warrior Jeffrey Sachs, is providing concrete examples of the benefits of such investment in 80 small villages clustered into about a dozen "Millennium Villages" scattered in hunger hot spots throughout Africa. With the help of a few rock stars and A-list actors, Sanchez and Sachs are spending $300,000 a year on each small village. That's one-third as much per person as Malawi's per capita GDP, leading many in the development community to wonder if such a program can be sustained over the long haul.

But is a reprise of the green revolution—with the traditional package of synthetic fertilizers, pesticides, and irrigation, supercharged by genetically engineered seeds—really the answer to the world's food crisis? Last year a massive study called the "International Assessment of Agricultural Knowledge, Science and Technology for Development" concluded that the immense production increases brought about by science and technology in the past 30 years have failed to improve food access for many of the world's poor. The six-year study, initiated by the World Bank and the UN's Food and Agriculture Organization and involving some 400 agricultural experts from around the globe, called for a paradigm shift in agriculture toward more sustainable and ecologically friendly practices that would benefit the world's 900 million small farmers, not just agribusiness.

Such a shift has already begun to small, underfunded projects scattered across Africa and Asia. Some call it agroecology, others sustainable agriculture, but the underlying idea is revolutionary: that we must stop focusing on simply maximizing grain yields at any cost and consider the environmental and social impacts of food production. Vandana Shiva is a nuclear physicist turned agroecologist who is India's harshest critic of the green revolution. "I call it monocultures of the mind," she says. "They just look at yields of wheat and rice, but overall the food basket is going down. There were 250 kinds of crops in Punjab before the green revolution." Shiva argues that small-scale, biologically diverse farms can produce more food

We're now poised to see probably the greatest period of fundamental scientific advance in the history of agriculture

with fewer petroleum-based inputs. Her research has shown that using compost instead of natural-gas-derived fertilizer increases organic matter in the soil, sequestering carbon and holding moisture—two key advantages for farmers facing climate change. "If you are talking about solving the food crisis, these are the methods you need," adds Shiva.

In northern Malawi one project is getting many of the same results as the Millennium Villages project, at a fraction of the cost. There are no hybrid corn seeds, free fertilizers, or new roads here in the village of Ekwendeni. Instead the Soils, Food and Healthy Communities (SFHC) project distributes legume seeds, recipes, and technical advice for growing nutritious crops like peanuts, pigeon peas, and soybeans, which enrich the soil by fixing nitrogen while also enriching children's diets. The program began in 2000 at Ekwendeni Hospital, where the staff was seeing high rates of malnutrition. Research suggested the culprit was the corn monoculture that had left small farmers with poor yields due to depleted soils and the high price of fertilizer.

The project's old pickup needs a push to get it going, but soon Boyd Zimba, the project's assistant coordinator, and Zacharia Nkhonya, its food-security supervisor, are rattling down the road, talking about what they see as the downside of the Malawi Miracle. "First, the fertilizer subsidy cannot last long," says Nkhonya, a compact man with a quick smile. "Second, it doesn't go to everyone. And third, it only comes once a year, while legumes are long-term—soils get improved every year, unlike with fertilizers."

At the small village of Encongolweni, a group of two dozen SFHC farmers greet us with a song about the dishes they make from soybeans and pigeon peas. We sit in their meetinghouse as if at an old-time tent revival, as they testify about how planting legumes has changed their lives. Ackim Mhone's story is typical. By

A farmer works in a barley field near an irrigation ditch. Increasing yields on existing farmland requires irrigation, yet new sources of fresh water can be as scarce as fertile land.

incorporating legumes into his rotation, he's doubled his corn yield on his small plot of land while cutting his fertilizer use in half. "That was enough to change the life of my family," Mhone says, and to enable him to improve his house and buy livestock. Later, Alice Sumphi, a 67-year-old farmer with a mischievous smile, dances in her plot of young knee-high tomatoes, proudly pointing out that they bested those of the younger men. Canadian researchers found that after eight years, the children of more than 7,000 families involved in the project showed significant weight increases, making a pretty good case that soil health and community health are connected in Malawi.

Which is why the project's research coordinator, Rachel Bezner Kerr, is alarmed that big-money foundations are pushing for a new green revolution in Africa. "I find it deeply disturbing," she says. "It's getting farmers to rely on expensive inputs produced from afar that are making money for big companies rather than on agroecological methods for using local resources and skills. I don't think that's the solution."

Regardless of which model prevails—agriculture as a diverse ecological art, as a high-tech industry, or some combination of the two—the challenge of putting enough food in nine billion mouths by 2050 is daunting. Two billion people already live in the driest parts of the globe, and climate change is projected to slash yields in these regions even further. No matter how great their yield

continued on page 158

continued from page 155

potential, plants still need water to grow. And in the not too distant future, every year could be a drought year for much of the globe.

New climate studies show that extreme heat waves, such as the one that withered crops and killed thousands in western Europe in 2003, are very likely to become common in the tropics and subtropics by century's end. Himalayan glaciers that now provide water for hundreds of millions of people, livestock, and farmland in China and India are melting faster and could vanish completely by 2035. In the worst-case scenario, yields for some grains could decline by 10 to 15 percent in South Asia by 2030. Projections for southern Africa are even more dire. In a region already racked by water scarcity and food insecurity, the all-important corn harvest could drop by 30 percent—47 percent in the worst-case scenario. All the while the population clock keeps ticking, with a net of 2.5 more mouths to feed born every second. That amounts to 4,500 more mouths in the time it takes you to read this article.

Which leads us, inevitably, back to Malthus.

On a brisk fall day that has put color into the cheeks of the most die-hard Londoners, I visit the British Library and check out the first edition of the book that still generates such heated debate. Malthus's *Essay on the Principle of Population* looks like an eighth-grade science primer. From its strong, clear prose comes the voice of a humble parish priest who hoped, as much as anything, to be proved wrong.

"People who say Malthus is wrong usually haven't read him," says Tim Dyson, a professor of population studies at the London School of Economics. "He was not taking a view any different than what Adam Smith took in the first volume of *The Wealth of Nations*. No one in their right mind doubts the idea that populations have to live within their resource base. And that the capacity of society to increase resources from that base is ultimately limited."

Though his essays emphasized "positive checks" on population from famine, disease, and war, his "preventative checks" may have been more important. A growing workforce, Malthus explained, depresses wages, which tends to make people delay marriage until they can better support a family. Delaying marriage reduces fertility rates, creating an equally powerful check on populations. It has now been shown that this is the basic mechanism that regulated population growth in western Europe for some 300 years before the industrial revolution—a pretty good record for *any* social scientist, says Dyson.

Yet when Britain recently issued a new 20-pound note, it put Adam Smith on the back, not T. R. Malthus. He doesn't fit the ethos of the moment. We don't want to think about limits. But as we approach nine billion people on the planet, all clamoring for the same opportunities, the same lifestyles, the same hamburgers, we ignore them at our risk.

None of the great classical economists saw the industrial revolution coming, or the transformation of economies and agriculture that it would bring about. The cheap, readily available energy contained in coal—and later in other fossil fuels—unleashed the greatest increase in food, personal wealth, and people the world has ever seen, enabling Earth's population to increase sevenfold since Malthus's day. And yet hunger, famine, and malnutrition are with us still, just as Malthus said they would be.

"Years ago I was working with a Chinese demographer," Dyson says. "One day he pointed out to me the two Chinese characters above his office door that spelled the word 'population.' You had the character for a person and the character for an open mouth. It really struck me. Ultimately there has to be a balance between population and resources. And this notion that we can continue to grow forever, well it's ridiculous."

Perhaps somewhere deep in his crypt in Bath Abbey, Malthus is quietly wagging a bony finger and saying, "Told you so."

Critical Responses

1. What is the gist of Thomas Malthus's argument about population and resources? Why have his views been ridiculed? What makes them reasonable? In what ways might they be accurate today?

2. What do high food prices indicate about supply and demand? Are prices always or necessarily an accurate index of quality of harvests? What do escalating food prices in grocery stores in well-off developed countries have to do with food production and consumption in poorer, under-developed ones?

3. What are the most important features and effects of the "green revolutions" described here? How is each one related to the other? How is each one distinct? Does the sequence represent a "progress"?

4. What is "agroecology," and what makes it so radical? What are the benefits of this approach? What negative impacts might it have? How does it compare to earlier "green revolutions"?

Writing Topics

1. From the point of view of strict dictionary definitions, what makes the phrase "perpetual crisis" a contradiction in terms? From the point of view of recent world history, what makes it an accurate description, nonetheless?

2. How are modern science and technology furthering progress in food production? How do they also contribute to the problems they intend to solve?

3. Continuing with this idea, consider whether and to what extent traditional and "low-tech" agricultural methods can help alleviate hunger. What does this suggest about how we might rethink ideas of what constitutes progress?

4. How is climate change affecting agriculture—and vice versa? When it comes to alleviating food shortages, where should reforms begin and what should they be?

Further Explorations

1. Insofar as small actions each of us take can have cumulative and far-reaching consequences, what can you do to contribute to alleviating hunger in some distant part of the globe?

2. If you were faced with a starving population, and if you knew of a short-term solution that could have negative consequences in the long run, what would you do? After formulating a brief response, debate the issue in class, and then write a paper reflecting your position.

OUR GOOD EARTH: SOIL

By Charles C. Mann

Photographs by Jim Richardson

OUR GOOD EARTH: SOIL

"The history of every nation is eventually written in the way in which it cares for its soil," observed Franklin Delano Roosevelt. The same might be said of the entire world today, as forces of globalization create greater interdependence between nations that are dirt poor and those that are rich. And with only 11 percent of the earth's land surface being in cultivation, and only three percent of that land being naturally fertile, an ever-growing world population has to make do with less, even as it needs more. As award-winning science writer Charles C. Mann follows these developments, he also suggests why we all need to care about soil in order to take care of ourselves.

A late-summer patchwork of trees, mowed hay fields, and standing corn follows the contours of Wisconsin's Coon Creek watershed. Once ravaged by erosion, its farms and streams became a national showcase for soil conservation strategies in 1933.

Staple food for half the people on Earth, rice has grown in paddies like this one in China's Yunnan Province for centuries. Within paddy walls standing water shields soil from drying and erosion. Protecting and improving soils becomes more crucial as world food needs grow.

RESTS ON THE SOIL BENEATH OUR FEET.

CAN WE SAVE IT?

On a warm September day, farmers from all over the state gather around the enormous machines. Combines, balers, rippers, cultivators, diskers, tractors of every variety—all can be found at the annual Wisconsin Farm Technology Days show. But the stars of the show are the great harvesters, looming over the crowd. They have names like hot rods—the Claas Jaguar 970, the Krone BiG X 1000—and are painted with colors bright as fireworks. The machines weigh 15 tons apiece and have tires tall as a tall man. When I visited Wisconsin Farm Technology Days last year, John Deere was letting visitors test its 8530 tractor, an electromechanical marvel so sophisticated that I had no idea how to operate it. Not to worry: The tractor drove itself, navigating by satellite. I sat high and happy in the air-conditioned bridge, while beneath my feet vast wheels rolled over the earth.

The farmers grin as they watch the machines thunder through the cornfields. In the long run, though, they may be destroying their livelihoods. Midwestern topsoil, some of the finest cropland in the world, is made up of loose, heterogeneous clumps with plenty of

> The farmers grin as they watch the machines thunder through the cornfields.

air pockets between them. Big, heavy machines like the harvesters mash wet soil into an undifferentiated, nigh impenetrable slab—a process called compaction. Roots can't penetrate compacted ground; water can't drain into the earth and instead runs off, causing erosion. And because compaction can occur deep in the ground, it can take decades to reverse. Farm-equipment companies, aware of the problem, put huge tires on their machines to spread out the impact. And farmers are using satellite navigation to confine vehicles to specific paths, leaving the rest of the soil untouched. Nonetheless, this kind of compaction remains a serious issue—at least in nations where farmers can afford $400,000 harvesters.

Unfortunately, compaction is just one, relatively small piece in a mosaic of interrelated problems afflicting soils all over the planet. In the developing world, far more arable land is being lost to human-induced erosion and desertification, directly

continued on page 166

Adapted from "Our Good Earth: Soil" by Charles C. Mann: National Geographic Magazine, September 2008.

Trailing puffs of silt, a cultivator prepares a Washington State field for planting. The Palouse Hills are "wheat country," says soil scientist John Reganold. Here large-scale intensive agriculture rules—and productivity depends on chemical pesticides and fertilizers.

continued from page 163

affecting the lives of 250 million people. In the first—and still the most comprehensive—study of global soil misuse, scientists at the International Soil Reference and Information Centre (ISRIC) in the Netherlands estimated in 1991 that humankind has degraded more than 7.5 million square miles of land. Our species, in other words, is rapidly trashing an area the size of the United States and Canada combined.

Journalists sometimes describe unsexy subjects as MEGO: My eyes glaze over. Alas, soil degradation is the essence of MEGO. Nonetheless, the stakes—and the opportunities—could hardly be higher, says Rattan Lal, a prominent soil scientist at Ohio State University. Researchers and ordinary farmers around the world are finding that even devastated soils can be restored. The payoff, Lal says, is the chance not only to fight hunger but also to attack problems like water scarcity and even global warming. Indeed, some researchers believe that global warming can be slowed significantly by using vast stores of carbon to reengineer the world's bad soils. "Political stability, environmental quality, hunger, and poverty all have the same root," Lal says. "In the long run, the solution to each is restoring the most basic of all resources, the soil."

When I met Zhang Liubao in his village in central China last fall, he was whacking the eroded terraces of his farm into shape with a shovel—something he'd been doing after every rain for more than 40 years. In the 1960s, Zhang had been sent to the village of Dazhai, 200 miles to the east, to learn the Dazhai Way—an agricultural system China's leaders believed would transform the nation. In Dazhai, Zhang told me proudly, "China learned everything about how to work the land." Which is true, but not, alas, in the way Zhang intended.

Dazhai is in a geological anomaly called the Loess Plateau. For eon upon eon winds have swept across the deserts to the west, blowing grit and sand into central China. The millennia of dust fall have covered the region with vast heaps of packed silt—loess, geologists call it—some of them hundreds of feet deep. China's Loess Plateau is about the size of France, Belgium, and the Netherlands combined. For centuries the silt piles have been washing away into the Yellow River—a natural process that has exacerbated, thanks to the Dazhai Way, into arguably the worst soil erosion problem in the world.

After floods ravaged Dazhai in 1963, the village's Communist Party secretary refused any aid from the state, instead promising to create a newer, more productive village. Harvests soared, and Beijing sent observers to learn how to replicate Dazhai's methods. What they saw was spade-wielding peasants terracing the loess hills from top to bottom, devoting their rest breaks to reading Mao Zedong's little red book of revolutionary proverbs. Delighted by their fervor, Mao bused thousands of village representatives to the settlement, Zhang among them. The atmosphere was cultlike; one group walked for two weeks just to view the calluses on a Dazhai laborer's hands. Mainly Zhang learned there that China needed him to produce grain from every scrap of land. Slogans, ever present in Maoist China, explained how to do it: Move Hills, Fill Gullies, and Create Plains! Destroy Forests, Open Wastelands! In Agriculture, Learn From Dazhai!

Zhang Liubao returned from Dazhai to his home village of Zuitou full of inspiration. Zuitou was so impoverished, he told me, that people ate just one or two good meals a year. Following Zhang's instructions, villagers fanned out, cutting the scrubby trees on the hillsides, slicing the slopes into earthen terraces, and planting millet on every newly created flat surface. Despite constant hunger, people worked all day and then lit lanterns and worked at night. Ultimately, Zhang said, they increased Zuitou's farmland by "about a fifth"—a lot in a poor place.

Alas, the actual effect was to create a vicious circle, according to Vaclav Smil, a University of Manitoba geographer who has long studied China's environment. Zuitou's terrace walls, made of nothing but packed silt, continually fell apart; hence Zhang's need to constantly shore up collapsing terraces. Even when the terraces didn't erode, rains sluiced away the nutrients and organic matter in the soil. After the initial rise, harvests started dropping. To maintain yields, farmers cleared and terraced new land, which washed away in turn.

The consequences were dire. Declining harvests on worsening soil forced huge numbers of farmers to become migrants. Partly for this reason, Zuitou lost half of its population. "It must be one of the greatest wastes of human labor in history," Smil says. "Tens of millions of people forced to work night and day on projects that a child could have seen were a terrible stupidity. Cutting down trees and planting grain on steep slopes—how could that be a good idea?"

Gaoxigou (Gaoxi Gully) is west of Dazhai, on the other side of the Yellow River. Its 522 inhabitants live in *yaodong*—caves dug like martin nests into the sharp pitches around the village. Beginning in 1953, farmers marched out from Gaoxigou and with heroic effort terraced not mere hillsides but entire mountains, slicing them one after another into hundred-tier wedding cakes iced with fields of millet and sorghum and corn. In a pattern that would become all too familiar, yields went up until sun and rain baked and blasted the soil in the bare terraces. To catch eroding loess, the village built earthen dams across gullies, intending to create new fields as they filled up with silt. But with little vegetation to slow the water, "every rainy season the dams busted," says Fu Mingxing, the regional head of education. Ultimately, he says, villagers realized that "they had to protect the ecosystem, which means the soil."

Today many of the terraces Gaoxigou laboriously hacked out of the loess are reverting to nature. In what locals call the "three-three" system, farmers replanted one-third of their

Even as humankind is ratchetting up its demands on soil, we are destroying it faster than ever before.

land—the steepest, most erosion-prone slopes—with grass and trees, natural barriers to erosion. They covered another third of the land with harvestable orchards. The final third, mainly plots on the gully floor that have been enriched by earlier erosion, was cropped intensively. By concentrating their limited supplies of fertilizer on that land, farmers were able to raise yields enough to make up for the land they sacrificed, says Jiang Liangbiao, village head of Gaoxigou.

In 1999 Beijing announced it would deploy a Gaoxigou Way across the Loess Plateau. The Sloping Land Conversion Program—known as "grain-for-green"—directs farmers to convert most of their steep fields back to grassland, orchard, or forest, compensating them with an annual delivery of grain and a small cash payment for up to eight years. By 2010 grain-for-green could cover more than 82,000 square miles, much of it on the Loess Plateau.

But the grand schemes proclaimed in faraway Beijing are hard to translate to places like Zuitou. Provincial, county, and village officials are rewarded if they plant the number of trees envisioned in the plan, regardless of whether they have chosen tree species suited to local conditions (or listened to scientists who say that trees are not appropriate for grasslands to begin with). Farmers who reap no benefit from their work have little incentive to take care of the trees they are forced to plant. I saw the entirely predictable result on the back roads two hours north of Gaoxigou: fields of dead trees, planted in small pits shaped like fish scales, lined the roads for miles. "Every year we plant trees," the farmers say, "but no trees survive."

Sometime in the 1970S, "Sahel" became a watchword for famine, poverty, and environmental waste. Technically, though, the name refers to the semiarid zone between the Sahara desert and the wet forests of central Africa. Until the 1950s the Sahel was thinly

continued on page 170

In the Amazon, excavations reveal fertile terra preta deposits, which archaeologist Eduardo Góes Neves (above, in blue) believes ancient people created by mixing charcoal from their fires with food and other wastes. Their low-tech strategy could offer farmers in the developing world a low-cost way to improve poor soils.

continued from page 167

settled. But when a population boom began, people started farming the region more intensively. Problems were masked for a long time by an unusual period of high rainfall. But then came drought. The worst effects came in two waves—one in the early 1970s and a second, even more serious, in the early 1980s—and stretched from Mauritania on the Atlantic to Chad, halfway across Africa. More than 100,000 men, women, and children died in the ensuing famine, probably many more.

"If people had the means to leave, they left," says Mathieu Ouédraogo, a development specialist in Burkina Faso, a landlocked nation in the heart of the Sahel. "The only people who stayed here had nothing—not enough to leave."

Scientists still dispute why the Sahel transformed itself from a savanna into a badland. Suggested causes include random changes in sea-surface temperatures, air pollution that causes clouds to form inopportunely, removal of surface vegetation by farmers moving into the desert periphery—and, of course, global warming. Whatever the cause, the consequences are obvious: Hammered by hot days and harsh winds, much of the soil turns into a stone-hard mass that plant roots and rainwater cannot penetrate, A Sahelian farmer once let me hack at his millet field with a pick. It was like trying to chop up asphalt.

When the drought struck, international aid groups descended on the Sahel by the score. (Ouédraogo, for instance, directed a project for Oxfam in the part of Burkina where he had been born and raised.) Many are still there now; half the signs in Niamey, capital of neighboring Niger, seem to be announcing a new program from the United Nations, a Western government, or a private charity. Among the biggest is the Keita project, established 24 years ago by the Italian government in mountainous central Niger. Its goal: bringing 1,876 square miles of broken, barren earth—now home to 230,000 souls—to ecological, economic, and social health. Italian agronomists and engineers cut

It must be one of the greatest wastes of human labor in history.

194 miles of road through the slopes, dug 684 wells in the stony land, constructed 52 village schools, and planted more than 18 million trees. With bulldozers and tractors, workers carved 41 dams into the hills to catch water from the summer rains. To cut holes in the ground for tree planting, an Italian named Venanzio Vallerani designed and built two huge plows—"monstrous" was the descriptor used by Amadou Haya, an environmental specialist with the project. Workers hauled the machines to the bare hills, filled their bellies full of fuel, and set them to work. Roaring across the plateaus for months on end, they cut as many as 1,500 holes an hour.

Early one morning Haya took us to a rainwater-storage dam outside the village of Koutki, about 20 minutes down a rutted dirt road from Keita project headquarters. The water, spreading oasis-like over several acres, was almost absurdly calm; birds were noisily in evidence. Women waded into the water to fill plastic jerry cans, their brilliant robes floating around their ankles. Twenty-five years ago Koutki was a bit player in the tragedy of the Sahel. Most of its animals had died or been eaten. There was not a scrap of green in sight. No birds sang. People survived on mouthfuls of rice from foreign charities. On the road to Koutki we met a former soldier who had helped distribute the aid. His face froze when he spoke about the starving children he had seen. Today there are barricades of trees to stop the winds, low terraces for planting trees, and lines of stone to interrupt the eroding flow of rainwater. The soil around the dam is still dry and poor, but one can imagine people making a living from it.

Budgeted at more than $100 million, however, the Keita project is expensive—Niger's per capita income, low even for the Sahel, is less than $800 a year. Keita boosters can argue that it costs two-thirds of an F-22 fighter jet. But the Sahel is vast—Niger alone is a thousand miles across. Reclaiming even part of this area would require huge sums if done by Keita methods. In consequence, critics have argued that soil-restoration efforts in the drylands are almost pointless: best turn to more promising ground.

Wrong, says Chris Reij, a geographer at VU (Free University) Amsterdam. Having worked with Sahelian colleagues for more than 30 years, Reij has come to believe that farmers themselves have beaten back the desert in vast areas. "It is one of Africa's greatest ecological success stories," he says, "a model for the rest of the world." But almost nobody outside has paid attention; if soil is MEGO, soil in Africa is MEGO squared.

In Burkina, Mathieu Ouédraogo was there from the beginning. He assembled the farmers in his area, and by 1981 they were experimenting together with techniques to restore the soil, some of them traditions that Ouédraogo had heard about in school. One of them was *cordons pier-reux*: long lines of stones, each perhaps the size of a big fist. Snagged by the cordon, rains washing over crusty Sahelian soil pause long enough to percolate. Suspended silt falls to the bottom, along with seeds that sprout in this slightly richer environment. The line of stones becomes a line of plants that slows the water further. More seeds sprout at the upstream edge. Grasses are replaced by shrubs and trees, which enrich the soil with falling leaves. In a few years a simple line of rocks can restore an entire field.

For a time Ouédraogo worked with a farmer named Yacouba Sawadogo. Innovative and independent-minded, he wanted to stay on his farm with his three wives and 31 children. "From my grandfather's grandfather's grandfather, we were always here," he says. Sawadogo, too, laid cordons pierreux across his fields. But during the dry season he also hacked thousands of foot-deep holes in his fields—*zaï*, as they are called, a technique he had heard about from his parents. Sawadogo salted each pit with manure, which attracted termites. The termites digested the organic matter, making its nutrients more readily available to plants. Equally important, the insects dug channels in the soil. When the rains came, water trickled through the termite holes into the ground. In each hole Sawadogo planted trees. "Without trees, no soil," he says. The trees thrived in the looser, wetter soil in each zaï. Stone by stone, hole by hole, Sawadogo turned 50 acres of wasteland into the biggest private forest for hundreds of miles.

Using the zaï, Sawadogo says, he became almost "the only farmer from here to Mali who had any millet." His neighbors, not surprisingly, noticed. Sawadogo formed a zaï association, which promotes the technique at an annual show in his family compound. Hundreds of farmers have come to watch him hack out zaï with his hoe. The new techniques, simple and inexpensive, spread far and wide. The more people worked the soil, the richer it became. Higher rainfall was responsible for part of the regrowth (though it never returned to the level of the 1950s). But mostly it was due to millions of men and women intensively working the land.

Wim sombroek learned about soil as a child, during the *hongerwinter*—the Dutch wartime famine of 1944-45, in which 20,000 or more people died. His family survived on the harvest from a minute plot of *plaggen* soil: land enriched by generations of careful fertilization. If his ancestors hadn't taken care of their land, he once told me, the whole family might have died.

In the 1950s, early in his career as a soil scientist, Sombroek journeyed to Amazonia. To his amazement, he found pockets of rich, fertile soil. Every Ecology 101 student knows that Amazonian rain forest soils are fragile and impoverished. If farmers cut down the canopy of trees overhead to clear cropland, they expose the earth to the pummeling rain and sun, which quickly wash away its small store of minerals and nutrients and bake what remains into something resembling brick—a "wet desert," as these ruined areas are sometimes called. The certainty of wrecking the land, environmentalists argue, makes large-scale agriculture impossible in the tropics. Nevertheless, scattered along the Amazon River, Sombroek discovered big patches of *terra preta do indio* (black Indian earth). As lush and dark as the plaggen of his childhood, it formed a rich base for agriculture in a land

continued on page 174

Tiny earthworks stipple bare slopes in China's Zizhou County, each intended to cradle a single sapling. Government-mandated reforestation programs are intended to halt erosion, but many earlier efforts here in the Loess Plateau failed when newly planted trees died.

continued from page 171

where it was not supposed to exist. Naturally, Sombroek paid attention. His 1966 book, *Amazon Soils*, included the first sustained study of terra preta.

Later Sombroek worked across the globe, eventually becoming director of ISRIC and secretary general of the International Society of Soil Science (now International Union of Soil Sciences), positions he used to convene the first ever world survey of human-induced soil degradation. All the while he never forgot the strange black earth in Brazil. Most restoration programs, like those in China and the Sahel, try to restore degraded soil to its previous condition. But in much of the tropics, its natural state is marginal—one reason so many tropical countries are poor. Sombroek came to believe that terra preta might show scientists how to make land richer than it ever had been, and thus help the world's most impoverished nations feed themselves.

Sombroek will never see his dream fulfilled—he died in 2003. But he helped to assemble a multinational research collaboration to investigate the origin and function of terra preta. Among its members is Eduardo Góes Neves, a University of São Paulo archaeologist whom I visited not long ago at a papaya plantation about a thousand miles up the Amazon, across the river from the city of Manaus. Beneath the trees was the unmistakable spoor of archaeological investigation: precisely squared off trenches, some of them seven feet deep. In the pits the terra preta, blacker than the blackest coffee, extended from the surface down as much as six feet. Top to bottom, the soil was filled with broken pre-Columbian pottery. It was as if the river's first inhabitants had thrown a huge, rowdy frat party, smashing every plate in sight, then buried the evidence.

Terra preta is found only where people lived, which means that it is an artificial, human-made soil, dating from before the arrival of Europeans. Neves and his colleagues have been

We have degraded an area of land the size of the United States and Canada combined.

trying to find out how the Amazon's peoples made it, and why. The soil is rich in vital minerals such as phosphorus, calcium, zinc, and manganese, which are scarce in most tropical soils. But its most striking ingredient is charcoal—vast quantities of it, the source of terra preta's color. Neves isn't sure whether Indians had stirred the charcoal into the soil deliberately, if they had done it accidentally while disposing of household trash, or even if the terra preta created by charcoal initially had been used for farming. Ultimately, though, it became a resource that could sustain entire settlements; indeed, Neves said, a thousand years ago two Indian groups may have gone to war over control of this terra preta.

Sombroek had wondered if modern farmers might create their own terra preta—*terra preta nova*, as he dubbed it. Much as the green revolution dramatically improved the developing world's crops, terra preta could unleash what the scientific journal *Nature* has called a "black revolution" across the broad arc of impoverished soil from Southeast Asia to Africa.

Key to terra preta is charcoal, made by burning plants and refuse at low temperatures. In March a research team led by Christoph Steiner, then of the University of Bayreuth, reported that simply adding crumbled charcoal and condensed smoke to typically bad tropical soils caused an "exponential increase" in the microbial population—kick-starting the underground ecosystem that is critical to fertility. Tropical soils quickly lose microbial richness when converted to agriculture. Charcoal seems to provide habitat for microbes—making a kind of artificial soil within the soil—partly because nutrients bind to the charcoal rather than being washed away. Tests by a U.S.-Brazilian team in 2006 found that terra preta had a far greater number and variety of microorganisms than typical tropical soils—it was literally more alive.

continued on page 176

After losing a foot of soil from parts of their Iowa corn farm, the Reed family changed the way they prepare fields for planting, to limit erosion. Cletus Reed, 80, hopes his grandson, Sam, will work these acres someday. "The land takes care of us as we care for it," he says.

continued from page 174

A black revolution might even help combat global warming. Agriculture accounts for more than one-eighth of humankind's production of greenhouse gases. Heavily plowed soil releases carbon dioxide as it exposes once buried organic matter. Sombroek argued that creating terra preta around the world would use so much carbon-rich charcoal that it could more than offset the release of soil carbon into the atmosphere. According to William I. Woods, a geographer and soil scientist at the University of Kansas, charcoal-rich terra preta has 10 or 20 times more carbon than typical tropical soils, and the carbon can be buried much deeper down. Rough calculations show that "the amount of carbon we can put into the soil is staggering," Woods says. Last year Cornell University soil scientist Johannes Lehmann estimated in *Nature* that simply converting residues from commercial forestry, fallow farm fields, and annual crops to charcoal could compensate for about a third of U.S. fossil-fuel emissions. Indeed, Lehmann and two colleagues have argued that humankind's use of fossil fuels worldwide could be wholly offset by storing carbon in terra preta nova.

Such hopes will not be easy to fulfill. Identifying the organisms associated with terra preta will be difficult. And nobody knows for sure how much carbon can be stored in soil—some studies suggest there may be a finite limit. But Woods believes that the odds of a payoff are good. "The world is going to hear a lot more about terra preta," he says.

Walking the roads on the farm hosting Wisconsin Farm Technology Days, it was easy for me to figure out what had worried Jethro Tull. Not Jethro Tull the 1970s rock band—Jethro Tull the agricultural reformer of the 18th century. Under my feet the prairie soil had been squashed by tractors and harvesters into a peculiar surface that felt like the poured-rubber flooring used around swimming pools. It was a modern version of a phenomenon

By 2030, 8.3 billion people will walk the Earth, and farmers will have to grow 30 percent more grain.

noted by Tull: When farmers always plow in the same path, the ground becomes "trodden as hard as the Highway by the Cattle that draw the Harrows."

Tull knew the solution: Don't keep plowing in the same path. In fact, farmers are increasingly not using plows at all—a system called no-till farming. But their other machines continue to grow in size and weight. In Europe, soil compaction is thought to affect almost 130,000 square miles of farmland, and one expert suggests that the reduced harvests from compaction cost midwestern farmers in the U.S. $100 million in lost revenue every year.

The ultimate reason that compaction continues to afflict rich nations is the same reason that other forms of soil degradation afflict poor ones: Political and economic institutions are not set up to pay attention to soils. The Chinese officials who are rewarded for getting trees planted without concern about their survival are little different from the farmers in the Midwest who continue to use huge harvesters because they can't afford the labor to run several smaller machines.

Next to the compacted road on the Wisconsin farm was a demonstration of horse-drawn plowing. The earth curling up from the moldboard was dark, moist, refulgent—perfect midwestern topsoil. Photographer Jim Richardson got on his belly to capture it. He asked me to hunker down and hold a light. Soon we drew a small, puzzled crowd. Someone explained that we were looking at the soil. "What are they doing that for?" one woman asked loudly. In her voice I could hear the thought: MEGO.

When I told this story over the phone to David Montgomery, the University of Washington geologist, I could almost hear him shaking his head. "With eight billion people, we're going to *have* to start getting interested in soil," he said. "We're simply not going to be able to keep treating it like dirt."

Critical Responses

1. While Mann acknowledges that soil can very well be a "MEGO" ("my eyes glaze over") topic, how does his writing style counter the "MEGO" effect and convey the urgency of paying attention to the subject? What, if any, suggestions would you offer to meet these aims more effectively?

2. How does climate change contribute to drought, erosion, and soil degradation? How can the improvement of soil contribute to reducing global warming?

3. What are the locations and time frames on which this article focuses? How does their sequence tie in with the main points being made? What do form and content suggest about the idea of "progress"?

4. Comparing the article on the seafood crisis to this one on soil, consider what "high-tech" large-scale fishing and "high-tech" large-scale farming have in common in terms of environmental costs. Can suggested solutions to problems in the ocean be applied to those on land and vice versa?

Writing Topics

1. What is the message of each of the photographs accompanying this article? What is their message cumulatively? How does the last one in particular tie in with the text, and what is their effect together?

2. This article has several examples of vicious cycles. Focusing on one, review and explain the dynamics involved and suggest ways that the negative effects might be halted if not reversed.

3. What can modern agriculture gain from traditional methods? Can techniques for improving soil fertility in poor and underdeveloped countries help do so in wealthy developed ones?

4. How do "Our Good Earth" and "The End of Plenty" complement one another? How, at the same time, do they differ?

Further Exploration

1. How would you go about convincing people who live in cities (and thus the majority of the world's population) to care about dirt?

2. Divide into groups to research the American Dust Bowl of the 1930s. One group (or more) can focus on its causes and effects; the other (or others) can examine the manner in which problems were addressed and the lessons that were learned. Together, all groups might consider their collective findings in relation to the trends discussed in "Our Good Earth."

© 1921 CHARLES MARTIN/National Geographic Image Collection

Studying the Image

1. The article "Rice: The Essential Harvest" explains that the reverence the people of Bali have for rice is based on their belief that the staple is the embodiment of the rice mother goddess, a deity that promotes life and fertility. How could this picture be seen as a representation of the spiritual relationship many cultures have with rice?

2. How would the landscape look without the rice paddies? In what ways do they destroy the natural environment? Do you think that more land should be used for this staple, or should other foods that cause less damage to the environment be promoted?

Writing Assignment

Research the history of golden rice and write an essay outlining the problems of its introduction into agrarian economies.

© 2004 IRA BLOCK/National Geographic Image Collection

Studying the Image

1. Why do you think the photographer chose these particular objects for the picture? What point is being made about the placement of the olive oil in this setting?

2. Write a caption for this picture.

Writing Assignment

"Olive Oil: Elixir of the Gods" describes the battle over which country produces the best olive oil. Design an advertisement that would promote a specific company and region's ability to produce superior olive oil.

© JULES GERVAIS COURTELLEMONT/National Geographic Image Collection

Studying the Image

1. What elements of the picture seem contradictory? How would you describe the look on her face? How is she responding to having her picture taken?

2. Why do you think that people ignore the health risks of caffeine, especially when it is coupled with tobacco? What alternatives could you suggest for the benefits the woman in the picture probably feels from this combination?

Writing Assignment

Conduct research to determine if there are any other health risks associated with the consumption of caffeine that the "Caffeine" article did not include, noting any that may be especially dangerous for women. Then write a persuasive letter to the woman in the picture, trying to convince her to stop drinking caffeine and smoking cigarettes.

© 1967 DAVID BOYER/National Geographic Image Collection

Studying the Image

1. How would you describe the tone of the picture? What statement does the picture make about fishing? About fishermen?

2. How does fishing become a part of the culture in places like Indonesia? How would regulating this livelihood impact the region's culture?

Writing Assignment

Write an essay that determines whether or not the ideas expressed in "Seafood Crisis: Time for a Sea Change" would help fishermen—like those depicted in the photograph—find alternative employment in the fishing industry. Argue whether or not this should be an important consideration in sustainability efforts.

© JODI COBB/National Geographic Image Collection

Studying the Image

1. Note the body language and expression on the boy's face in the picture. What is he thinking? What attitude is he trying to express to the viewer?

2. Scientists have determined that eating meat and poultry is an inefficient way of feeding people since it takes so much grain to feed livestock. Should the United States regulate fast food companies that help promote this inefficiency? Should other countries ban KFC and McDonald's, along with other fast food chains?

Writing Assignment

Choose a fast food chain and investigate the food production process for the most popular item on its menu. Write an essay that explores the sustainability of that process.

© 1984 CHRIS JOHNS/National Geographic Image Collection

Studying the Image

1. How does the way the photographer framed the shot contribute to its tone? What important settling elements did he include in the frame?

2. How do you think dust storms change people's attitude toward nature?

Writing Assignment

The experiences of people who lived through the Dust Bowl inspired many stories and songs, including John Steinbeck's *The Grapes of Wrath* and Woody Guthrie's ballad "Dust Bowl Refugee." Choose Guthrie's or another Dust Bowl ballad and write an analysis of its point of view about this period in American history. Does the song make a political statement?

SECTION B
Work, Play, Love

*A glittering slide and whirling amusement ride
light up a fair in Alabama.*

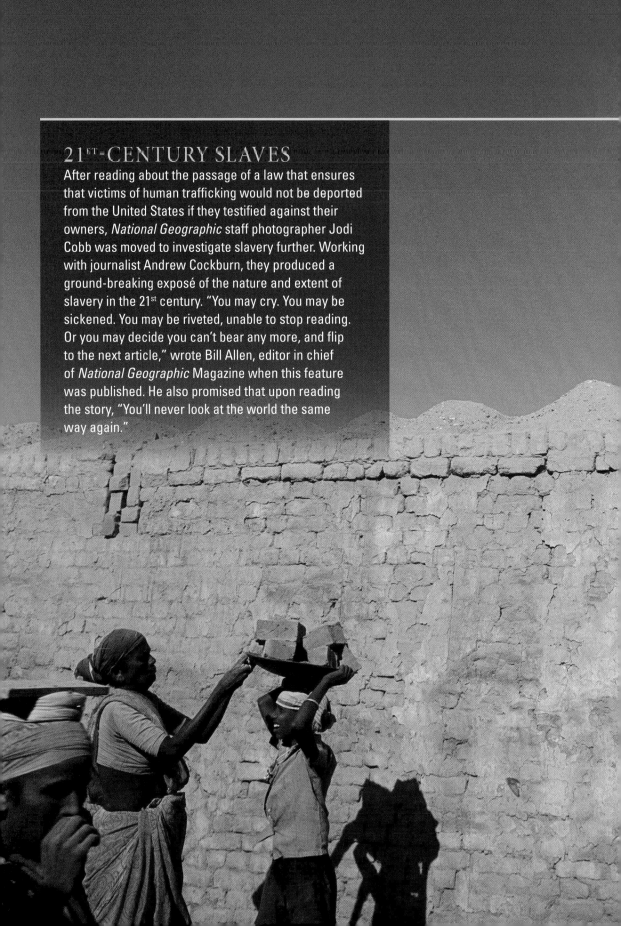

21ST-CENTURY SLAVES

After reading about the passage of a law that ensures that victims of human trafficking would not be deported from the United States if they testified against their owners, *National Geographic* staff photographer Jodi Cobb was moved to investigate slavery further. Working with journalist Andrew Cockburn, they produced a ground-breaking exposé of the nature and extent of slavery in the 21st century. "You may cry. You may be sickened. You may be riveted, unable to stop reading. Or you may decide you can't bear any more, and flip to the next article," wrote Bill Allen, editor in chief of *National Geographic* Magazine when this feature was published. He also promised that upon reading the story, "You'll never look at the world the same way again."

21ST-CENTURY SLAVES

By Andrew Cockburn

Photographs by Jodi Cobb

Debt traps entire families in bondage for generations.
*Mothers and daughters haul handmade bricks at a southeast
India kiln while fathers and sons stoke the fires. Kiln owners
acquire workers by loaning poor families money for expenses
far beyond their means: medical care or a funeral. Despite
years of work to pay these loans, exorbitant interest and
dishonest accounting perpetuate the debts, and parents pass
the burdens on to their children. Roughly two-thirds of the
world's captive laborers—15 to 20 million people—are debt
slaves in India, Pakistan, Bangladesh, and Nepal.*

Each woman's home is a 4-by-6-foot pinjara—Hindi for cage. Brothels line Falkland Road in Mumbai, with the youngest, prettiest women displayed in street level cages to attract customers day and night. Many women are delivered into these ramshackle hives by traffickers: many others are sold outright by parents or husbands. Some 50,000 women—nearly half shipped a thousand miles across India from Nepal—work as prostitutes in this city. Violence, disease, malnutrition, and lack of medical care reduce their life expectancy to less than 40 years.

THE TITLE IS NOT A METAPHOR.

THIS STORY IS ABOUT SLAVES. NOT PEOPLE LIVING *LIKE* SLAVES, WORKING HARD FOR LOUSY PAY. NOT PEOPLE 200 YEARS AGO.

IT'S ABOUT 27 MILLION PEOPLE WORLDWIDE WHO ARE BOUGHT AND SOLD, HELD CAPTIVE, BRUTALIZED, EXPLOITED FOR PROFIT.

Sherwood Castle, headquarters to Milorad Milakovic, the former railway official who rose to become a notorious slave trafficker in Bosnia, looms beside the main road just outside the northwest Bosnian town of Prijedor. Under stucco battlements, the entrance is guarded by well-muscled, heavily tattooed young men, while off to one side Milakovic's trio of pet Siberian tigers prowl their caged compound. I arrived there alone one gray spring morning—alone because no local guide or translator dared accompany me—and found my burly 54-year-old host waiting for me at a table set for lunch beside a glassed-in aquamarine swimming pool.

The master of Sherwood has never been shy about his business. He once asked a dauntless human rights activist who has publicly detailed his record of buying women for his brothels in Prijedor: "Is it a crime to sell women? They sell footballers, don't they?"

> **Is it a crime to sell women? They sell footballers, don't they?**

Milakovic threatened to kill the activist for her outspokenness, but to me he sang a softer tune. Over a poolside luncheon of seafood salad and steak, we discussed the stream of young women fleeing the shattered economies of their home countries in the former Soviet bloc. Milakovic said he was eager to promote his scheme to legalize prostitution in Bosnia—"to stop the selling of people, because each of those girls is someone's child."

One such child is a nearsighted, chain-smoking blonde named Victoria, at 20 a veteran of the international slave trade. For three years of her life she was among the estimated 27 million men, women, and children in the world who are enslaved—physically confined or restrained and forced to work, or

Adapted from "21ˢᵗ-Century Slaves" by Andrew Cockburn: National Geographic Magazine, September 2003.

controlled through violence, or in some way treated as property.

Victoria's odyssey began when she was 17, fresh out of school in Chisinau, the decayed capital of the former Soviet republic of Moldova. "There was no work, no money," she explained simply. So when a friend—"at least I thought he was a friend"—suggested he could help her get a job in a factory in Turkey, she jumped at the idea and took up his offer to drive her there, through Romania. "But when I realized we had driven west, to the border with Serbia, I knew something was wrong."

It was too late. At the border she was handed over to a group of Serb men, who produced a new passport saying she was 18. They led her on foot into Serbia and raped her, telling her that she would be killed if she resisted. Then they sent her under guard to Bosnia, the Balkan republic being rebuilt under a torrent of international aid after its years of genocidal civil war.

Victoria was now a piece of property and, as such, was bought and sold by different brothel owners ten times over the next two years for an average price of $1,500. Finally, four months pregnant and fearful of a forced abortion, she escaped. I found her hiding in the Bosnian city of Mostar, sheltered by a group of Bosnian women.

In a soft monotone she recited the names of clubs and bars in various towns where she had to dance seminaked, look cheerful, and have sex with any customer who wanted her for the price of a few packs of cigarettes. "The clubs were all awful, although the Artemedia, in Banja Luka, was the worst—all the customers were cops," she recalled.

Victoria was a debt slave. Payment for her services went straight to her owner of the moment to cover her "debt"—the amount he had paid to buy her from her previous owner. She was held in servitude unless or until the money she owed to whomever controlled her had been recovered, at which point she would be sold again and would begin to work off the purchase price paid by her new owner. Although slavery in its traditional form survives in many parts of the world, debt slavery of this kind, with variations, is the most common form of servitude today.

According to Milorad Milakovic, such a system is perfectly aboveboard, "There is the problem of expense in bringing a girl here," he had explained to me. "The plane, transport, hotels along the way, as well as food. That girl must work to get that money back."

In November 2000 the UN-sponsored International Police Task Force (IPTF) raided Milakovic's nightclub-brothels in Prijedor, liberating 34 young women who told stories of servitude similar to Victoria's. "We had to dance, drink a lot, and go to our rooms with anyone," said one. "We were eating once a day and sleeping five to six hours. If we would not do what we were told, guards would beat us."

Following the IPTF raids, Milakovic complained to the press that the now liberated women had cost a lot of money to buy, that he would have to buy more, and that he wanted compensation. He also spoke openly about the cozy relations he had enjoyed with the IPTF peacekeepers, many of whom had been his customers.

But there were no influential friends to protect him in May this year, when local police finally raided Sherwood Castle and arrested Milakovic for trafficking in humans and possessing slaves.

We think of slavery as something that is over and done with, and our images of it tend to be grounded in the 19th century: black field hands in chains. "In those days slavery thrived on a shortage of person power," explains Mike Dottridge, former director of Anti-Slavery International, founded in 1839 to carry on the campaign that had already abolished slavery in the British Empire. The average slave in 1850, according to the research of slavery expert Kevin Bales, sold for around $40,000 in today's money.

I visited Dottridge at the organization's headquarters in a small building in Stockwell, a nondescript district in south London. "Back then," said Dottridge, "black people were kidnapped and forced to work as slaves. Today vulnerable people are lured into debt slavery in the expectation of a better life. There are so many of them because there are so many desperate people in the world."

The offices are festooned with images of contemporary slavery—forced labor in West Africa, five- and six-year-old Pakistani children delivered to the Persian Gulf to serve as jockeys on racing camels, Thai child prostitutes. File cabinets bulge with reports: Brazilian slave gangs hacking at the Amazon rain forest to make charcoal for the steel industry, farm laborers in India bound to landlords by debt they have inherited from their parents and will pass on to their children.

The buying and selling of people is a profitable business because, while globalization has made it easier to move goods and money around the world, people who want to move to where jobs are face ever more stringent restrictions on legal migration.

Almost invariably those who cannot migrate legally or pay fees up front to be smuggled across borders end up in the hands of trafficking mafias. "Alien smuggling [bringing in illegal aliens who then find paying jobs] and human trafficking [where people end up enslaved or sold by the traffickers] operate exactly the same way, using the same routes," said a veteran field agent from the U.S. Immigration and Naturalization Service (INS). "The only difference is what happens to people at the other end." As the fees people must pay for transport rise in step with tightening border controls, illegal immigrants are ever more likely to end up in debt to the traffickers who have moved them—and are forced to work off their obligations as slaves.

The tiny Guatemalan town of Tecún Umán lies on the bank of the Suchiate River. Here migrants from Central America gather to cross into Mexico on their way north. Those with valid travel documents for Mexico cross the bridge over the river; those without them pay a few cents to be ferried across on rafts made from tractor inner tubes.

No matter where they come from, a great majority of migrants arrive in Tecún Umán penniless, easy prey for the local hoteliers, bar owners, and people smugglers—known as coyotes—who live off the flow of humanity. It is a town where, in the words of one former resident, "everything and everyone is for sale."

Some of the luckier migrants find a temporary safe haven at Casa del Migrante, a walled compound just a few yards from the muddy riverbank. "Every day, morning and night, I give a speech here, "says the Casa's director, Father Ademar Barilli, a Brazilian Jesuit who remains surprisingly buoyant despite the surrounding misery. "I talk about the dangers of the trip north and urge them to go back. It's a bad choice to go home, but a worse one to try to go on to the U.S."

Barilli warns migrants about the bosses in Mexico who may take their precious documents and force them into slavery on remote plantations. He tells them about the brothels in Tapachula, the Mexican town across the river, where girls are forced into prostitution. Most, remembering the misery they have left behind, disregard his warnings. As Adriana, a 14-year-old prostitute in a Tapachula bar, exclaimed when asked if she would consider going home to Honduras: "No, there you die of hunger!"

Despite Barilli and Casa del Migrante, Tecún Umán itself is hardly safe. The week before I arrived, a dead coyote had been dumped just outside the gates of the compound with a hundred bullets in his body. "People are killed here because of the traffic in people and babies. There are many mafias involved in the business of this town. *Aquí uno no sale en la noche*—Here you don't go out at night," Barilli said.

continued on page 194

After work in tomato fields and citrus groves, farmworkers gather to tackle another job: ending labor abuses in South Florida agriculture. The Coalition of Immokalee Workers (CIW), mostly immigrants from Mexico, Guatemala, and Haiti, has rescued many of its own 2,000-plus members from five large-scale Florida slave-labor operations in the past six years. CIW estimates that up to 10 percent of U.S. farm laborers are enslaved. The rest are earning sweatshop wages.

continued from page 191

As I calculated the amount of daylight left, Barilli explained what local bar owners say to girls from the buses that roll in every day from the south. "They talk about a job working in a restaurant. But the job is in a bar. After the girl has worked for a while just serving drinks, the owner denounces her to the police and gets her arrested because she has no documents. She is jailed; he bails her out. Then he tells her she is in his debt and must work as a prostitute. The debt never ends, so the girl is a slave."

Barilli cited a recent case involving a bar named La Taverna on the highway out of town. The owner, a woman, had duped six girls in this fashion. "Some of them got pregnant, and she sold the babies," he said. Thanks partly to the efforts of a Casa del Migrante lay worker (who afterward went into hiding in response to a flood of very credible death threats), the bar owner was finally arrested and jailed.

Stepped-up security in the wake of 9/11 has made the major obstacle on the road from the south, the border between Mexico and the U.S., more difficult than ever to clear. With heightened control has come a commensurate increase in the price charged by smuggling gangs to take people across: up from an average of about $1,000 a person to $2,000. Survivors of the journey arrive deeply indebted and vulnerable to slavers.

In Immokalee, Florida, I sat in a room full of men and women with the same Maya features I had last seen on the faces of the people in Tecún Umán. Almost all of them were farm laborers, toiling on Florida's vast plantations to pick fruit and vegetables consumed all over the U.S. They were meeting at the headquarters of a farmworker organization, the Coalition of Immokalee Workers (CIW), to discuss ways of improving conditions in their ill-paid occupation. When the rapid-fire Spanish conversation died away, an elderly man picked up a guitar and began to sing about Juan Muñoz, who left Campeche, Mexico, "to seek his fortune in the U.S." but ended up in Lake Placid, Florida, working "as a slave" for a cruel boss who stole all his money.

Blues singers composed similar laments about the miseries of plantation life in the Old South, and we think of those songs as part of our heritage. But this song was not about the past. Juan Muñoz is a real person, a 32-year-old who left his small farm in Campeche because he couldn't earn enough money to feed his family. He made his way across the border to Marana, Arizona, where a coyote promised him a ride all the way to a job picking oranges in Florida. The ride cost $1,000, which Muñoz was told he could pay off over time. On arrival he found he had in fact joined the modern slave economy.

Highway 27 runs through citrus country in the heart of Florida, which supplies 80 percent of U.S. orange juice. The pickers in the fields that line the highway are overwhelmingly immigrants, many undocumented and all poor. They earn an average $7,500 a year for work that is hard and unhealthy, toiling for bosses who contract with growers to supply crews to pick crops. The law generally leaves these people alone so long as they stick to low-paid but necessary work in the fields.

Sweatshop conditions in the fields are almost inevitable, since the corporations that buy the crops have the power to keep the prices they pay low, thus ensuring that wages paid by harvesting companies to pickers stay low too. These conditions lead to a high turnover in the workforce, since anyone with a prospect of alternative work swiftly moves on. Hence the appeal to crew bosses of debt-slave crews, whose stability and docility are assured. That is how Juan Muñoz found himself held captive along with at least 700 others in the well-guarded camps operated by the Ramos family in and around the little town of Lake Placid.

"They had almost all been picked up in Arizona by coyotes who offered to take them to Florida and then sold them to the crew bosses," says Romeo Ramirez, a 21-year-old Guatemalan who went undercover to investigate the Ramoses' operation on behalf of the CIW.

Captives in eight camps in and around Lake Placid were living "four to a room, which stank, sleeping on box springs." Not surprisingly, the

One U.S. shelter has rescued 10,000 child prostitutes.
Sociologist Lois Lee, right, has spent 24 years working with children from 11 to 17 years old who've been trafficked by pimps. One young resident, left, at her Children of the Night shelter in southern California was forced to work as a prostitute in Oregon, Washington, Idaho, and Nevada before escaping her captor. "The sexual exploitation of American children cuts across every economic, ethnic, and social line," Lee says. "This is not just a Third World problem."

workers were terrified of their bosses. "People knew they would be beaten for trying to get away," said Ramirez, citing the rumor about one would-be escapee who "had his knees busted with a hammer and then was thrown out of a car moving 60 miles an hour.

"The workers were paid by the growers every Friday," Ramirez continued, "but then they would all be herded to the Ramoses' stores in Lake Placid and forced to sign over their checks. By the time they had paid for rent and food, their debt was as high as ever." One such store, Natalie's Boutique, is a block from the police station.

In April 2001 a team from the CIW helped four of the captive laborers, including Muñoz, to make a break. Spurred to action by the unequivocal testimony of the escapees, the FBI and INS mounted a raid—although the prominent "INS Deportation Service" sign on the side of the bus accompanying the raiding party gave the crew bosses enough warning to send the workers out into the orange groves around Lake Placid to hide. Nevertheless, the brothers Ramiro and Juan Ramos, along with their cousin José Luis Ramos, were eventually charged with trafficking in slaves, extortion, and possession of firearms.

continued on page 198

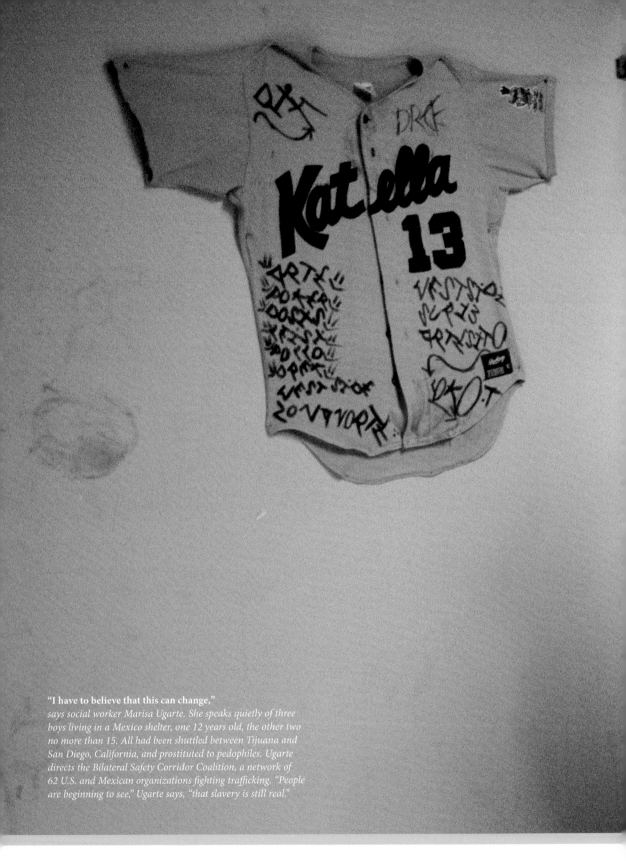

"I have to believe that this can change," *says social worker Marisa Ugarte. She speaks quietly of three boys living in a Mexico shelter, one 12 years old, the other two no more than 15. All had been shuttled between Tijuana and San Diego, California, and prostituted to pedophiles. Ugarte directs the Bilateral Safety Corridor Coalition, a network of 62 U.S. and Mexican organizations fighting trafficking. "People are beginning to see," Ugarte says, "that slavery is still real."*

continued from page 195

In June 2002 the three Ramoses were convicted on all counts and received prison sentences totaling 34 years and 9 months.

This 21st-century slave operation may have been ignored by the Ramoses' corporate clients; and federal agencies may have been slow to react to prodding by the CIW. But the slave crews were hardly out of sight. The main camp in which the Ramoses confined their victims was just on the edge of town right beside a Ramada Inn. On the other side of the compound a gated community, Lakefront Estates, offered a restful environment for seniors.

"The slaves in Lake Placid were invisible, part of our economy that exists in a parallel universe," points out Laura Germino of the CIW. "People were playing golf at the retirement community, and right behind them was a slave camp. Two worlds, speaking different languages."

The Department of State puts the number of people trafficked into the U.S. every year at close to 20,000. Many end up as prostitutes or farm laborers. Some work in nursing homes. Others suffer their servitude alone, domestic slaves confined to private homes.

The passage by Congress in 2000 of the Victims of Trafficking and Violence Protection Act, which protects such slaves against deportation if they testify against their former owners, perhaps has helped dispel some fearfulness. The growth of organizations ready to give help, like the CIW or the Coalition to Abolish Slavery and Trafficking, a southern California group that has assisted more than 200 trafficked people, means that victims are not alone. Public scrutiny in general is rising.

Still, such captives the world over are mostly helpless. They are threatened; they live in fear of deportation; they are cut off from any source of advice or support because they cannot communicate with the outside world. And the harsh fact remains that this parallel universe, as Laura Germino called it, can be a very profitable place to do business. Before sentencing the Ramoses, U.S. District Court Judge K. Michael Moore ordered the confiscation of three million dollars the brothers had earned from their operation, as well as extensive real estate and other property.

Moore also pointed a finger at the agribusiness corporations that hired the Ramoses' picking crews. "It seems," he said, "that there are others at another level in this system of fruit picking—at a higher level—that to some extent are complicit in one way or another in how these activities occur."

A former slave named Julia Gabriel, now a landscape gardener in Florida and a member of CIW, remembers her arrival in the U.S. from Guatemala at the age of 19. She picked cucumbers under armed guard in South Carolina for 12 to 14 hours a day; she saw fellow captives pistol-whipped into unconsciousness. "Maybe this is normal in the U.S.," she thought. Then a friend told her, "no, this is not normal here," so Gabriel found the courage to escape.

"This is meant to be the country to which people come fleeing servitude, not to be cast into servitude when they are here," says Attorney General John Ashcroft. But some historians argue that the infamous trans-Atlantic slave trade that shipped millions of Africans to the New World was abolished only when it had outlived its economic usefulness. Now slave traders from Sherwood Castle to sunny Florida—and at hundreds of points in between—have rediscovered the profitability of buying and selling human beings. Which means that, in the 21st century, slavery is far from gone.

Critical Responses

1. What was your initial reaction to this article? What revelations were most shocking to you, and why?

2. How do Jodi Cobb's photographs and Andrew Cockburn's text supplement and complement one another?

3. According to Kevin Bayles, a prominent U.S.-based slavery investigator, modern slaves are controlled not by legal ownership but by "the final authority of violence." What does this phrase mean?

4. What makes slavery so difficult to detect? How can it be distinguished from other forms of exploitation?

Writing Topics

1. Debt slavery, according to this article, is the most common form of 21st-century bondage. What does its extent suggest about contemporary social and economic values?

2. What do you make of Milakovic's view that selling women is no different from selling athletes? What about his advocating the legalization of prostitution in order "to stop the selling of people, because each of these girls is someone's child"?

3. Compare enslavement as described in this article to labor as described in the article on "The Price of Gold." In attending to similarities and differences, take gender and age into account as well.

4. While *National Geographic* Magazine is published across the world, the cover of the edition in which "21st-Century Slaves" was printed varied from country to country. In the United States, for example, zebras, which were the subject of another article, were featured. By contrast, an image from the slavery article appeared on the cover of the U.K. edition. What kinds of considerations might have been involved in these editorial decisions? What are some effects and some further implications?

Further Explorations

1. After this article appeared, the magazine received more letters from readers than it had for any story in over fifteen years. Write your own letter to the editor about "21st-Century Slaves," commenting on your reaction, on the value of the article, and on the effect of publishing it in such a widely read magazine.

2. Returning to the topic of debt highlighted in this article, divide into groups that focus on common forms of debt such as student loans, home mortgages, and credit card debt. What are the reasons and incentives for accruing these kinds of debt? How do such debts affect one's life in the present and in the future?

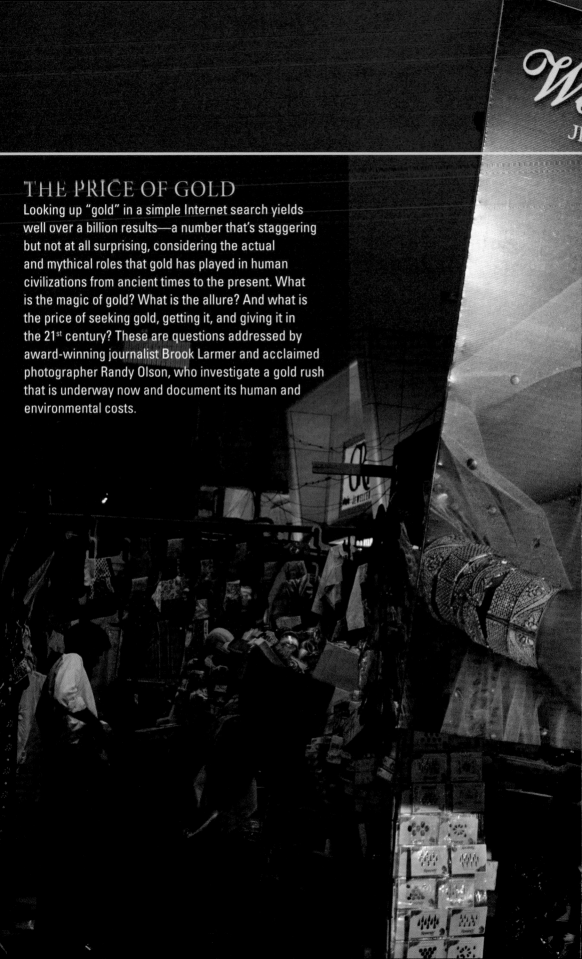

THE PRICE OF GOLD

Looking up "gold" in a simple Internet search yields
well over a billion results—a number that's staggering
but not at all surprising, considering the actual
and mythical roles that gold has played in human
civilizations from ancient times to the present. What
is the magic of gold? What is the allure? And what is
the price of seeking gold, getting it, and giving it in
the 21st century? These are questions addressed by
award-winning journalist Brook Larmer and acclaimed
photographer Randy Olson, who investigate a gold rush
that is underway now and document its human and
environmental costs.

THE PRICE OF GOLD

By Brook Larmer

Photographs by Randy Olson

The allure of gold dominates a Chennai street in September, just before India's wedding season, when jewelry sales soar. India is the top gold consumer, its citizens buying as much for investment as adornment.

At recent prices, one 28-pound gold bar held by the Federal Reserve Bank of New York is worth more than $335,000. Inside the vault officials transfer dozens of bars in a transaction between clients.

THE PRICE OF GOLD IN DOLLARS AND SUFFERING,
IT'S NEVER BEEN HIGHER.

Like many of his Inca ancestors, Juan Apaza is possessed by gold. Descending into an icy tunnel 17,000 feet up in the Peruvian Andes, the 44-year-old miner stuffs a wad of coca leaves into his mouth to brace himself for the inevitable hunger and fatigue. For 30 days each month Apaza toils, without pay, deep inside this mine dug down under a glacier above the world's highest town, La Rinconada. For 30 days he faces the dangers that have killed many of his fellow miners—explosives, toxic gases, tunnel collapses—to extract the gold that the world demands. Apaza does all this, without pay, so that he can make it to today, the 31st day, when he and his fellow miners are given a single shift, four hours or maybe a little more, to haul out and keep as much rock as their weary shoulders can bear. Under the ancient lottery system that still prevails in the high Andes, known as the *cachorreo*, this is what passes for a paycheck: a sack of rocks that may contain a small fortune in gold or, far more often, very little at all.

Apaza is still waiting for a stroke of luck. "Maybe today will be the big one,"

> This is what passes for a paycheck: a sack of rocks that may contain a small fortune in gold or, far more often, very little at all.

he says, flashing a smile that reveals a single gold tooth. To improve his odds, the miner has already made his "payment to the Earth": a bottle of pisco, the local liquor, placed near the mouth of the mine; a few coca leaves slipped under a rock; and, several months back, a rooster sacrificed by a shaman on the sacred mountaintop. Now, heading into the tunnel, he mumbles a prayer in his native Quechua language to the deity who rules the mountain and all the gold within.

"She is our Sleeping Beauty," says Apaza, nodding toward a sinuous curve in the snowfield high above the mine. "Without her blessing we would never find any gold. We might not make it out of here alive."

It isn't El Dorado, exactly. But for more than 500 years the glittering seams trapped beneath the glacial ice here, three miles above sea level, have drawn people to this place in Peru. Among the first were the Inca, who

Adapted from "The Price of Gold" by Brook Larmer: National Geographic Magazine, January 2009.

saw the perpetually lustrous metal as the "sweat of the sun"; then the Spanish, whose lust for gold and silver spurred the conquest of the New World. But it is only now, as the price of gold soars—it has risen 235 percent in the past eight years—that 30,000 people have flocked to La Rinconada, turning a lonely prospectors' camp into a squalid shantytown on top of the world. Fueled by luck and desperation, sinking in its own toxic waste and lawlessness, this no-man's-land now teems with dreamers and schemers anxious to strike it rich, even if it means destroying their environment—and themselves—in the process.

The scene may sound almost medieval, but La Rinconada is one of the frontiers of a thoroughly modern phenomenon: a 21st-century gold rush.

No single element has tantalized and tormented the human imagination more than the shimmering metal known by the chemical symbol Au. For thousands of years the desire to possess gold has driven people to extremes, fueling wars and conquests, girding empires and currencies, leveling mountains and forests. Gold is not vital to human existence; it has, in fact, relatively few practical uses. Yet its chief virtues—its unusual density and malleability along with its imperishable shine—have made it one of the world's most coveted commodities, a transcendent symbol of beauty, wealth, and immortality. From pharaohs (who insisted on being buried in what they called the "flesh of the gods") to the forty-niners (whose mad rush for the mother lode built the American West) to the financiers (who, following Sir Isaac Newton's advice, made it the bedrock of the global economy): Nearly every society through the ages has invested gold with an almost mythological power.

Humankind's feverish attachment to gold shouldn't have survived the modern world.

It's never been clear if we have gold—or gold has us.

Few cultures still believe that gold can give eternal life, and every country in the world—the United States was last, in 1971—has done away with the gold standard, which John Maynard Keynes famously derided as "a barbarous relic." But gold's luster not only endures; fueled by global uncertainty, it grows stronger. The price of gold, which stood at $271 an ounce on September 10, 2001, hit $1,023 in March 2008, and it may surpass that threshold again. Aside from extravagance, gold is also reprising its role as a safe haven in perilous times. Gold's recent surge, sparked in part by the terrorist attack on 9/11, has been amplified by the slide of the U.S. dollar and jitters over a looming global recession. In 2007 demand outstripped mine production by 59 percent. "Gold has always had this kind of magic," says Peter L. Bernstein, author of *The Power of Gold*. "But it's never been clear if we have gold—or gold has us."

For all of its allure, gold's human and environmental toll has never been so steep. Part of the challenge, as well as the fascination, is that there is so little of it. In all of history, only 161,000 tons of gold have been mined, barely enough to fill two Olympic-size swimming pools. More than half of that has been extracted in the past 50 years. Now the world's richest deposits are fast being depleted, and new discoveries are rare. Gone are the hundred-mile-long gold reefs in South Africa or cherry-size nuggets in California. Most of the gold left to mine exists as traces buried in remote and fragile corners of the globe. It's an invitation to destruction. But there is no shortage of miners, big and small, who are willing to accept.

At one end of the spectrum are the armies of poor migrant workers converging on small-scale mines like La Rinconada. According to the United Nations Industrial Development Organization (UNIDO), there are between 10 million and 15 million so-called artisanal miners around the world, from Mongolia to Brazil. Employing crude methods that have hardly changed in centuries, they produce about 25 percent of the world's gold and support a total of 100 million people. It's a vital activity for these people—and deadly too.

In the Democratic Republic of the Congo in the past decade, local armed groups fighting for control of gold mines and trading routes have routinely terrorized and tortured miners and used profits from gold to buy weapons and fund their activities. In the Indonesian province of East Kalimantan, the military, along with security forces of an Anglo-Australian gold company, forcibly evicted small-scale miners and burned their villages to make way for a large-scale mine. Thousands of protestors against expansion of a mine in Cajamarca, Peru, faced tear gas and police violence.

The deadly effects of mercury are equally hazardous to small-scale miners. Most use mercury to separate gold from rock, spreading poison in both gas and liquid forms. UNIDO estimates that one-third of all mercury released by humans into the environment comes from artisanal gold mining. This turns places like La Rinconada into a sort of Shangrila in reverse: The pursuit of a metal linked to immortality only serves to hasten the miners' own mortality.

At the other end of the spectrum are vast, open-pit mines run by the world's largest mining companies. Using armadas of supersize machines, these big-footprint mines produce three-quarters of the world's gold. They can also bring jobs, technologies, and development to forgotten frontiers. Gold mining, however, generates more waste per ounce than any other metal, and the mines' mindbending disparities of scale show why: These gashes in the Earth are so massive they can be seen from space, yet the particles being mined in them are so microscopic that, in many cases, more than 200 could fit on the head of a pin. Even at showcase mines, such as Newmont Mining Corporation's Batu Hijau

operation in eastern Indonesia, where $600 million has been spent to mitigate the environmental impact, there is no avoiding the brutal calculus of gold mining. Extracting a single ounce of gold there—the amount in a typical wedding ring—requires the removal of more than 250 tons of rock and ore.

As a girl growing up on the remote Indonesian island of Sumbawa, Nur Piah heard tales about vast quantities of gold buried beneath the mountain rain forests. They were legends—until geologists from an American company, Newmont Mining Corporation, discovered a curious green rock near a dormant volcano eight miles from her home. The rock's mossy tint meant it contained copper, an occasional companion to gold, and it wasn't long before Newmont began setting up a mine named Batu Hijau, meaning "green rock."

Nur Piah, then 24, replied to a Newmont ad seeking "operators," figuring her friendly manner would get her a job answering phones. When the daughter of a Muslim cleric arrived for training, though, her boss showed her a different operating booth—the cab of a Caterpillar 793 haul truck, one of the world's largest trucks. Standing 21 feet tall and 43 feet long, the truck was bigger than her family home. Its wheels alone were double her height. "The truck terrified me," Nur Piah recalls. Another shock soon followed when she saw the first cut of the mine itself. "They had peeled the skin off the Earth!" she says. "I thought, whatever force can do that must be very powerful."

Ten years later, Nur Piah is part of that force herself. Pulling a pink head scarf close around her face, the mother of two smiles demurely as she revs the Caterpillar's 2,337-horsepower engine and rumbles into the pit at Batu Hijau. Her truck is part of a 111-vehicle fleet that hauls close to a hundred million tons of rock out of the ground every year. The 1,800-foot volcano that stood here for millions of years? No hint of it remains. The space it once occupied has been turned into a mile-wide pit that

continued on page 208

Indonesian farmers turn their hoes to mining, illegally digging for gold on a tornup riverbank in Borneo. For the chance to make five dollars a day, thousands have left their fields to join Indonesia's gold rush.

continued from page 205

reaches 345 feet below sea level. By the time the seam at Batu Hijau is exhausted in 20 years or so, the pit will bottom out at 1,500 feet below sea level. The environmental wreckage doesn't concern Nur Piah anymore. "I only think about getting my salary," she says.

There is one thing, however, that Nur Piah finds curious: In a decade at Batu Hijau, she has never seen a speck of the gold she has helped mine. The engineers monitoring the process track its presence in the copper compounds to which it adheres. And since the gold is shipped out to smelters overseas in copper concentrate, nobody on Sumbawa ever sees the hidden treasure that has transformed their island.

The gold ornaments come out of the velvet boxes one by one, family heirlooms that Nagavi, a 23-year-old Indian bride, always knew she would wear on her wedding day. The eldest daughter of a coffee plantation owner in the southern Indian state of Karnataka, Nagavi grew up marveling at the weddings that mark the merger of two wealthy Indian families. But not until the morning of her own arranged wedding to the only son of another coffee plantation family does she understand just how achingly beautiful the golden tradition can be.

By the time Nagavi is ready for her wedding, the university graduate with a predilection for jeans and T-shirts has been transformed into an Indian princess, shimmering in gold. An exquisitely crafted hairpiece is so heavy— five and a half pounds of gold—that it pulls her head back. Three gold necklaces and a dozen bangles act as effective counterweights. Wrapped in an 18-foot-long sari woven with thread dipped in gold, Nagavi walks slowly out of her home, trying to keep her balance as she tosses rice over her head in a traditional gesture of farewell.

There are some ten million weddings in India every year, and in all but a few, gold is crucial both to the spectacle and to the culturally freighted transaction between families and generations.

The gold treasures Nagavi wears—along with the jewelry and saris packed in the trunk of the SUV taking her to the wedding hall—are not a traditional dowry. In this circle of coffee growers around the town of Chikmagalur, unlike in many poorer parts of the country, it is considered unseemly for a groom's family to make explicit demands. "This is seen as my 'share' of the family wealth," says Nagavi, gazing at the millions of dollars of gold jewelry. As with any Indian wedding, the gold also serves to display the value she brings to the union. "With daughters, you have to start saving gold from the day they are born," says Nagavi's father, C. P. Ravi Shankar. "It's important to marry them off well."

Nowhere is the gold obsession more culturally entrenched than it is in India. Per capita income in this country of a billion people is $2,700, but it has been the world's runaway leader in gold demand for several decades. In 2007, India consumed 773.6 tons of gold, about 20 percent of the world gold market and more than double that purchased by either of its closest followers, China (363.3 tons) and the U.S. (278.1 tons). India produces very little gold of its own, but its citizens have hoarded up to 18,000 tons of the yellow metal—more than 40 times the amount held in the country's central bank.

India's fixation stems not simply from a love of extravagance or the rising prosperity of an emerging middle class. For Muslims, Hindus, Sikhs, and Christians alike, gold plays a central role at nearly every turning point in life—most of all when a couple marries. There are some ten million weddings in India every year, and in all but a few, gold is crucial both to the spectacle and to the culturally freighted transaction between families and generations. "It's written into our DNA," says K. A. Babu,

Manpower at an improvised mine in Ghana includes a 13-year-old boy put to work sluicing for gold. Large mining firms control just 4 percent of Ghana's territory, but a landgrab by those firms evicted thousands of villagers from their homes, forcing many to survive by poaching gold. Illegal mining produces 25 percent of the world's gold.

a manager at the Alapatt jewelry store in the southwestern city of Cochin. "Gold equals good fortune."

This equation manifests itself most palpably during the springtime festival of Akshaya Tritiya, considered the most auspicious day to buy gold on the Hindu calendar. The quantity of gold jewelry Indians purchase on this day—49 tons in 2008—so exceeds the amount bought on any other day of the year throughout the world that it often nudges gold prices higher.

Throughout the year, though, the epicenter of gold consumption is Kerala, a relatively prosperous state on India's southern tip that claims just 3 percent of the country's population but 7 to 8 percent of its gold market. It's an unusual distinction for

a region that has one of the world's only democratically elected Marxist governments, but it is rooted in history. A key port in the global spice trade, Kerala gained an early exposure to gold, from the Romans who offered coins in exchange for pepper, cardamom, and cinnamon to subsequent waves of colonizers, the Portuguese, Dutch, English. But local historians say it was the region's revolt against the Hindu caste system (before which the lowest castes were allowed to adorn themselves only with polished stones and bones), and the mass conversion to Christianity and Islam that followed, that turned gold into something more than commerce: a powerful symbol of independence and upward mobility.

Despite the long history, no era in Kerala has been hungrier for gold than the present. The road from the airport to Cochin is lined with billboards showing women adorned in gold wedding jewelry. India's biggest gold retailers all come from Kerala, and 13 large gold showrooms clog a two-mile stretch of Cochin's main thoroughfare, Mahatma Gandhi Road. (What would the ascetic Mahatma have thought?) Among the upper classes and younger consumers in Delhi and Mumbai, gold may be starting to lose ground to more understated—and expensive—materials like platinum and diamonds. But even as Kerala grows in wealth (thanks to a large number of workers in the Persian Gulf) and education (it boasts a 91 percent literacy rate), the attachment to gold persists. Dowries, though officially banned, dominate most wedding proceedings in India, and in Kerala, the largest portion of the dowry is usually gold.

As the price of the metal goes up, however, poor Indian families are having a harder time raising the gold they need for dowries. Though the dowry retains a social function—balancing the wealth between the families of bride and groom—the rising price of gold has only fueled its abusive side. In the neighboring state of Tamil Nadu, the struggle to acquire gold has led to dowry-related domestic violence (usually when grooms' families beat the brides for bringing too little gold) and selective abortions (committed by families desperate to avoid the financial burden of a daughter).

Even in Kerala, the pressure is sometimes too much for the poor to take. Rajam Chidambaram, a 59-year-old widow living in a slum on the outskirts of Cochin, recently found a young man to marry her only daughter, age 27. The groom's family, however, demanded a dowry far out of her reach: 25 sovereigns, or 200 grams, of gold (worth $1,650 eight years ago, but more than $5,200 today). Chidambaram, a cleaning woman, has only the two earrings she wears; the gold necklace she once owned went to pay off her deceased husband's hospital bills. "I had to agree to the groom's demand," Chidambaram says, wiping away tears. "If I refuse, my daughter will stay home forever."

In the end, local financiers advanced a loan for her daughter's dowry. Chidambaram may have averted the shame of an unmarried daughter, but she is now burdened with a debt that she may spend the rest of her life trying to repay.

Rosemery sánchez condori is just nine years old, but the backs of her hands are burnished like aged leather. That's what happens when a girl spends time pounding rocks under the Andean sun. Ever since Rosemery's father fell ill in the mines of La Rinconada eight years ago, her mother has worked 11-hour days collecting rocks near the mines and hammering them into smaller bits to find flecks of overlooked gold. On school holidays, Rosemery sometimes helps her mother on the mountain. It is child labor, perhaps, but for a girl whose family is living hand to mouth, it also qualifies as her proudest achievement. "Last year I found two grams of gold," Rosemery says, almost giddily. "It was enough to buy my schoolbooks and uniform."

In small-scale mines around the globe, searching for gold is a family affair. Of the world's 12 to 15 million artisanal gold miners, an estimated 30 percent are women and children. On the mountain above La Rinconada, men disappear into the mines, while their wives sit near piles of discarded rock, swinging four-pound mallets in a syncopated rhythm. With no child care at home and a need for extra income, the women in their long traditional skirts and bowler hats sometimes bring their children along. It is the uncertainty of the mines' lottery system—and the perfidy of many men here—that compels the women to come to the mountain. At least they know that the six or eight grams of gold they find each month, worth about $200, will go to the family—not to the dingy bars and brothels that line the town's red-light district.

Only gold, that object of desire and destruction, could have conjured up a place of such startling contradictions as La Rinconada. Remote and inhospitable—at 17,000 feet, even oxygen is in short supply—the town is, nevertheless, growing at a furious pace. Approaching the settlement from across the high plains, a visitor first sees the glint of rooftops under a magnificent glacier draped like a wedding veil across the mountain. Then comes the stench. It's not just the garbage dumped down the slope, but the human and industrial waste that clogs the settlement's streets. For all its growth—the number of mines perforating the glacier has jumped in six years from 50 to around 250—La Rinconada has few basic services: no plumbing, no sanitation, no pollution control, no postal service, not even a police station. The nearest one, with a handful of cops, is an hour down the mountain. This is a place that operates, quite literally, above the law.

Many miners at La Rinconada don't officially exist. There are no payrolls—just those bags of rocks—and some mine operators don't even bother writing down workers' names. Bosses, of course, can get rich on this kind of indentured servitude. The manager of one of La Rinconada's larger operations says his mine yields 50 kilos (110 pounds) every three months—more than $5 million worth of gold each year. His workers, on their monthly cachorreo, each pull in an average of about ten grams (two-tenths of a pound) of gold, or around $3,000 a year. Despite the disparity, the miners do not rebel against the system; in fact, they seem to prefer the slim chance of winning big once a month in the mines to the dull certainty of low wages and chronic poverty in the fields. "It's a cruel lottery," says Juan Apaza, the gold-toothed miner up on the glacier. "But at least it gives us hope."

The more unforgiving lottery may be the one miners and their families face just trying to survive in such a dangerous and despoiled place. Life expectancy in La Rinconada is a mere 50 years, 21 years fewer than the national average. Fatal mine accidents are common, often caused by crude explosives handled by inexperienced or inebriated miners. If the blast doesn't kill, the carbon monoxide fumes may. Peru has strict laws governing mine safety, but there's little oversight in La Rinconada. "Of the 200 mining companies here, only five make a full set of safety equipment obligatory," says Andrés Paniura Quispe, a safety engineer who works with one of the few companies that maintains high standards but still requires miners to buy their own equipment.

Miners cope with the drumbeat of death with a reflexive fatalism. The local saying—"Al labor me voy, no sé si volveré"—translates as "Off to work I go, I don't know if I'll make it back." A death in the mine, in fact, is considered a good omen for those left behind. Human sacrifices, practiced in the Andes for centuries, are still considered the highest form of offering to the mountain deity. According to local beliefs, the chemical process by which the mountain absorbs a human brain brings gold ore closer to the surface, making it easier to extract.

But the gods surely can't be happy with how poisoned La Rinconada's environment has become. The raw sewage and garbage on the overcrowded streets are minor nuisances compared with the tons of mercury released during the process of separating gold from rock. In small-scale gold mining, UNIDO estimates, two to five grams of mercury are released into the environment for every gram of gold recovered—a staggering statistic, given that mercury poisoning can cause severe damage to the nervous system and all major organs. According to Peruvian environmentalists, the mercury released at La Rinconada and the nearby mining town of Ananea is contaminating rivers and lakes down to the coast of Lake Titicaca, more than a hundred miles away.

Residents around La Rinconada suffer the brunt of the destruction. Rosemery's father,

continued on page 214

In Chennai, Dilli Bai joins other sweepers who pan for flecks from neighborhood jewelry workshops, prospecting at dawn, before official trash collectors arrive. Bai collects about a gram a week from the dust of the city streets. Wherever there is gold, people will seek it.

continued from page 211

Esteban Sánchez Mamani, has worked here for 20 years, though he rarely enters the mines these days because of a chronic illness that has sapped his energy and raised his blood pressure. Sánchez isn't sure what the ailment is—his lone visit to the doctor was inconclusive—but he suspects it originated in the polluted environment. "I know the mines have taken years away from me," says Sánchez, whose hunched frame makes him seem decades older than his 40 years. "But this is the only life we know."

The family's fate now depends on the ore that Sánchez's wife, Carmen, hauls down from the mountain. Sitting on the floor of the family's stone hut, Sánchez spends most of his days pounding the rock into smaller pieces, keeping the gold-flecked shards in a blue coffee cup. Rosemery does her homework on a sack of rice, peppering a visitor with questions about life outside La Rinconada: "Do you chew coca leaves in your country? Do you own alpaca?" Though just a first grader, she has decided that she'd like to be an accountant and live in the U.S. "I want to go far from here," she says.

Rosemery tags along as her father delivers two sacks of ore—the weekly haul—to the tiny mill above their home. This is part of the endless routine, but each time Sá can't help hoping he's hit the jackpot. At the very least, he hopes there is enough gold to keep his two children in school. "I want them to study so they can leave this place," says Sánchez, who never completed the seventh grade.

Together, father and daughter watch the miller perform his ancient art. Using his bare hands, the man swirls several pounds of liquid mercury into a wooden pan to separate the gold from the rock, dumping the mercury-tainted waste into a stream beneath the shed. Thirty feet down stream a young girl is filling up a plastic bottle in the rancid water. But inside the miller's shed all eyes are focused on the marble-size silvery nugget the miller produces: its mercury-coated exterior hides an unknown quantity of gold.

Stuffing the nugget into his pocket, Sánchez trudges up the hill to a gold-buying shop. The merchant, one of several hundred in town, burns off the mercury with a blowtorch, releasing the toxic gas through an exhaust pipe into the cold, thin air. As the merchant works, Sánchez paces the room, his frayed gray cap in hand.

After ten minutes, a tiny kernel of gold emerges from the flame. Sánchez frowns. It weighs only 1.1 grams, about one-thirtieth of an ounce. The merchant peels off a few bills and, with a shrug of his shoulders, hands Sánchez a sum that, once the miller's fee is deducted, leaves the family with less than $20.

"Better luck next time," the merchant says. Maybe next month, or the next. Eking out a living sky-high on a glacier, Sánchez knows that luck is all he can ever hope for.

Critical Responses

1. What makes a substance like gold, which has very few practical applications, so important and alluring in so many cultures?

2. "It's never been clear if we have gold—or gold has us," observes Peter L. Bernstein, author of the book *The Power of Gold*. How does Brook Larmer, who quotes this remark, navigate the ambiguity in the article?

3. What are some of the dangers faced by small-scale miners? What accounts for their taking the risks that they do?

4. While gold represents wealth, what else does it represent? Can the economic value of gold be separated from its other attributes and values?

Writing Topics

1. Look up the word "fortune" and, taking into account its many and various definitions, consider how these figure implicitly and explicitly in this article.

2. Given both the human toll and the environmental impact of gold mining, do you think that people should abstain from buying gold, whether for jewelry or for investment? Further, should governments have a role in addressing this question?

3. Compare the gold workers described in this article to the debt slaves described in "21st-Century Slaves."

Are similarities or differences more prominent? Which seem to be more critical, and why?

4. One of the photographs in this article features a billboard advertising gold jewelry. What else is represented in the photograph? How do those details that are in the background provide a perspective on the billboard that is in the foreground, and vice versa? And how do you read this photograph in relation to the others that accompany the article?

Further Explorations

1. Continuing with the subject of advertising, select two or three examples of ads for gold jewelry in magazines, on the Internet, or wherever you encounter them, and analyze these ads, individually and comparatively. Pay attention to the images and the text, to the context in which they appear and their targeted audience, and to anything else that contributes to or conveys their messages.

2. Myths and fairy tales centered on gold, such as those involving King Midas, Rumpelstiltskin, and legions of others, have abounded around the world and over time. Choose one such gold story to research, investigate its origins insofar as possible, and consider ways in which the story can be interpreted.

COUNTY FAIRS

By John McCarry

Photographs by Randy Olson

COUNTY FAIRS

When county fairs were first held in the United States in the early 19th century, their aim was forward-looking and progressive. Nowadays, though, many fairs are on the verge of being consigned to an antique shop of American history—unless they can adapt to new circumstances and audiences and become local attractions once more. Visiting several fairs around the country, John McCarry looks at what makes some endure and others fade, and ponders what it would take to revive county fairs.

Appetites undampened by rain, visitors to Iowa's Clay County Fair graze among scores of food stands in a straw-slurping, chocolate-coated, on-a-stick, nine-day snack marathon.

A century ago a parading brass band and 83 yoke of oxen opened the Tunbridge World's Fair. These days stock showing, pony pulling, midway glitter, and big-name grandstand acts fill this quiet Vermont valley with bumper-to-bumper crowds. Blending community traditions with entertainment spectacles, county fairs thrive across the United States.

FAIR TIME: THE MOMENT BETWEEN SUMMER AND FALL WHERE THE BEST OF THE BEST ARE JUDGED, AUCTIONED, AND PRIZED.

AND THE KID IN EVERYONE LOSES THEMSELVES IN THE FANTASY WORLD OF THE CARNIVAL.

On a brilliantly sunny day in August several dozen Future Farmers of America and 4-H'ers struggled, one by one, to get their lambs and steers and hogs to walk in a circle at the swine barn of the Kitsap County Fair in Bremerton, Washington. An auctioneer perched atop a platform made from bales of hay was selling off the animals by the pound.

A hog had just sold for top dollar to Safeway when Matt Muzzy, a skinny 12-year-old with cropped blond hair, yanked his lamb, Butthead, into the arena.

"Now, who's going to help this young man out?" the auctioneer asked from his lofty perch. "He needs the money so he can go to the National Boy Scout Jamboree in Virginia next summer and get a badge."

And the auction began. Speaking at 78 rpm, the auctioneer launched into an alliterative litany of numbers. His voice grew tenser, his breath shorter as the numbers pushed upward. And then his voice hesitated, briefly, at $6.50 per pound. The auctioneer scanned the group of people crowded around until, finally, from the corner of his eye he saw a hand furtively rise from the back of some

County fairs give us a chance to glimpse the American past.

rickety bleachers. "Sold!" the auctioneer cried.

I caught up with Matt outside the sheep barn. He was breathless; his cheeks were flush. The throaty protests of the animals were joined by the crowd noises drifting over from the midway. The breeze rolling in off Puget Sound carried the edgy sweet smell of fair food all jumbled up with the rich odors of the barnyard.

I asked Matt if he was happy the way things had turned out. He smiled, a glinting semicircle of orthodontia.

"You bet!" he said. "Last year I only got $3.11 a pound."

But wasn't he going to be a little sad to see his lamb go? Matt rolled his eyes. "It's hard to get attached to a lamb called Butthead," he said and, giving me an "Are you done?" look, sprinted off toward the lights and music of the midway.

Fair time: That moment between summer and fall when young 4-H'ers sell off their lambs, when proud farmers bring in their

Adapted from "County Fairs" by John McCarry: National Geographic Magazine, October 1997.

fattest pumpkins or prettiest ears of corn and let them be judged against the efforts of their neighbors, when kids across the country lose themselves in the fantasy world of the carnival.

County fairs give us a chance to glimpse the American past. Yet they have lasted not by being annual historical reenactments but by evolving as American society evolves and becomes more urban.

In the summer and fall of 1996 I visited four county fairs scattered across the U.S.—in the Northwest, New England, the Midwest, and California. Whether in farm country or areas with more diverse economies, most of these fairs thrived as local people got together to reward one another for their small accomplishments, to celebrate their subtle regional differences, to compete gently. If a fair had momentarily faltered, it was perhaps because it was struggling to understand what kind of community it had found itself in.

I spent the latter part of my childhood in Northampton, Massachusetts, a city of 30,000 people in the western part of the state. My three brothers and I would eagerly await fair time—my eldest brother so he could show his Morgan horses, the rest of us just to spend the five bucks our parents gave each of us for the event. What I remember most was the elusive promise of winning the big stuffed Tweety Bird from the carny who kept urging, "Just give her one more try, kid; you'll be sure to get it next turn. Thataboy." I never won the Tweety Bird, although each year I would blow my money—25 cents at a time—trying.

For the first time since I was a kid, I returned to the Three County Fair in Northampton. I bought a ticket—entry alone was now five dollars—from Gordon Shoro, a local man in

T his used to be more of a family fair. Can't get the kids to come nowadays.

his 60s who has worked at the fair the past couple of years. I asked Shoro why he decided to help out at the fair.

"It takes me back," Shoro said. "I remember coming here when I was ten years old with only 52 cents in my pocket. I used to sneak in through a hole in the fence and then run like heck." Shoro, a gentle, quiet-voiced man, shook his head. "I don't know. It kind of seems to me there was more to see then. The chance booths were easier to win. And I knew everyone by sight. Now I hardly know anybody. This used to be more of a family fair. Can't get the kids to come nowadays."

One reason may be that Northampton, a market town with limited agriculture around it, has a lot of the upscale amenities of a big city. Young people, mostly students from the five nearby colleges, drift in and out of the ethnic restaurants, espresso bars, cybercafés, and pricey boutiques along Main Street. Very few are aware that less than a 15-minute walk away lie the grounds where one of the oldest continuous county fairs in the U.S. has been operating since 1818.

For years the biggest draw at the fair was the racetrack, but these days it's hard to get enough horses together to run the races. Passing through the entrance gates, I immediately came upon the track. Knots of people pored over racing forms, smoking cigarettes down to the filters, or sat on lawn chairs facing TV monitors, drinking beer from big plastic cups. There appeared to be more losers than winners on this gray day: A woman in a pair of stretchy lime green pants, a scarf knotted under her chin, kicked angrily at the litter of empty plastic cups and discarded racing forms scattered across the asphalt; another, lugging an outsize plastic shopping bag, muttered to herself, "Worse than a house of pain."

Winner of more than five dozen Humboldt County, California, gardening prizes, 93-year-old Mary Coppini has now retired from competition, making way for other ribbon-hungry green thumbs.

I walked along a muddy lane where a handful of pitchmen were trying to get the attention of a thin stream of passersby. I saw a woman hawking some sort of 20th-century snake oil and a man demonstrating an Electrolux vacuum cleaner.

At the far end of the fairgrounds, back near the rest rooms, Capt. Russell J. Myette stood at attention. Dressed in Union blue with a red stripe running down his pant leg to identify him as an artilleryman, Myette posed next to a reproduction of a 19th-century cannon, arms folded squarely across his barrel chest.

Born and raised in Northampton, Myette had worked as a maintenance supervisor for 38 years. After retiring in 1995, he devoted himself full-time to his living-history project. Taking their encampment all over the state, he and 13 other history buffs visit schools and teach young people about the Ninth Massachusetts Light Artillery, which suffered 37 casualties while making a valiant stand at Gettysburg.

Myette has invested $55,000 in his living-history display, which fills three trailers and takes four and a half hours to set up.

Here in Northampton all of this effort appeared to be almost for naught. "I don't know what's happened to us," Myette said, his voice sinking to a husky whisper. "Our sense of community seems to be gone. This fair here should be a reason for us all to come together, to teach one another things. But all anybody cares about are those horse races. The old-timers just don't care anymore. I see people I've known since I was a kid walk by and not even bother to take a look at my exhibit."

I left the fairgrounds through a modest wooden gate that was once the fair's main entrance. Is this what's happened to the fair of my childhood? Is this what's happened to America? I wondered as I walked along Route 9 toward Main Street and its crowds, feeling as dark as the ribbon of blacktop that stretched before me.

Just inside the entrance to the Clay County Fair in Spencer, Iowa, a semicircle of a hundred or so John Deere tractors glinted yellow and green in the dying afternoon light. Stationed at the top of this enormous horseshoe were Edward Morisch and his son, Michael. I asked Edward, a solidly built man with green suspenders and a John Deere cap, how they had gotten involved in the Northwest Iowa Two-Cylinder Club.

"Memories," Edward replied. "A few years back I saw an old B-John Deere advertised in the paper, and I recalled that back in the 1940s my dad traded in his pair of horses for his first tractor. It was a B-John Deere."

Michael added, "A lot of people did that, traded in their horses for B-John Deeres because they worked better with horse-drawn implements than other tractors. And maybe because of that, people are very close to their John Deeres. Just like people and horses, there's that deep kind of connection."

I asked the Morisches if they took their club's tractors to other fairs. "Nope," Michael said. "This is the only fair we do because this is the only fair in the area worth doing."

After five days in Spencer, I concluded that it would be near impossible to find anyone who would disagree. Just like farmers and their John Deeres, there's a deep kind of connection between the people of Clay County and their fair.

Although the population of Spencer is only about 12,000, the fair draws some 300,000 visitors. Once a year, rising from the endless flatness of the Iowa countryside, a crowd forms—to stroll, to hear big country music acts like the Statler Brothers, to sell a grand champion boar, to buy a new silo.

Like most county fairs, the Clay County Fair is a not-for-profit endeavor that relies on volunteers like Mary Christensen, who lives on a nearby farm. Christensen stood behind a display case of cookies and pies. An old woman was peering inside the case, her nose against the glass, intently examining a cake baked to look like a loaf of Wonder Bread in its wrapper. She looked up at Christensen and said, somewhat testily, "Back in 1930 they used to sell the cakes after they were judged," and shuffled off.

Christensen seemed unfazed. I asked how long she had been coming to the fair. "Forty-five years." And how long had she been volunteering? "Fifteen." Did she enjoy working at the fair? "We all come back. I guess something must bite ya." Preparing myself for a telegraphic reply, I asked why she volunteered.

Christensen looked at me for a long moment: "We're proud of our fair. We want to keep it going. People start talking 'fair' months in advance. The 1980s were hard on farmers. The fair forces us to stick together."

The Los Angeles County Fair evolved from a commercial-industrial show first held along the Southern Pacific Railroad siding in downtown Pomona in 1921. In 1996, more than a million people visited, making it the largest county fair in the United States. With eight hangar-size pavilions, a grandstand, a major horse-racing facility, 12 acres of carnival

continued on page 224

Amid the midway glitz at Los Angeles County's mammoth Fairplex, teenagers line up for snapshots of family and friends when fair time comes to city streets as well as country lanes.

continued from page 222

grounds, and an eight-story hotel, the fair has remained faithful to its commercial origins.

Before the Second World War, dairies and orchards flourished in L.A. County. Now, amid the urban sprawl, only a few farmers with tiny specialized plots remain. Yet the fair survives—not so much as an agricultural event but as a buoyant celebration of the diversity and energy of Los Angeles County.

To stroll through the Fairplex is to stroll through L.A., if such a thing were possible. Passing among the palm trees, I saw grab joints selling not only funnel cakes and corn dogs but also vegetarian tacos and Indian fry bread. To wash it down, I could certainly get a Coke—but why not a microbrew? Or a glass of Chardonnay from the Sonoma Valley?

In Fiesta Village, a re-creation of a plaza in a Latin American town, I watched a band perform Latin jazz. Poking around the shops on the square, I saw "Brown Power" T-shirts and Hispanic family shields. In the youth pavilion, Kids on Stage for a Better World—an outreach program of the Church of Scientology—sang a song by L. Ron Hubbard.

Back outside I wandered through the crowd, admiring the mission architecture, feeling the sun. A woman on stilts loped past, and a man riding a unicycle zipped by in the other direction. Someone handed me a flyer: "Don't let negative karma and experiences of a past life affect you in your present incarnation." I examined incense being sold by a Rasta with impressively long dreadlocks and thought about getting my picture taken astride a Harley-Davidson. "Only five bucks for a memory—what a deal!" the biker babe with the tattoos said.

I walked over to the High Tech Expo, where scores of computer monitors glowed, luring passersby into cyberspace. Like a great post-modern bazaar, the pavilion was a crush of activity as computer wonks shouted for attention and fairgoers elbowed their way onto the information highway.

Although agriculture continues to provide a motif, county fairs today are less about farming than they are about community—however it may define itself. They are where we Americans can go, in our ever increasing diversity, and feel that we belong.

Critical Responses

1. What is the tone of this article? What is the author's attitude toward fairs? What are some of the nuances and their effects?

2. What is the dominant mood of each of the accompanying photographs? How do the photographs interact with the text?

3. What makes some regional fairs thrive and some decline? Are the circumstances strictly local, or are broader cultural factors involved?

4. What makes county fairs "attractions"? To whom? Do they hold an attraction for you? Why or why not? How do they compare with your choices?

Writing Topics

1. "Community" is a word that comes up often in this article. What does it mean in each context? Are virtual communities included—or at least compatible? Or, if they're opposed, how so?

2. What is nostalgia, literally and figuratively? How and to what extent does this feeling inform this article? How do you respond, and why?

3. Focusing on two images in this feature, describe and compare the mood and the message each conveys.

4. Compare county fairs to carnivals, such as Mardi Gras. What do they have in common and how do they differ, particularly in the way each is related to the everyday working world?

Further Explorations

1. Describe a family tradition. What makes it endure?

2. What regions of the country are represented in your classroom? What special events are associated with those regions? What are some of the aims of these events and the values they foster? How do these events compare to county fairs, if at all?

THE BEAUTIFUL GAME: WHY SOCCER RULES THE WORLD

By Sean Wilsey

THE BEAUTIFUL GAME: WHY SOCCER RULES THE WORLD

Soccer is a game that unites and divides, brings out the best and the worst. Its global appeal is unflagging. Its fans grow in number all the time. What makes soccer so popular all over the world? Here, several journalists and novelists look at soccer from distinct national points of view and offer perspectives on what makes soccer a beautiful game.

Rain and mud can't hide the muscle and grace of a player during a match in Belgium.
Jimmy Bolcina/Photonews/Getty Images

English goalkeeper Joe Hart jumps for the ball during a Euro 2012 championship quarter-final match.

CARL DE SOUZA/AFP/Getty Images

SOCCER:
A GAME THAT UNITES—
AND DIVIDES—
COUNTRIES AROUND THE GLOBE.

There are many beautiful things about being an American fan of men's World Cup soccer—foremost among them is ignorance. The community in which you were raised did not gather around the television set every four years for a solid, breathless month. Your country has never won. You can pick whatever team you like best and root for it without shame or fear of reprisal. You have not been indoctrinated into unwanted-yet-inescapable tribal allegiances by your soccer-crazed countrymen. You are an amateur, in the purest sense of the word. So with the World Cup taking place this month in Germany—and the World Cup is the only truly international sporting event on the planet (no, the Olympics, with their overwhelming clutter of boutique athletics, do not matter in the same way)—you can expect to spend the month in paradise.

I am ready.

Soccer's worldwide popularity isn't surprising when you look at what has always motivated humanity: money and God. There's lots of money in soccer, of course. Club soccer

> **S**occer's popularity isn't surprising when you look at what has always motivated humanity; money and God.

(like capitalism) is basically the childlike desire to make dreams come true, no matter what the cost, realized by men with enough money to combine such commodities as the best Brazilian attacker, Dutch midfielder, British defender, and German goalie and turn them loose on whatever the other billionaires can put together—an unfair situation that describes much of the world these days. But the divine's there, too.

What is soccer if not everything that religion should be? Universal yet particular, the source of an infinitely renewable supply of hope, occasionally miraculous, and governed by simple, uncontradictory rules ("laws," officially) that everyone can follow. Soccer's laws are laws of equality and nonviolence and restraint, and free to be reinterpreted at the discretion of a reasonable arbiter. What the ref says goes, no matter how flagrantly in violation of dogma his decisions may be. My

Adapted from "The Beautiful Game: Why Soccer Rules the World" by Sean Wilsey: National Geographic Magazine, June 2006.

official rule book, after presenting a detailed enumeration of soccer's 17 laws, concludes that the ref can throw out any of them in order to apply what it rather mystically calls "the spirit of fair play."

The religious undercurrent in soccer runs especially deep in World Cup years. Teams from across the globe converge on the host nation in something of an unarmed, athletic crusade. As in the Crusades, the host nation tends to repel them. There's a weird power in home-team advantage. Hosts find a level of success disproportionate to their talents on paper, triumphing over stronger teams, as if exerting a gravitational pull on the game, causing it to be played the way they want to play it, as if, to carry this metaphor to its inevitable conclusion, God were on their side.

It's well-known that soccer, like religion, can provoke violence—hooliganism and tramplings at overcrowded, Mecca-mid-hajj-like stadiums are what many Americans assume about the game. But soccer has also proved unique in its ability to bridge differences and overturn national prejudices. The fact that the World Cup could even take place in South Korea and in Japan, as it did in 2002, was a victory for tolerance and understanding. In less than half a century South Korea had gone from not allowing the Japanese national team to cross its borders for a World Cup qualifier, to co-hosting the tournament with the former occupier. Give the world another 50 years and we might see the Cup co-hosted by Israel and Palestine.

And why not? Soccer's universality is its simplicity—the fact that the game can be played anywhere with anything. Urban children kick the can on concrete and rural kids kick a rag wrapped around a rag wrapped around a rag, barefoot, on dirt. Soccer is something to believe in now, perhaps empty at its core, but not a stand-in for anything else.

The beautiful game—let's call it business and religion combined—will be at its most unfair, frustrating, and magnificent this month in unified Germany's first World Cup.

And what makes the World Cup most beautiful is the world, all of us together. The joy of being one of the billion or more people watching 32 countries abide by 17 rules fills me with the conviction, perhaps ignorant, but like many ignorant convictions, fiercely held, that soccer can unite us all.

ENGLAND
Faded Glory: Taming the Hooligans
By Nick Hornby

It was all so straightforward back in the '60s, when I started to watch soccer. England had just won the 1966 World Cup and, therefore, unarguably, were the best team in the world: fact, period, end of story. Then everything went wrong, pretty much forever. For a start, I became a grown-up and much more troubled about what it meant to belong to a country; meanwhile England's soccer team was hopeless. (I may not have been so conflicted about the subject of patriotism if they'd been any good.) The team didn't even qualify for the World Cup of 1974 and 1978; the world-class players we'd been blessed with in the '60s had gone, and by the '80s, the whole subject of patriotism and soccer had become much more complicated.

In the mind's eye now, England games during that decade were only just visible through a cloud of tear gas, used by European police to disperse our rioting hooligans. England fans were fast becoming a pretty sinister bunch. If you went to see England play at Wembley, you could observe people around you making the Nazi salute during the national anthem, and abuse of black players—even those playing for the home team—was commonplace. Sometimes it seemed as though the thousand worst scumbag fans from every single league club were gathered at Wembley so they could make monkey noises and sing anti-IRA songs. If you saw someone coming toward you in a T-shirt sporting the Union Jack, you'd have been best advised to cross the street. The T-shirt was a graphic alternative to a slogan that might say something like, "I'm a racist, but I hate you no matter what color you are."

And so some soccer fans started to feel a little conflicted about the national team. In 1990, when England played Cameroon in the quarterfinals of the World Cup, it wasn't hard to find people in England—middle-class, liberal people, admittedly, but people nonetheless—who wanted Cameroon to win. I watched that game with some of them, and when England went 2-1 down (they eventually won 3-2 in extra time), these people cheered. I understood why, but I couldn't cheer with them, much to my surprise. Those drunk, racist thugs draped in the national colors.... They were, it turned out, my people, not the nice liberal friends I was watching the game with, and England was my soccer team. I mean, you can't choose stuff like that, right? The 1990 World Cup turned out to be a turning point. The team wasn't embarrassing. The fans weren't embarrassing either. After a horrendous couple of decades, the national team once again basked in the warmth of the nation's affections.

The rebirth lasted about five minutes. There was a disastrous managerial appointment, which resulted in yet another failure to qualify. And by 1998 soccer was a different game. Many of the players in our top division came from outside the British Isles. The globalization of the transfer market was beginning to rob international football of much of its point. In the old days, you'd look at the best players in the club teams and think, What would they be like if they played together? And the answer was they looked like the national team. Now, Chelsea, Manchester United, Real Madrid, Juventus, AC Milan, and Barcelona have replaced the national teams as fantasy soccer teams.

In 1989 England played out a goalless draw against Sweden, helping to ensure qualification for the 1990 World Cup. The enduring image of that game is of the England captain, Terry Butcher, swathed in a bandage, his white England shirt and shorts covered in blood that had pumped steadily out of a head wound throughout the game. "Off the pitch I was always an ordinary, mild-mannered bloke," said Butcher in an interview. "But put me in a football shirt and it was tin hats and fixed bayonets. Death or glory."

That was the old England: the war imagery, the crucial nil-nil draw against modest opposition, the unavoidable replacement of style and talent with blood and graft. Those who loathe David Beckham, the current England captain, would claim that he will wear a tin hat and bandages only when tin hats and bandages become de rigueur in some ludicrously fashionable European nightclub. That's not fair, because despite his looks and his cash, he has worked hard to compensate for things he lacks as a player, notably pace. But there's no doubt he is brilliantly illustrative of a new kind of English sportsman: professional, media-aware, occasionally petulant, and very, very rich.

The England fans who went to the 2005 friendly match against Argentina (resulting in a meaningless but enthralling last-minute win) were still singing their "No surrender to the IRA" song, and there's more than a suspicion that they'd rather be watching Terry Butcher and his fixed bayonets than David Beckham, a man who, after all, has been photographed wearing a sarong. But then, that's England all over at the moment. We'd still rather be bombing the Germans; but after 60 years, there's a slowly dawning suspicion that those days aren't coming back any time soon, and in the meantime we must rely on sarong-wearing, multimillionaire pretty boys to kick the Argies for us. We're not happy about it, but what can we do?

BRAZIL
Ballet with the Ball: A Love Story
By John Lanchester

Why do we fall in love with soccer? What happens? At some deep level the reason soccer snags us is that good soccer is beautiful, and it's difficult, and the two are related. A team kicking the ball to each other,

continued on page 234

Founding Fathers
Players at England's prestigious Harrow School pose in the late 1860s, shortly after the world's first football association formed in London. Though "Harrow football," like rugby, permits catching the ball, soccer (as the game is called in the U.S.) evolved into the hands-off kicker's sport it is today. In all, more than 200 countries now field national soccer teams.

Bob Thomas/Popperfoto/Getty Images

continued from page 231

passing into empty space that is suddenly filled by a player who wasn't there two seconds ago and who is running at full pelt and whom without looking or breaking stride knocks the ball back to a third player who he surely can't have seen, who, also at full pelt and without breaking stride, then passes the ball, at say 60 miles an hour, to land on the head of a fourth player who has run 75 yards to get there and who, again all in stride, jumps and heads the ball with, once you realize how hard this is, unbelievable power and accuracy toward a corner of the goal just exactly where the goalkeeper, executing some complex physics entirely without conscious thought and through muscle-memory, has expected it to be, so that all this grace and speed and muscle and athleticism and attention to detail and power and precision will never appear on a score sheet and will be forgotten by everybody a day later—this is the strange fragility, the evanescence of soccer. It's hard to describe and it is even harder to do, but it does have a deep beauty, a beauty hard to talk about and that everyone watching a game discovers for themselves, a secret thing, and this is the reason why soccer, which has so much ugliness around it and attached to it, still sinks so deeply into us: Because it is, it can be, so beautiful.

No country tries as hard or as consistently to play beautiful soccer as Brazil. It's an ideological thing. That is why Brazilian players are so loved. Not in South America, of course, where they have the status of a regional sporting superpower, but by pretty much everyone else in the world. In fact, the Brazil soccer team is unique in sports in being an example of a beloved overdog. In general, sports fans, and especially soccer fans, hate the overdogs (Real Madrid in Spain, Juventus in Italy, Manchester United/Chelsea in England). But Brazil, the only team to have won five World Cups, the only team to have won it playing away from its own continent, is loved. So

> **S**o a great many soccer fans have, at the national level, two teams: their own, and Brazil. It is the only favorite that's a favorite.

a great many soccer fans have, at the national level, two teams: their own, and Brazil. It is the only favorite that's a favorite.

SPAIN
Morality Play: Soccer as Theater
By Robert Coover

Spain, summer of '82. The smog cap over Barcelona is like the lid of a pressure cooker, ablaze with sunlight, and up here on the top tier of the little Sarriá soccer stadium, where Brazil, Italy, and Argentina are meeting in a World Cup knockout round-robin, they seem to have sold ten tickets for every square foot of space. We have to go an hour and a half early just to squeeze in at all. No way to sit, no chance to go for drinks, by the time the matches start it's hard to breathe. My teenage son spends one entire game hanging over an exit from a stair railing. Each day we say: If it's not bloody sensational, we'll go to a bar and watch it on TV, this is crazy. And each day we stay.

We've been here before. The other time, in 1977, two years after the death of the dictator Franco, it was raining and dark and turning cold. We stayed that time, too, huddled under an umbrella high up on the roof under the floodlights in the blustery winds and pouring rain in the only seats we could get, and happy to have them. That night we were watching a late autumn Spanish league match between the two archrivals of this city, FC (Fútbol Club) Barcelona and Real Club Deportivo Español (the Spanish Royal Sports Club), a match that was more like a reenactment of the Spanish Civil War than a mere athletic event.

There are, it sometimes seems, only two universal games: war and soccer. War is perhaps closer to the realm of fantasy, soccer to that of the real, but both share this ubiquity and centrality, as though arising from some collective libidinous source, primary and intuitive.

Dust flies as boys play a pickup match in southern Yemen, once a protectorate of the British Empire. In colonial days, British soldiers and missionaries spread the game to the empire's remotest corners. Today rivalries between colonized countries and their former overlords give World Cup matches added drama.

Marco Di Lauro/Getty Images

Perhaps they are simply variations of the same game, modern industrial-era ritualizations of some common activity from the Dreamtime of the species, back when both used the same players and the same field—which is to say, all the men of the tribe and all of nature. Still today, they often fade into one another. Soccer managers "declare war," generals apply soccer tactics and terminology, warlike violence invades the soccer field, spreads into the stands and out into the communities, soldiers wear their team colors into battle, fan clubs are known as "armies."

The explanations advanced for soccer's intense mysterious power, the trancelike quality of great matches, its worldwide domination over all other sports, have been many. There is the game's inherent theatricality— not the razzmatazz of an American halftime, but the inner dramas of sin and redemption, the testing of virtue, the pursuit of pattern and cohesion, the collision of paradoxical forces. Soccer has often been compared to Greek tragedy, or seen as a kind of open-ended morality play. Perhaps the difficulty in scoring (and thus the usual narrowness of margins of victory, even between teams of markedly unequal ability) intensifies this sense of theater, causing the denouement— or the collective catharsis—to be withheld almost always until the final whistle. Nor, until that whistle, is there relief from the tyranny of time's ceaseless flow: Once you've fallen into a game, there is no getting out. The player must stay with that flow, maintain the rhythm, press for advantage, preserving all his skills, his mind locked into the shifting patterns; and the spectator, though less arduously, shares this experience.

continued on page 237

A fan of Ghana's team waves their national flag during the team's match against Australia during the 2010 FIFA World Cup.
PABALLO THEKISO/AFP/Getty Images

continued from page 235

One is left at the end, not with data, but with impressionistic images of bodies in motion. Nothing of importance can be statistically recorded about a match except corners, shots, goals, and saves (the American effort to record assists is admirable but—since it's often a complete mystery, even with TV replays, who's scored the goal—a bit desperate), and these will tell you almost nothing about the game itself. The player who actually wins the game may be the one who moves into space at the opposite side of the field, drawing a defender, forcing a new configuration upon the defense and making virtually inevitable a goal that was before impossible, but no one—not even he—may be aware of this. It's all narrative, and thus subjective: Each game is a story, a sequence of ambivalent metaphors, a personal revelation couched in the idiom of the faith. No game I know of is so dependent upon such flowing intangibles as "pattern" and "rhythm" and "vision" and "understanding." Which may all be illusions. And at the same time it is a very simple game; like dreams, almost childlike.

ANGOLA
Greater Goal: Healing a War-Torn Land
By Henning Mankell

The first time I visited Angola I was not aware that I was in that country. It was 1987 and I was living in the northwestern corner of Zambia, near the Angolan border. Narrow sand roads twisted through the endless bush. It was easy to get stuck while driving, and I often lost my bearings on my way to some distant village. When I'd stop to ask for directions, if the person I spoke to answered in Portuguese then it was imperative to get back to the right side of the invisible border quickly. Angola, so deeply wounded by its long colonial period, was throttled after liberation from Portugal by a violent civil war. The rebel leader Jonas Savimbi's warriors, infamous for indiscriminate violence, were everywhere. A generation of Angolans did not know what it was to live in a country where peace reigned.

But there was also something magical about that land beyond the invisible border: Soccer was everywhere. On gravel pitches and sandy beaches, on sidewalks and city squares, the ball was played back and forth between hordes of young men. The balls were made of the most remarkable materials, an old T-shirt or fishing net or woman's handbag filled up with paper and grass. But they rolled and bounced, and you could do headers with them and make goals with them. War could never kill soccer in Angola. The soccer fields were demilitarized zones, and the face-off between teams conducting an intense yet essentially friendly battle served as a defense against the horrors that raged all around. It is harder for people who play soccer together to go out and kill each other.

Angola has seen many of its soccer players leave the country to seek their livelihood, mostly in Portugal. But they have not given up their citizenship. And when they are called home to put on black shorts and red socks and jerseys, their national team colors, they do not hesitate. They are known fondly as Palancas Negras, the "black antelopes."

On the eighth of October 2005, Angola arrives at Amahoro Stadium in Kigali. At that moment the astonishing situation is that if Angola can beat Rwanda by even a single goal, it will qualify for the World Cup ahead of Nigeria—no matter what happens in Nigeria's game against Zimbabwe. It is a nightmarish wait for all the Angolans who sit with their ears glued to radios. Luanda stands still, Huambo, Lubango, Namibe, Lobito, Benguela, Malanje, every city, every village is gathered at radios. Perhaps even the antelopes themselves stand out on the savanna with pricked ears.

When the first half ends, the score is tied at zero. Meanwhile, Nigeria is on its way to victory over Zimbabwe. But in Kigali the game continues without a goal. It all seems to be ending badly for Angola. One wonders what the players and coaches said to each other at the half. Nervousness spreads among the players. Rwanda, playing only for its honor, comes close to scoring on several occasions. Everyone agrees that Angola is playing miserably. It is a team at the edge of a breakdown, missing passes and misunderstanding each other. There are ten minutes left. The Angolans are almost unconscious in their desperation. Then the last-minute replacement Zé Kalanga makes a cross pass that is as surprising as it is brilliant. Fabrice "Akwa" Maieco is in the right place. With a header he perfectly launches the game's only goal, past Rwanda's goalie, one bounce on the ground, and then the ball flies up into the net.

A person would have to live for a long time in Africa to understand what this victory means. Of course no one imagines today that Angola will get very far in the tournament. But it is in the very nature of soccer to be unpredictable. If it were not the case that underdogs can sometimes defeat the predicted winners, soccer would be uninteresting.

But a great victory has already been won. It brought no gleaming cup. This triumph exists first of all in the hearts and minds of the Angolan people. To go to the finals of the World Cup in soccer means an enormous amount to the self-confidence of a country that has been ravaged by war and deprivation. A country, battered for so long, will be built up again.

Critical Responses

1. "Soccer can unite us all," writes Sean Wilsey in the introduction to the article. In what ways and to what extent do the descriptions of soccer by other contributors support this idea? Are there ways in which they do not?

2. What makes soccer beautiful? Are the qualities apparent in other games? Do other games have different characteristics of beauty?

3. How does soccer transcend national identity? How does soccer reinforce it? Are internationalism and nationalism at odds when it comes to soccer? Or are they complementary?

4. Reading this article, one would never know that a Women's World Cup championship has been held every four years since 1991. What do you make of the omission?

Writing Topics

1. Select two of the four descriptions of soccer in this article and compare them, paying particular attention to the cultural contexts of the descriptions and the metaphors and analogies used.

2. Money and religion, war and peace, tragedy and triumph, beauty and bloodshed—these themes recur in each section of the article. Follow the thread of one of them, elaborating on it in your own ways as well.

3. Choose a sport or recreation with which you're familiar, and write an essay in which you demonstrate its attractions to your audience and try to persuade them to participate.

4. Over the last few decades, soccer has become increasingly popular in the United States—so much so that almost 10 percent of the population watched the 2010 World Cup. What accounts for Americans' growing enthusiasm for playing as well as watching the sport?

Further Explorations

1. What are some characteristics of a sports fan? Are you one? What sport is your favorite, and why? If you're not a sports fan, you can still suggest answers to the first question. And whether you are or not, you might consider connections between the characteristics of the fan and that of the sport.

2. As of this writing, the most recent Men's World Cup championship was held in 2010 and the most recent Women's World Cup championship was held in 2011. Whether individually or in groups, research media representations of the two events and of the teams. How and to what extent does gender come into play?

THE ENIGMA OF BEAUTY

Like love, beauty moves us, and in ways we don't fully understand. Like love, beauty is a quality, a condition, even a force, and one that we've never quite pinned down. "I'll know it when I see it" is one way of answering the question, "What is beauty?" Here, *National Geographic* senior writer Cathy Newman and staff photographer Jodi Cobb look at some other questions and give us a glimpse of beauty, in its surfaces and its depths, as well as its ineffable mystery.

THE ENIGMA OF BEAUTY

By Cathy Newman

Photographs by Jodi Cobb

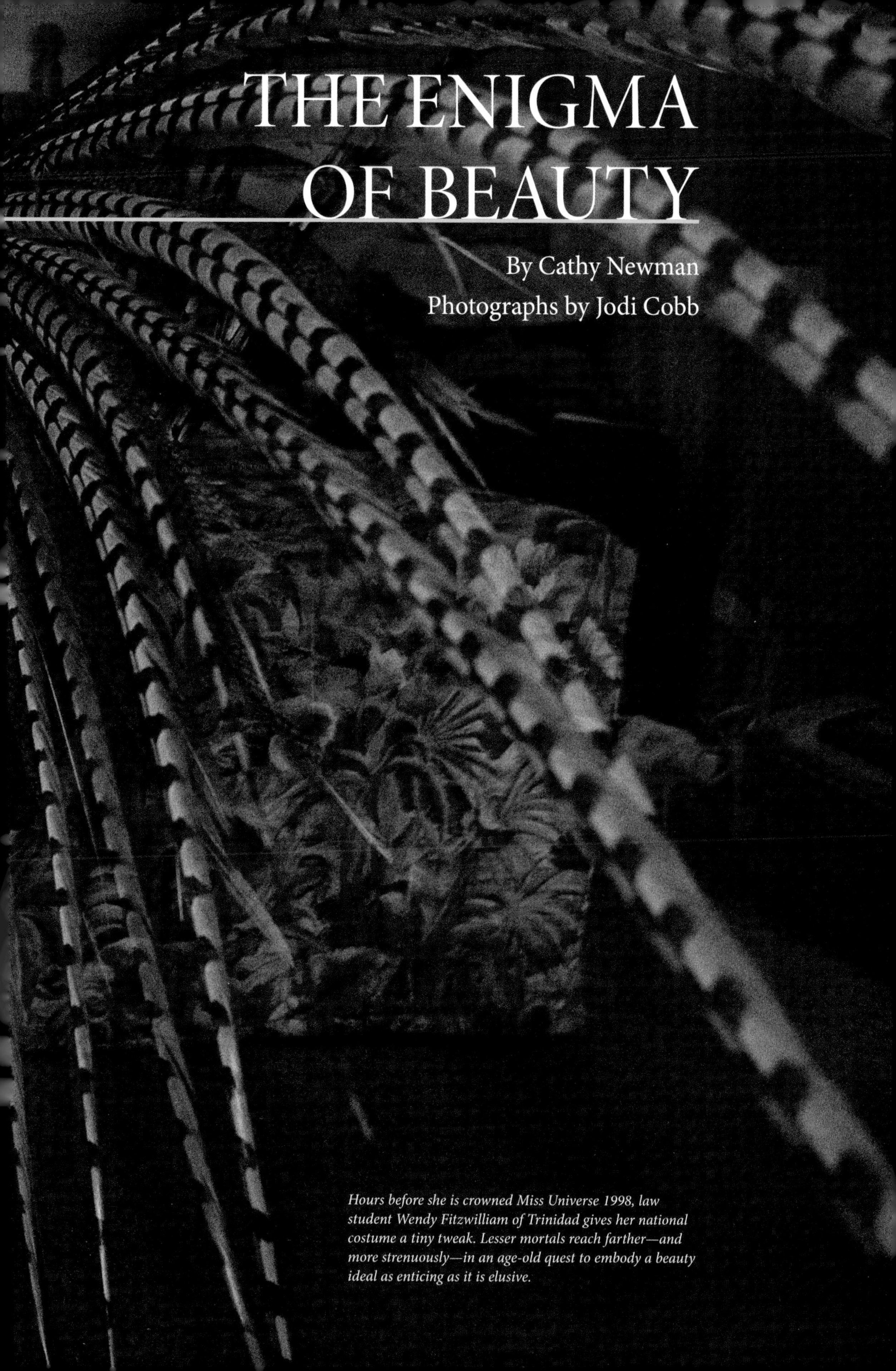

Hours before she is crowned Miss Universe 1998, law student Wendy Fitzwilliam of Trinidad gives her national costume a tiny tweak. Lesser mortals reach farther—and more strenuously—in an age-old quest to embody a beauty ideal as enticing as it is elusive.

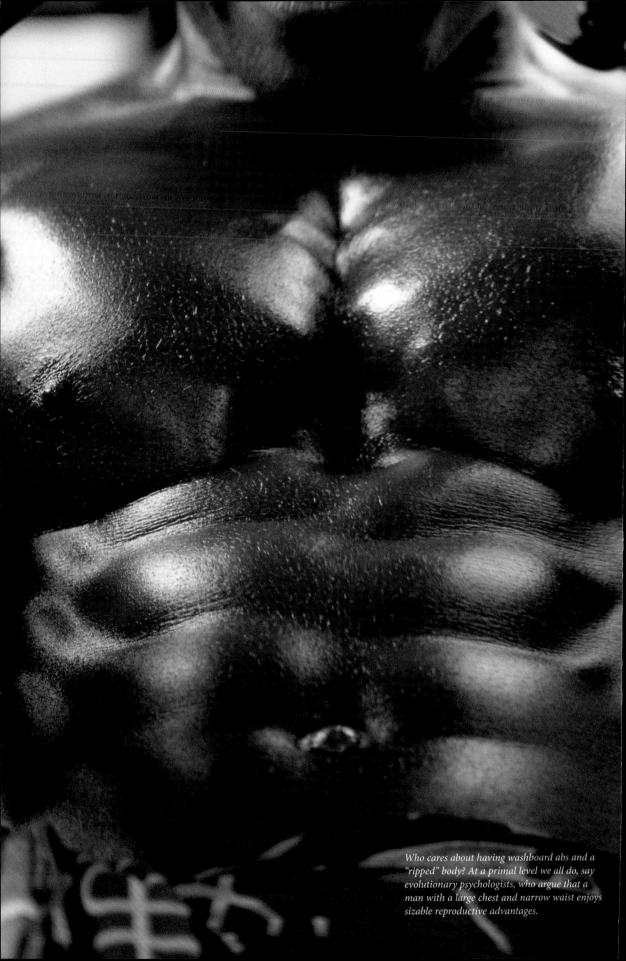

Who cares about having washboard abs and a "ripped" body? At a primal level we all do, say evolutionary psychologists, who argue that a man with a large chest and narrow waist enjoys sizable reproductive advantages.

SHELI JEFFRY IS SEARCHING FOR BEAUTY. AS A SCOUT FOR FORD, ONE OF THE WORLD'S TOP MODEL AGENCIES, JEFFRY SCANS UP TO 200 YOUNG WOMEN EVERY THURSDAY AFTERNOON. INSIDE AGENCY HEADQUARTERS IN NEW YORK, EXQUISITE FACES STARE DOWN FROM THE COVERS OF *VOGUE, GLAMOUR,* AND *HARPER'S BAZAAR.* OUTSIDE, YOUNG HOPEFULS WAIT FOR THEIR BIG CHANCE.

You're not what we're looking for right now.

Jeffry is looking for height: at least five feet nine. She's looking for youth: 13 to 19 years old. She's looking for the right body type.

What is the right body type?

"Thin," she says. "You know, the skinny girls in school who ate all the cheeseburgers and milk shakes they wanted and didn't gain an ounce. Basically, they're hangers for clothes."

In a year, Jeffry will evaluate several thousand faces. Of those, five or six will be tested. Beauty pays well. A beginning model makes $1,500 a day; those in the top tier, $25,000; stratospheric supermodels, such as Naomi Campbell, four times that.

Jeffry invites the first candidate in.

"Do you like the camera?" she asks Jessica from New Jersey.

"I love it. I've always wanted to be a model," Jessica says, beaming like a klieg light.

Others seem less certain. Marsha from California wants to check out the East Coast vibes, while Andrea from Manhattan works on Wall Street and wants to know if she has what it takes to be a runway star. (Don't give up a sure thing like a well-paying Wall Street job for this roll of the dice, Jeffry advises.)

The line diminishes. Faces fall and tears well as the refrain "You're not what we're looking for right now" extinguishes the conversation—and hope.

You're not what we're looking for. . . .

Confronted with this, Rebecca from Providence tosses her dark hair and asks: "What are you looking for? Can you tell me exactly?"

continued on page 246

Adapted from "The Enigma of Beauty" by Cathy Newman: National Geographic Magazine, January 2000.

It's a feast for the eyes backstage at the finals of the Elite Model Look competition in Nice, France. Some 350,000 girls from 55 countries compete in this search, which helps satisfy the advertisers and fashion mavens with their never ending demands for a new look, a fresh face.

continued from page 243

Jeffry meets the edgy, almost belligerent, tone with a composed murmur. "It's hard to say. I know it when I see it."

What is beauty? We grope around the edges of the question as if trying to get a toehold on a cloud.

"I'm doing a story on beauty," I tell a prospective interview. "By whose definition?" he snaps.

Define beauty? One may as well dissect a soap bubble. We know it when we see it—or so we think. Philosophers frame it as a moral equation. What is beautiful is good, said Plato. Poets reach for the lofty. "Beauty is truth, truth beauty," wrote John Keats, although Anatole France thought beauty "more profound than truth itself."

Others are more concrete. "People come to me and say: 'Doctor, make me beautiful,'" a plastic surgeon reveals. "What they are asking for is high cheekbones and a stronger jaw."

Science examines beauty and pronounces it a strategy. "Beauty is health," a psychologist tells me. "It's a billboard saying 'I'm healthy and fertile. I can pass on your genes.'"

At its best, beauty celebrates. From the Txikao warrior in Brazil painted in jaguar-like spots to Madonna in her metal bra, humanity revels in the chance to shed its everyday skin and masquerade as a more powerful, romantic, or sexy being.

At its worst, beauty discriminates. Studies suggest attractive people make more money, get called on more often in class, receive lighter court sentences, and are perceived as friendlier. We do judge a book by its cover.

We soothe ourselves with clichés. It's only skin-deep, we cluck. It's only in the eye of the beholder. Pretty is as pretty does.

In an era of feminist and politically correct values, not to mention the closely held belief that all men and women are created equal, the fact that all men and women are not—and that some are more beautiful than others—disturbs, confuses, even angers.

Beauty is health. It's a billboard saying "I'm healthy and fertile. I can pass on your genes."

For better or worse, beauty matters. How much it matters can test our values. With luck, the more we live and embrace the wide sweep of the world, the more generous our definition becomes.

The search for beauty spans centuries and continents. A relief in the tomb of the Egyptian nobleman Ptahhotep, who lived around 2400 B.C., shows him getting a pedicure. Cleopatra wore kohl, an eyeliner made from ground-up minerals.

Love of appearance was preeminent among the aristocracy of the 18th century. Montesquieu, the French essayist, wrote: "There is nothing more serious than the goings-on in the morning when Madam is about her toilet." But monsieur, in his wig of cascading curls, scented gloves, and rouge, was equally narcissistic. "They have their color, toilet, powder puffs, pomades, perfumes," noted one lady socialite, "and it occupies them just as much as or even more than us."

The search for beauty could be macabre. To emphasize their noble blood, women of the court of Louis XVI drew blue veins on their necks and shoulders.

The search for beauty could be deadly. Vermilion rouge used in the 18th century was made of a sulfur and mercury compound. Men and women used it at the peril of lost teeth and inflamed gums. They sickened, sometimes died, from lead in the white powder they dusted on their faces. In the 19th century women wore whalebone and steel corsets that made it difficult to breathe, a precursor of the stomach-smooshing Playtex Living Girdle.

The search for beauty is costly. In the United States last year people spent six billion dollars on fragrance and another six billion on makeup. Hair- and skin-care products drew eight billion dollars each, while fingernail items alone accounted for a billion. In the mania to lose weight 20 billion was spent on diet products and services—in addition to the billions that were paid out for health club memberships and cosmetic surgery.

Despite the costs, the quest for beauty prevails, an obsession once exemplified by the taste of Copper Eskimo women for a style of boot that let in snow but was attractive to men because of the waddle it inflicted on the wearer—a fashion statement not unlike the ancient Chinese custom of foot binding or the 20th-century high heel shoe.

I am standing behind a one-way mirror watching a six-month-old baby make a choice. The baby is shown a series of photographs of faces that have been rated for attractiveness by a panel of college students. A slide is flashed; a clock ticks as the baby stares at the picture. The baby looks away; the clock stops. Then it's on to the next slide.

After more than a decade of studies like these, Judith Langlois, professor of psychology at the University of Texas in Austin, is convinced that this baby, like others she has tested, will spend more time looking at the attractive faces than the unattractive ones.

What's an attractive face? It's a symmetrical face. Most important, it's an averaged face, says Langlois. Averaged, that is, in terms of position and size of all the facial features. As the slides flash in front of the baby, I see what she means. Some faces are more pleasing to look at than others. It's a question of harmony and the placement of features. The picture of the young girl with wide-set eyes and a small nose is easier on the eye than the one of the young girl with close-set eyes and a broad nose. Extremes are off-putting and generally not attractive, Langlois says.

The idea that even babies can judge appearance makes perfect sense to Don Symons, an anthropologist at the University of California at Santa Barbara.

"Beauty is not whimsical. Beauty has meaning. Beauty is functional," he says. Beauty, his argument goes, is not so much in the eye as in the brain circuitry of the beholder.

In the scenario envisioned by Symons and other evolutionary scientists, the mind unconsciously tells men that full lips and clear skin equal health, fertility, and genetic soundness. It's an instinct honed over a hundred thousand years of selection, Symons believes. Because we are mortgaged to our evolutionary history, the instinct persists.

Not everyone agrees. "Our hardwiredness can be altered by all sorts of expectations—predominantly cultural," says C. Loring Brace, an anthropologist at the University of Michigan. "The idea that there is a standard desirable female type tells you more about the libidinous fantasies of aging male anthropologists than anything else."

Douglas Yu, a biologist from Great Britain, and Glenn Shepard, an anthropologist at the University of California at Berkeley, found that indigenous peoples in southeast Peru preferred shapes regarded as overweight in Western cultures: "A fuller evolutionary theory of human beauty must embrace variation," Yu says.

In the world of beauty there are many variations on a theme, but one thing seems clear. Every culture has its bad hair day. In central Australia balding Aranda Aborigines once wore wigs made of emu feathers. Likewise, the Azande in Sudan wore wigs made of sponge. To grow long hair among the Ashanti in Nigeria made one suspect of contemplating murder, while in Brazil the Bororo cut hair as a sign of mourning.

Hair has other shades of meaning. Although the archetypal male hero in Western civilization is tall, dark, and handsome like Cary Grant, blond women have sometimes been imagined as having more fun.

What other signals does hair send? In most societies, short hair means restraint and discipline: Think West Point, Buddhist monks, and prison. Long hair means freedom and unconventional behavior: Think Lady Godiva and Abbie Hoffman. Hair says I'm grown-up, and let's get that first haircut. It's the stages of life, from pigtails to ponytail to gray hair.

continued on page 250

continued from page 247

"This is what I looked like at age five," Noliwe Rooks, a visiting assistant professor of history and African-American studies at Princeton, tells me.

We're at her dining table drinking tea and talking about hair—specifically African-American hair—and how it defines culture, politics, and the tension between generations. The photograph she shows me is of a little girl with a big puff ball of an Afro staring up at the camera.

"My mother was a political activist, and so I wore my hair like this until I was 13," Rooks says, smiling.

"My grandmother had this huge issue with it. I was her only grandchild, and she couldn't stand it. It wasn't cute. It wasn't feminine. You couldn't put little bows in it. Every summer my mother would take me down to Florida to stay with her. As soon as my mother left, my grandmother would take me to Miss Ruby's beauty parlor and straighten my hair. Issues between my mother, my grandmother, and me got worked out around my hair."

While in college Rooks decided to let her hair "lock," or grow into a mass of pencil-thin dreadlocks.

"Before I was able to tell my grandmother, she had a stroke. I found myself on a plane flying to her bedside, rehearsing how I was going to explain the locks. The doctors didn't know the extent of the damage. She hadn't spoken. All she could make were garbled sounds. I couldn't wear a hat to hide my hair. It was Florida. It was 80 degrees. I walked into her hospital room, expecting the worst, when all of a sudden she opened her eyes and looked at me."

"'What did you do to your hair?' she said, suddenly regaining the power of speech."

After her grandmother died, Rooks found herself in front of the mirror cutting her hair in a gesture of mourning.

"When my grandmother was in the hospital, I'd brushed her hair. I pulled the gray hairs out of the brush, put them in a plastic bag, and put it in front of her picture. That was hair for me. There was so much about it that defined our relationship. It meant closeness, and then, finally, acceptance."

Gravity takes its toll on us all. That, along with time, genetics, and environment, is what beauty's archenemy, aging, is about. "The bones stay upright until you go permanently horizontal," says Dr. Linton Whitaker, chief of plastic surgery at the University of Pennsylvania Medical Center. "As the soft tissue begins to sag off the bones, the rosy cheeks of childhood become the sallow jowls of the elderly. What was once jawline becomes a wattle."

Blame the vulnerability of flesh on collagen and elastin—materials found in the second layer of our skin that give it elasticity.

"Collagen under a microscope is like a knit sweater," Whitaker explains. "After the 10,000th wearing and stretching, it becomes baggy, and the same with skin. When the knit of collagen and elastin begins to fragment, skin loses its elasticity." Then gravity steps in.

"If aging is a natural process, isn't there something unnatural about all this surgical snipping and stitching to delay the inevitable?" I ask.

"I guess it's not natural, but what is?" Whitaker sighs. "It's the world we live in. Right or wrong, it's a judgment. But it's doable and makes people happy."

At 48, gravity has taken its toll on me. I look at the mirror and note the delta of wrinkles starting to branch from the corners of my eyes. My chin has begun to blur into my neck. There is a suggestion of jowliness.

Of course I could consult a plastic surgeon like Dr. Sherwood Baxt. On the day I visit his office in Paramus, New Jersey, Baxt, a tall man with a sweep of graying hair, is dressed in a well-cut charcoal double-breasted suit with a pinstripe shirt, yellow silk tie affixed by a gold safety pin, and a pair of black tasseled calf loafers.

You might say that Baxt, who has not one but three different lasers for sculpting, peeling, and taming the bumps and wrinkles of imperfect flesh, offers one-stop shopping for cosmetic surgery. The centerpiece of his office complex is an operating suite that would be the envy of a small community hospital.

"Plastic surgery is exciting," Baxt tells me in calm, reassuring tones. "We're lifting, tightening, firming. We change people's lives."

"How and why?" I want to know.

"Most of my patients work," he says. "I see a lot of high-power women who can't fit into a suit anymore because of hormonal changes and pregnancies. They're in a competitive world. Liposuction is the most common procedure. The face is the next order of business—the eyes, double chins. All of that says to the workforce, 'You look a bit tired. You're a bit over the hill. You're having trouble keeping up.'"

Wondering how I'd fare with a nip and tuck of my own, I've asked for a consultation. Thanks to computer imaging, I can get a preview. An assistant takes front and side views of my face with a Polaroid camera and scans them into a computer. As I watch, my face pops up on the screen and then morphs as Baxt manipulates the image. The softness under my chin retracts into firmness; the circles under my eyes disappear; wrinkles smooth out. I'm looking younger—not the hard, stiff, pulled-tight mask-look that screams "face-lift! face-lift!"—but more subtly younger.

The tab? About nine or ten thousand dollars. Of course my insurance would never pay this bill. It's strictly out-of-pocket. No problem. Baxt offers an installment plan.

Back home, I stare at myself in the mirror. I've always scoffed at plastic surgery. Then 50 loomed into view. Now I'm more tolerant. We are living longer. We are healthier. Today the average life expectancy is 76 years. Fifty years ago it was 68. One hundred years ago it was 48. The face in the mirror doesn't always reflect how old or young we feel.

The sad, sometimes ugly, side of beauty: In a 1997 magazine survey, 15 percent of women and 11 percent of men sampled said they'd sacrifice more than five years of their life to be at their ideal weight. Others were prepared to make other sacrifices. One 25-year-old Maryland woman said: "I love children and would love to have one more—but only if I didn't have to gain the weight."

Is life not worth living unless you're thin?

"Girls are literally weighing their self-esteem." says Catherine Steiner Adair, a psychologist at the Harvard Eating Disorders Center in Boston. "We live in a culture that is completely bonkers. We're obsessed with sylphlike slimness, yet heading toward obesity. According to one study, 80 percent of women are dissatisfied with their bodies. Just think about how we talk about food: 'Let's be really bad today and have dessert.' Or: 'I was good. I didn't eat lunch.'"

In one of its worst manifestations, discontent with one's body can wind up as an eating disorder, such as anorexia, a self-starvation syndrome, or bulimia, a binge-and-purge cycle in which people gorge and then vomit or use laxatives. Both can be fatal.

Today eating disorders, once mostly limited to wealthy Western cultures, occur around the world. "I was in Fiji the year television was introduced," says Dr. Anne Becker, director of research at the Harvard center. "Eating disorders were virtually unknown in Fiji at that time." When she returned three years later, 15 percent of the girls she was studying had tried vomiting to lose weight.

In Japan anorexia was first documented in the 1960s. It now affects an estimated one in one hundred Japanese women and has spread to other parts of Asia, including Korea, Singapore, and Hong Kong. In the U.S., according to the Menninger Clinic in Topeka, Kansas, the proportion of females affected by eating disorders is around 5 to 10 percent.

To say that all women with eating disorders want to look like runway models is to gloss over a complex picture that weaves biology and family dynamics in with cultural

> The face in the mirror doesn't always reflect how old or young we feel.

influences. One thing can be said: Eating disorders are primarily a disease of women.

"It's easy to be oversimplistic in defining causes," says Emily Kravinsky, medical director at the Renfrew Center in Philadelphia, a treatment center for women with eating disorders. "Some of these women don't know how to cope or soothe themselves. They have low self-esteem. Also, there's increasing evidence that biology and genetics play a role. Finally, the distance between the cultural ideal of what we would like to look like and the reality of what we actually look like is becoming wider. If Marilyn Monroe walked into Weight Watchers today, no one would bat an eye. They'd sign her up."

The preoccupation with beauty can be a neurosis, and yet there is something therapeutic about paying attention to how we look and feel.

One day in early spring, I went to Bliss, a spa in New York. It had been a difficult winter, and I needed a bit of buoyancy. At Bliss I could sink back in a sand-colored upholstered chair, gaze at the mural of the seashore on the walls, and laugh as I eased my feet into a basin of warm milk. I could luxuriate in the post-milk rubdown with sea salts and almond oil. Beauty can be sheer self-indulgent pleasure as well as downright fun, and it's best not to forget it.

"People are so quick to say beauty is shallow," says Ann Marie Gardner, beauty director of *W* magazine. "They're fearful. They say: 'It doesn't have substance.' What many don't realize is that it's fun to reinvent yourself, as long as you don't take it too seriously. Think of the tribesmen in New Guinea in paint and feathers. It's mystical. It's a transformation. That's what we're doing when we go to a salon. We are transforming ourselves."

Until she was a hundred years old, my grandmother Mollie Spier lived in a condominium in Hallandale, Florida, and had a "standing," a regular appointment, at the beauty salon down the street. Every Friday she would drive, then later be driven, for a shampoo, set, and manicure.

This past year, too frail to live on her own, she moved to a nursing home and away from her Friday appointment.

A month before she died, I went to visit her. Before I did, I called to ask if she wanted me to make an appointment for her at the salon.

"I could drive you, Grandma. We could take your nurse and wheelchair. Do you think you could handle it?"

"Of course," she replied, as if I'd asked the silliest question in the world. "What's the big deal? All I have to do is sit there and let them take care of me."

On a Friday afternoon I picked my grandmother up at the nursing home and drove her to the salon she hadn't visited in more than a year. I wheeled her in and watched as she was greeted and fussed over by Luis, who washed and combed her fine pewter gray hair into swirls, then settled a fog of hair spray over her head.

When he was finished, Yolanda, the manicurist, appeared. "Mollie, what color would you like your nails?"

"What's new this year? I want something no one else has," she shot back, as if in impossibly fast company at the Miami Jewish Home for the Aged.

Afterward I drove my grandmother back to the nursing home. She admired her fire engine red nails every quarter mile. Glancing in the car mirror, she patted her cloud of curls and radiated happiness.

"Mollie," said the nurse behind the desk when I brought her back. "You look absolutely beautiful."

Critical Responses

1. What is enigmatic about beauty? In what ways does the article affirm this enigmatic quality? In what ways does the article dispel it?

2. What is ugliness? Is that enigmatic, too? Can ugliness be attractive? Or does it always repel?

3. Although beauty exists in innumerable forms—take the article on soccer, "The Beautiful Game," as just one example—here beauty is described and defined predominantly in terms of women's appearances, and mostly in the United States. Does this perspective shed light on beauty itself?

4. On the other hand, photographs accompanying the text are confined neither to women nor to the West. How do you see these images? How do they further an understanding of beauty? What do they convey?

Writing Topics

1. "For better or for worse, beauty matters," writes Cathy Newman. Using your own examples, consider how and why it does.

2. Compare the account of love in the article entitled "This Thing Called Love" with the account of beauty in this one. How are love and beauty related? To what extent does one depend on the other or not?

3. What is the price of beauty, according to this article? Is beauty worth the price? In pursuing these questions, look at the article on "The Price of Gold" in this reader as well.

4. When it comes to the physical appearance of American women, what type or types of body image does the U.S. media promote? Do these representations contribute to an appreciation for diversity, or the reverse?

Further Explorations

1. It has been over a decade since this feature was published. What does female beauty look like these days in the United States? Have ideas of beauty changed in any significant ways in recent years?

2. Individually or in groups, examine some popular representations of male beauty, and compare what makes a man good looking to what makes a woman look good.

THIS THING
CALLED LOVE

By Lauren Slater

Photographs by Jodi Cobb

THIS THING CALLED LOVE

"Fondness," "infatuation," "attachment," "adoration," "passion," "affection"—all of these and many more words are associated with love, but none is quite a synonym for it. Does love encompass all these feelings? Is love something else in itself? Why is love, which is so powerful and prevalent, so hard to define? Can science grasp what it is? In the feature below, author and psychologist Lauren Slater looks at some recent research that scrutinizes this thing called love—which may or may not help explain what it is.

What's kept Emily and Marion Grillot married for 58 years? It may be the bond forged by having children—20 of them, plus 77 grandkids, many pictured in the Grillots' Ohio home. It could be the calming effect of oxytocin, a chemical thought to be plentiful in long-term couples. For Mr. Grillot, a farmer, "it's our commitment and concern for one another. Some call it love."

Sometimes love appears when it's least expected. By the time Jodi Cobb arrived in Florence, Italy, she'd already rounded the globe photographing courtship and marriage rituals. Wandering the streets on a hot summer afternoon, her eyes were drawn to the scene of a lone woman at a café. "I started taking pictures, thinking to myself, 'This is great, but it has nothing to do with the story.' Then I noticed the headline and thought, 'Yes!'" A phonetic rendering of "I love you," the headline tops an elaborate greeting card in the guise of a newspaper proclaiming the sender's passionate devotion.

SCIENTISTS ARE DISCOVERING THAT

THE COCKTAIL OF BRAIN CHEMICALS THAT SPARKS ROMANCE IS TOTALLY DIFFERENT FROM THE BLEND THAT FOSTERS LONG-TERM ATTACHMENT.

SO WHAT, REALLY, IS THIS THING CALLED LOVE?

For the first time, new research has begun to illuminate where love lies in the brain, the particulars of its chemical components.

In the Western world we have for centuries concocted poems and stories and plays about the cycles of love, the way it morphs and changes over time, the way passion grabs us by our flung-back throats and then leaves us for something saner. If *Dracula*—the frail woman, the sensuality of submission—reflects how we understand the passion of early romance, the *Flintstones* reflects our experiences of long-term love: All is gravel and somewhat silly, the song so familiar you can't stop singing it, and when you do, the emptiness is almost unbearable.

We have relied on stories to explain the complexities of love, tales of jealous gods and arrows. Now, however, these stories—so much a part of every civilization—may be changing as science steps in to explain what we have always felt to be myth, to be magic. For the first time, new research has begun to illuminate where love lies in the brain, the particulars of its chemical components.

Anthropologist Helen Fisher may be the closest we've ever come to having a doyenne of desire. At 60 she exudes a sexy confidence, with corn-colored hair, soft as floss, and a willowy build. A professor at Rutgers University, she lives in New York City, her book-lined apartment near Central Park, with its green trees fluffed out in the summer season, its paths crowded with couples holding hands.

One of Fisher's central pursuits in the past decade has been looking at love, quite literally, with the aid of an MRI machine. Fisher and her colleagues Arthur Aron and Lucy Brown recruited subjects who had been "madly in love" for an average of seven months. Once

Adapted from "This Thing Called Love" by Lauren Slater: National Geographic Magazine, February 2006.

inside the MRI machine, subjects were shown two photographs, one neutral, the other of their loved one.

What Fisher saw fascinated her. When each subject looked at his or her loved one, the parts of the brain linked to reward and pleasure—the ventral tegmental area and the caudate nucleus—lit up. What excited Fisher most was not so much finding a location, an address, for love as tracing its specific chemical pathways. Love lights up the caudate nucleus because it is home to a dense spread of receptors for a neurotransmitter called dopamine, which Fisher came to think of as part of our own endogenous love potion. In the right proportions, dopamine creates intense energy, exhilaration, focused attention, and motivation to win rewards. It is why, when you are newly in love, you can stay up all night, watch the sun rise, run a race, ski fast down a slope ordinarily too steep for your skill. Love makes you bold, makes you bright, makes you run real risks, which you sometimes survive, and sometimes you don't.

I first fell in love when I was only 12, with a teacher. His name was Mr. McArthur, and he wore open-toed sandals and sported a beard. I had never had a male teacher before, and I thought it terribly exotic. Mr. McArthur did things no other teacher dared to do. He explained to us the physics of farting. He demonstrated how to make an egg explode. He smoked cigarettes at recess, leaning languidly against the side of the school building, the ash growing longer and longer until he casually tapped it off with his finger.

What unique constellation of needs led me to love a man who made an egg explode is interesting, perhaps, but not as interesting, for me, as my memory of love's sheer physical facts. I had never felt anything like it before. I could not get Mr. McArthur out of my mind. I was anxious; I gnawed at the lining of my cheek until I tasted the tang of blood. School became at once terrifying and exhilarating. Would I see him in the hallway? In the cafeteria? I hoped. But when my wishes were granted, and I got a glimpse of

my man, it satisfied nothing; it only inflamed me all the more. Had he looked at me? Why had he not looked at me? When would I see him again? At home I looked him up in the phone book; I rang him, this in a time before caller ID. He answered.

"Hello?" Pain in my heart, ripped down the middle. Hang up.

Call back. "Hello?" I never said a thing.

Once I called him at night, late, and from the way he answered the phone it was clear, even to a prepubescent like me, that he was with a woman. His voice fuzzy, the tinkle of her laughter in the background. I didn't get out of bed for a whole day.

Sound familiar? Maybe you were 30 when it happened to you, or 8 or 80 or 25. Maybe you lived in Kathmandu or Kentucky; age and geography are irrelevant. Donatella Marazziti is a professor of psychiatry at the University of Pisa in Italy who has studied the biochemistry of lovesickness. Having been in love twice herself and felt its awful power, Marazziti became interested in exploring the similarities between love and obsessive-compulsive disorder.

She and her colleagues measured serotonin levels in the blood of 24 subjects who had fallen in love within the past six months and obsessed about this love object for at least four hours every day. Serotonin is, perhaps, our star neurotransmitter, altered by our star psychiatric medications: Prozac and Zoloft and Paxil, among others. Researchers have long hypothesized that people with obsessive-compulsive disorder (OCD) have a serotonin "imbalance." Drugs like Prozac seem to alleviate OCD by increasing the amount of this neurotransmitter available at the juncture between neurons.

Marazziti compared the lovers' serotonin levels with those of a group of people suffering from OCD and another group who were free from both passion and mental illness. Levels of serotonin in both the obsessives' blood and the lovers' blood were 40 percent lower than those in her normal subjects. Translation: Love and obsessive-compulsive disorder could have a similar chemical profile. Translation: Love and mental illness may be difficult to tell apart. Translation: Don't be a fool. Stay away.

Psychoanalysts have concocted countless theories about why we fall in love with whom we do. Freud would have said your choice is influenced by the unrequited wish to bed your mother, if you're a boy, or your father, if you're a girl. Jung believed that passion is driven by some kind of collective unconscious. Today psychiatrists such as Thomas Lewis from the University of California at San Francisco's School of Medicine hypothesize that romantic love is rooted in our earliest infantile experiences with intimacy, how we felt at the breast, our mother's face, these things of pure unconflicted comfort that get engraved in our brain and that we ceaselessly try to recapture as adults. According to this theory we love whom we love not so much because of the future we hope to build but because of the past we hope to reclaim. Love is reactive, not proactive, it arches us backward, which may be why a certain person just "feels right." Or "feels familiar." He or she is familiar. He or she has a certain look or smell or sound or touch that activates buried memories.

When I first met my husband, I believed this psychological theory was more or less correct. My husband has red hair and a soft voice. A chemist, he is whimsical and odd. One day before we married he dunked a rose in liquid nitrogen so it froze, whereupon he flung it against the wall, spectacularly shattering it. That's when I fell in love with him. My father, too, has red hair, a soft voice, and many eccentricities. He was prone to bursting into song, prompted by something we never saw.

However, it turns out my theories about why I came to love my husband may be just so much hogwash. Evolutionary psychology has said good riddance to Freud and the Oedipal complex and all that other transcendent stuff and hello to simple survival skills. It hypothesizes that we tend to see as attractive, and

Love and mental illness may be difficult to tell apart.

thereby choose as mates, people who look healthy. And health, say these evolutionary psychologists, is manifested in a woman with a 70 percent waist-to-hip ratio and men with rugged features that suggest a strong supply of testosterone in their blood. Waist-to-hip ratio is important for the successful birth of a baby, and studies have shown this precise ratio signifies higher fertility. As for the rugged look, well, a man with a good dose of testosterone probably also has a strong immune system and so is more likely to give his partner healthy children.

Perhaps our choice of mates is a simple matter of following our noses. Claus Wedekind of the University of Lausanne in Switzerland did an interesting experiment with sweaty T-shirts. He asked 49 women to smell T-shirts previously worn by unidentified men with a variety of the genotypes that influence both body odor and immune systems. He then asked the women to rate which T-shirts smelled the best, which the worst. What Wedekind found was that women preferred the scent of a T-shirt worn by a man whose genotype was most different from hers, a genotype that, perhaps, is linked to an immune system that possesses something hers does not. In this way she increases the chance that her offspring will be robust.

It all seems too good to be true, that we are so hardwired and yet unconscious of the wiring. Because no one to my knowledge has ever said, "I married him because of his B.O." No. We say, "I married him (or her) because he's intelligent, she's beautiful, he's witty, she's compassionate." But we may just be as deluded about love as we are when we're *in* love. If it all comes down to a sniff test, then dogs definitely have the edge when it comes to choosing mates.

Why doesn't passionate love last? How is it possible to see a person as beautiful on Monday, and 364 days later, on another Monday, to see that beauty as bland? Surely the object of your affection could not have changed that much. She still has the same shaped eyes. Her

continued on page 262

"I'd do anything for you," whispers Blair Witherspoon to girlfriend Erica Hoskey. That includes giving her the Tweety Bird he won shooting baskets at the Butler County Fair in Pennsylvania. Sweet talk and gifts fuel romantic passion. But biochemists say this feverish stage of love typically burns out after a few years. Why? Perhaps the brain can't maintain the intense neural activity of infatuation.

continued from page 259

voice has always had that husky sound, but now it grates on you—she sounds like she needs an antibiotic. Or maybe you're the one who needs an antibiotic, because the partner you once loved and cherished and saw as though saturated with starlight now feels more like a low-level infection, tiring you, sapping all your strength.

Studies around the world confirm that, indeed, passion usually ends. Its conclusion is as common as its initial flare. No wonder some cultures think selecting a life-long mate based on something so fleeting is folly. Helen Fisher has suggested that relationships frequently break up after four years because that's about how long it takes to raise a child through infancy. Passion, that wild, prismatic insane feeling, turns out to be practical after all. We not only need to copulate; we also need enough passion to start breeding, and then feelings of attachment take over as the partners bond to raise a helpless human infant. Once a baby is no longer nursing, the child can be left with sister, aunts, friends. Each parent is now free to meet another mate and have more children.

Biologically speaking, the reasons romantic love fades may be found in the way our brains respond to the surge and pulse of dopamine that accompanies passion and makes us fly. Cocaine users describe the phenomenon of tolerance: The brain adapts to the excessive input of the drug. Perhaps the neurons become desensitized and need more and more to produce the high—to put out pixie dust, metaphorically speaking.

Maybe it's a good thing that romance fizzles. Would we have railroads, bridges, planes, faxes, vaccines, and television if we were all always besotted? In place of the ever evolving technology that has marked human culture from its earliest tool use, we would have instead only bonbons, bouquets, and birth control. More seriously, if the chemically altered state induced by romantic love is akin to a mental illness or a drug-induced euphoria, exposing yourself for too long could result in psychological damage. A good sex life can be as strong as Gorilla Glue, but who wants that stuff on your skin?

Once upon a time, in India, a boy and a girl fell in love without their parents' permission. They were from different castes, their relationship radical and unsanctioned. Picture it: the sparkling sari, the boy in white linen, the clandestine meetings on tiled terraces with a fat, white moon floating overhead. Who could deny these lovers their pleasure, or condemn the force of their attraction?

Their parents could. In one recent incident a boy and girl from different castes were hanged at the hands of their parents as hundreds of villagers watched. A couple who eloped were stripped and beaten. Yet another couple committed suicide after their parents forbade them to marry.

Anthropologists used to think that romance was a Western construct, a bourgeois byproduct of the Middle Ages. Romance was for the sophisticated, took place in cafés, with coffees and Cabernets, or on silk sheets, or in rooms with a flickering fire. It was assumed that non-Westerners, with their broad familial and social obligations, were spread too thin for particular passions. How could a collectivist culture celebrate or in any way sanction the obsession with one individual that defines new love? Could a lice-ridden peasant really feel passion?

Easily, as it turns out. Scientists now believe that romance is panhuman, embedded in our brains since Pleistocene times. In a study of 166 cultures, anthropologists William Jankowiak and Edward Fischer observed evidence of passionate love in 147 of them. In another study men and women from Europe, Japan, and the Philippines were asked to fill out a survey to measure their experiences of passionate love. All three groups professed feeling passion with the same searing intensity.

But though romantic love may be universal, its cultural expression is not. To the Fulbe tribe of northern Cameroon, poise matters more than passion. Men who spend too much time with their wives are taunted, and those who are weak-kneed are thought to have fallen under a dangerous spell. Love may be inevitable, but for the Fulbe its manifestations are shameful, equated with sickness and social impairment.

In India romantic love has traditionally been seen as dangerous, a threat to a well-crafted caste system in which marriages are arranged as a means of preserving lineage and bloodlines. Thus the gruesome tales, the warnings embedded in fables about what happens when one's wayward impulses take over.

Today love marriages appear to be on the rise in India, often in defiance of parents' wishes.

Studies around the world confirm that passion usually ends.

No wonder some cultures think selecting a lifelong mate based on something so fleeting is folly.

The triumph of romantic love is celebrated in Bollywood films. Yet most Indians still believe arranged marriages are more likely to succeed than love marriages. In one survey of Indian college students, 76 percent said they'd marry someone with all the right qualities even if they weren't in love with the person (compared with only 14 percent of Americans). Marriage is considered too important a step to leave to chance.

Renu Dinakaran is a striking 45-year-old woman who lives in Bangalore, India. When I meet her, she is dressed in Western-style clothes—black leggings and a T-shirt. Renu lives in a well-appointed apartment in this thronging city, where cows sleep on the highways as tiny cars whiz around them, plumes of black smoke rising from their sooty pipes.

Renu was born into a traditional Indian family where an arranged marriage was expected. She was not an arranged kind of person, though, emerging from her earliest days as a fierce tennis player, too sweaty for saris, and smarter than many of the men around her. Nevertheless at the age of 17 she was married off to a first cousin, a man she barely knew, a man she wanted to learn to love, but couldn't. Renu considers many arranged marriages to be acts of "state-sanctioned rape."

Renu hoped to fall in love with her husband, but the more years that passed, the less love she felt, until, at the end, she was shrunken, bitter, hiding behind the curtains of her in-laws' bungalow, looking with longing at the couple on the balcony across from theirs. "It was so obvious to me that couple had married for love, and I envied them. I really did. It hurt me so much to see how they stood together, how they went shopping for bread and eggs."

Exhausted from being forced into confinement, from being swaddled in saris that made it difficult to move, from resisting the pressure to eat off her husband's plate, Renu did what traditional Indian culture forbids one to do. She left. By this time she had had two children. She took them with her. In her mind was an old movie she'd seen on TV, a movie so strange and enticing to her, so utterly confounding and comforting at the same time, that she couldn't get it out of her head. It was 1986. The movie was *Love Story*.

"Before I saw movies like *Love Story*, I didn't realize the power that love can have," she says.

Renu was lucky in the end. In Mumbai she met a man named Anil, and it was then, for the first time, that she felt passion. "When I first saw Anil, it was like nothing I'd ever experienced. He was the first man I ever had an orgasm with. I was high, just high, all the time. And I know it wouldn't last, couldn't last, and so that infused it with a sweet sense of longing, almost as though we were watching the end approach while we were also discovering each other."

When Renu speaks of the end, she does not, to be sure, mean the end of her relationship with Anil; she means the end of a certain stage. The two are still happily married, companionable, loving if not "in love," with a playful black dachshund they bought together. Their relationship, once so full of fire, now seems to simmer along at an even temperature, enough to keep them well fed and warm. They are grateful.

"Would I want all that passion back?" Renu asks. "Sometimes, yes. But to tell you the truth, it was exhausting."

From a physiological point of view, this couple has moved from the dopamine-drenched state of romantic love to the relative quiet of an oxytocin-induced attachment. Oxytocin is a hormone that promotes a feeling of connection, bonding. It is released when we hug our long-term spouses, or our children. It is released when a mother nurses her infant. Prairie voles, animals with high levels of oxytocin, mate for life. When scientists block oxytocin receptors in these rodents, the animals don't form monogamous bonds and tend to roam. Some researchers speculate that autism, a disorder marked by a profound inability to forge and maintain social connections, is linked to an oxytocin deficiency. Scientists have been experimenting by treating autistic people with oxytocin, which in some cases has helped alleviate their symptoms.

In long-term relationships that work—like Renu and Anil's—oxytocin is believed to be abundant in both partners. In long-term relationships that never get off the ground, like Renu and her first husband's, or that crumble once the high is gone, chances are the couple has not found a way to stimulate or sustain oxytocin production.

Arthur Aron, a psychologist at Stony Brook University in New York, conducted an experiment that illuminates some of the mechanisms by which people become and stay attracted. He recruited a group of men and women and put opposite sex pairs in rooms together, instructing each pair to perform a series of tasks, which included telling each other personal details about themselves. He then asked each couple to stare into each other's eyes for two minutes. After this encounter, Aron found most of the couples, previously strangers to each other, reported feelings of attraction. In fact, one couple went on to marry.

Fisher says this exercise works wonders for some couples. Aron and Fisher also suggest doing novel things together, because novelty triggers dopamine in the brain, which can stimulate feelings of attraction. In other words, if your heart flutters in his presence, you might decide it's not because you're anxious but because you love him. Carrying this a step further, Aron and others have found that even if you just jog in place and then meet someone, you're more likely to think they're attractive. So first dates that involve a nerve-racking activity, like riding a roller coaster, are more likely to lead to second and third dates. That's a strategy worthy of posting on Match.com. Play some squash. And in times of stress—natural disasters, blackouts, predators on the prowl—lock up tight and hold your partner.

Critical Responses

1. The scientific findings reported here are not especially romantic. But do they dampen romance? To what extent do they affect your idea of love, if at all?

2. Conversely, would learning more about the chemistry of love make a difference to your falling in love or being in love—or to the "chemistry," figuratively speaking, between you and another person?

3. In what ways does this article substantiate the cliché "madly in love"? Does being in love mean being a fool?

4. What roles do chance and fate play in ideas of romantic love? How does science treat chance and fate, and how does this affect ideas of romantic love?

Writing Topics

1. "The lunatic, the lover, and the poet/ Are of imagination all compact." What do these lines from Shakespeare suggest? How might the scientist fit in—if at all?

2. In what ways is scientific research of love useful to online dating services? Would research into falling out of love be useful as well? Who stands to gain, either way?

3. Choose one of the images that accompany this article and, focusing on details in the picture as well as the overall impression, construct an account of the relationship being represented.

4. Write an essay in which you analyze a popular contemporary love song, paying attention to the music as well as the lyrics, to the sound as well as the sense. What feelings does the song express? What feelings does it stir? What kind of love is the song about? What message about love does it convey?

Further Explorations

1. Recently, there has been a spate of television shows about brides, weddings, and the like. After watching an episode of one of these shows, consider what makes it appealing, and to whom. What does the popularity of this show say about the audience? What does the popularity of the genre say about our society?

2. What sorts of ideas and expectations do you have about romantic love? How do these compare with the ideas and expectations of your classmates? Are cultural differences apparent, and if so, what are they? What about generational differences within your family, as well as the families of your classmates?

© JODI COBB/National Geographic Image Collection

Studying the Image

1. The article "21ˢᵗ-Century Slaves" provides vivid details about the lives of children who are forced into labor. What do you think are the psychological and physical damages children—like those depicted in the photograph—will experience after working for years under these brutal conditions?

2. Do you think that companies should outsource production to countries that have been known to use slave or child labor? Should they take the responsibility of finding out about labor practices before they outsource work?

Writing Assignment

What do you think is behind the rug in the picture? Imagine the setting details and the children behind the rug and write a detailed description about one day of their lives in that room.

© 1974 JAMES L. STANFIELD/National Geographic Image Collection

Studying the Image

1. Why do you think the photographer focused on the man at the center of the picture and left the other figures blurry? What effect does this technique have on the viewer? What point do you think the photographer is trying to make?

2. What kind of relationships do you think miners—like those depicted in the photograph— forge with each other? Do you think their relationships are similar to that of other groups who are placed in dangerous positions?

Writing Assignment

Research how miners during the California Gold Rush in the mid-1800s extracted gold, and in an essay, compare their methods to those in the article "The Price of Gold." Did the Gold Rush miners experience the same type of dangerous conditions? Were any measures taken to ensure their safety?

© 1997 RANDY OLSON/National Geographic Image Collection

Studying the Image

1. What emotion is the boy expressing in the picture? What do you think has caused this emotion?

2. How could a child's participation in animal husbandry, such as raising chickens, help him or her forge a relationship with nature?

Writing Assignment

Write a short description from the boy's point of view about his rooster winning the top prize at a county fair.

© SARAH LEEN/National Geographic Image Collection

Studying the Image

1. Notice that there are no women surrounding the casket in the picture. Why do you think they are absent, at least from the inner circle? Why do you think that men are more devoted soccer fans than women?

2. Why do you think soccer is not as popular in the United States as it is in other countries?

Writing Assignment

Some soccer fans have an almost religious devotion to their team, as is suggested in the photograph. Why do you think their devotion is so strong? What elements in the picture illustrate the depth of connection men can have to a soccer team? What other cultural institutions inspire a similar kind of group devotion? Compare and contrast followers of one other institution to soccer fans, determining the similarities and differences in the reasons for their devotion.

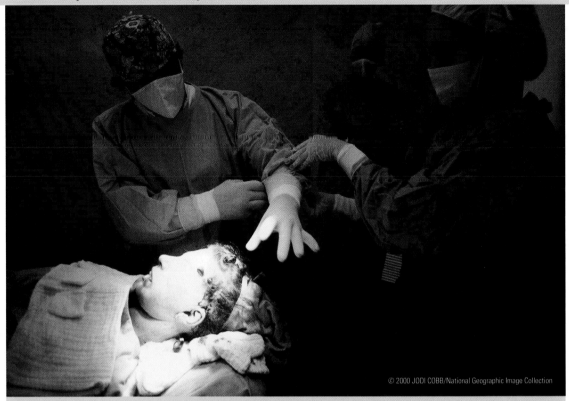

© 2000 JODI COBB/National Geographic Image Collection

Studying the Image

1. How does the photographer guide our focus to the surgeons' hands in this picture? Why do you think that the picture was snapped just at this moment?

2. How important is physical appearance to you? How much pain would you endure to make yourself more attractive?

Writing Assignment

Imagine that a close female friend of yours has decided to get a specific type of plastic surgery on her face. After researching the procedure, noting the details of the operation, the recovery, and the possible side effects, write a letter to her, either supporting her decision or trying to convince her not to have the operation.

Studying the Image

1. The article "This Thing Called Love" states that certain activities can "trigger dopamine in the brain, which can stimulate feelings of attraction." How does this scene depict an example of one of those activities?

2. Focus on the setting details and technique in the picture. How do these elements contribute to its romantic tone?

Writing Assignment

The romantic feelings that the couple in the picture is probably experiencing will not last, according to the biological studies outlined in the article. Write a description of what you think the couple's relationship will be like five years in the future.

SECTION C
People and Places

Eight lanes of traffic course between a mile of skyscrapers on Dubai's Sheikh Zayed Road.
© 2007 MAGGIE STEBER/National Geographic Image Collection

INTO THE
AMAZON

By Scott Wallace

INTO THE AMAZON

From the time that Europeans first began exploring the Amazon, the consequences for indigenous people have been dire. European diseases have decimated populations; even the common cold can have deadly effects on a tribe. Under the circumstances, the best-intentioned contact with indigenous peoples can involve grave risks, which is why Sydney Possuelo, who once sought out isolated tribes, now works to protect their isolation. In this article, *National Geographic* journalist Scott Wallace accompanies Possuelo on a mission to avoid the tribe whom he seeks.

Snaking deep into remote territory, stretches of the Itaquai River have not yet been plundered, as have more accessible parts of the Amazon, where gold and oil, rubber and timber, slaves and souls have fueled 500 years of conquest, disease, and devastation. Brazil's Indian population, once in the millions, is now roughly 350,000, including a few uncontacted tribes like the Flecheiros—the Arrow People.

© MICHAEL NICHOLS/National Geographic Image Collection

*Indigenous people in a canoe on the river.
Possuelo is sure that once you make contact with
the Indians, you begin the process of destroying
their universe.*

DEEP IN THE JUNGLES OF BRAZIL, INDIAN RIGHTS ADVOCATE, SYDNEY POSSUELO,

RACES TO SAVE THE PEOPLE IIE HOPES NEVER TO MEET:

THE UNCONTACTED FLECHEIROS.

We found fresh human tracks this morning. They all pointed in the same direction that we're walking through the virgin jungle of Brazil's westernmost Amazon Basin. Woolly monkeys hoot and chatter somewhere in the distance, their banter punctuated by the occasional zing of a machete and the shrill cries of screaming piha birds high in the canopy overhead. Our column of 34 men proceeds in silence, string out single file far back into the forest. Only one or two companions are visible at any time in the blur of electric greens and rain-soaked browns. The rest are swallowed from view by a spray of overhanging branches and vines as thick as anacondas dangling a hundred feet from the treetops to the forest floor. Just ahead of me, Sydney Possuelo strides double-time across a stretch of level ground, a welcome break from the steep hillsides we've been scrambling over for days. "We're probably the only ones who have ever walked here," he tells me. "Us and the Indians."

A cantankerous iconoclast with bulging hazel eyes, scraggly salt-and-pepper beard, and wild locks flowing from beneath a floppy camouflage jungle hat, Possuelo, 63, is widely

> We're probably the only ones who have ever walked here. Us and the Indians.

considered one of the Amazon's last great wilderness scouts and the leading authority on Brazil's remaining pockets of isolated Indians. After two weeks of river travel and 20 days of steady bushwhacking, Possuelo has led us into one of the most remote and uncharted places left on the planet, near the headwaters of two adjacent rivers, the Itaquai and the Jutai. This is the land of the mysterious Flecheiros, or Arrow People, a rarely glimpsed Indian tribe known principally as deft archers disposed to unleashing poison-tipped projectiles to defend their territory against all intruders, then melting away into the forest.

Suddenly Possuelo stops in his tracks. A freshly hacked sapling, still dangling by a shred of bark, lies across the path in front of us. In itself, the makeshift gate could not halt a toddler, much less a column of nearly three dozen armed men. But still, it bears a message—and a warning—that Possuelo instantly recognizes and respects. "This is universal language in

continued on page 280

Adapted from "Into the Amazon" by Scott Wallace: National Geographic Magazine, August 2003.

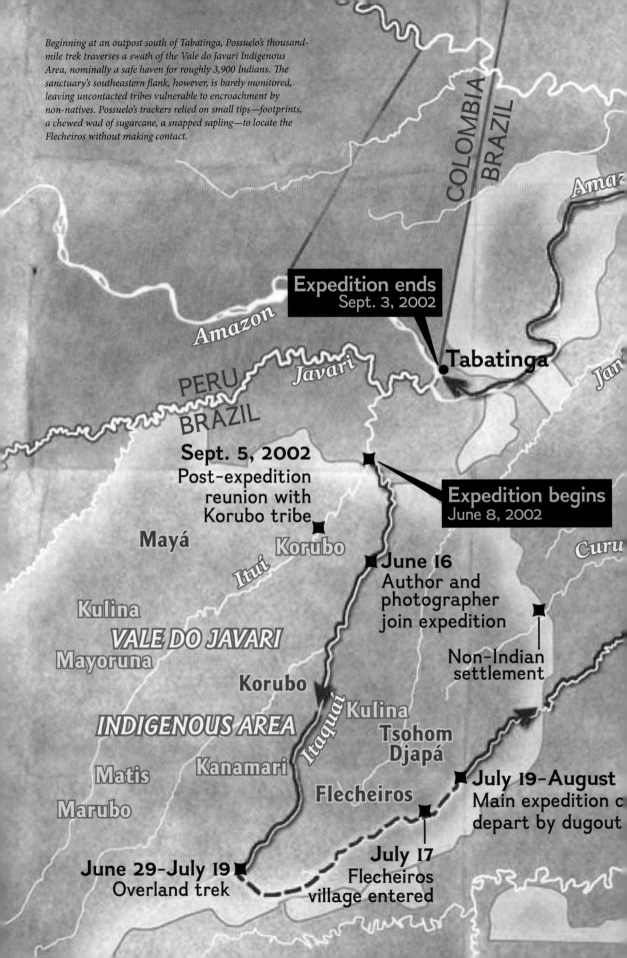

Beginning at an outpost south of Tabatinga, Possuelo's thousand-mile trek traverses a swath of the Vale do Javari Indigenous Area, nominally a safe haven for roughly 3,900 Indians. The sanctuary's southeastern flank, however, is barely monitored, leaving uncontacted tribes vulnerable to encroachment by non-natives. Possuelo's trackers relied on small tips—footprints, a chewed wad of sugarcane, a snapped sapling—to locate the Flecheiros without making contact.

COLOMBIA
BRAZIL

Amaz

Amazon

PERU

Javari

BRAZIL

Jan

Expedition ends
Sept. 3, 2002

Tabatinga

Sept. 5, 2002
Post-expedition
reunion with
Korubo tribe

Expedition begins
June 8, 2002

Mayá

Korubo

Ituí

Curu

June 16
Author and
photographer
join expedition

Kulina

VALE DO JAVARI

Mayoruna

Non-Indian
settlement

Korubo

Itaquaí

Kulina
Tsohom
Djapá

INDIGENOUS AREA

Matis

Kanamari

July 19-August
Main expedition c
depart by dugout

Flecheiros

Marubo

July 17
Flecheiros
village entered

June 29-July 19
Overland trek

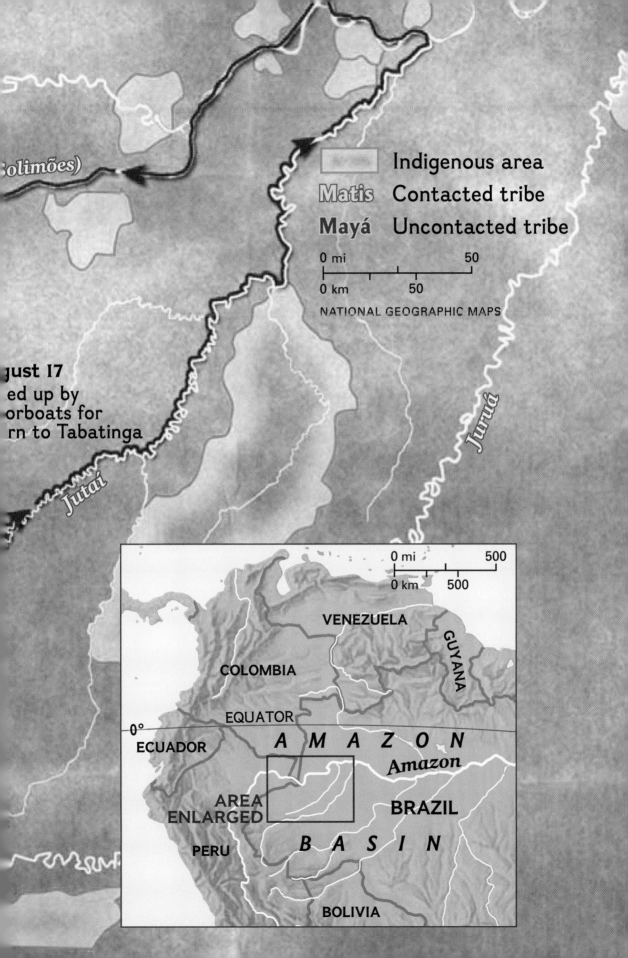

olimões)

Indigenous area
Matis   Contacted tribe
Mayá   Uncontacted tribe

0 mi   50
0 km   50

NATIONAL GEOGRAPHIC MAPS

just 17
ed up by
orboats for
rn to Tabatinga

Juruá

Jutaí

0 mi   500
0 km   500

VENEZUELA

GUYANA

COLOMBIA

EQUATOR

0°

A M A Z O N

ECUADOR

Amazon

AREA
ENLARGED

BRAZIL

B A S I N

PERU

BOLIVIA

continued from page 277

the jungle," he whispers. "It means 'Stay Out. Go No Farther.' We must be getting close to their village."

Which is something Possuelo wants to avoid. He wheels around and with a silent, dramatic wave directs our column to veer off the path into the dense undergrowth on our flanks. A half hour later, after slogging through boot-sucking mud and dodging branches that swarm with fire ants, we arrive by the steep banks of a clear, narrow creek, where Possuelo orders a halt to the march while we wait for stragglers to catch up.

The Flecheiros figure among 17 so-called uncontacted tribes living in the far recesses of the Brazilian Amazon. In this part of the rain forest, the Vale do Javari Indigenous Area, there may be as many as 1,350 uncontacted indigenous people—perhaps the largest such concentration anywhere in the world. Most of them are descendants of the survivors of massacres perpetrated by white intruders over the centuries. The Indians then scattered into the rugged folds of the region's headwaters and continue to shun contact with the outside world.

But violent clashes account for only a fraction of the deaths suffered by native communities at the hands of outsiders. Most died from epidemic diseases, including the common cold, for which they had no biological defenses. Ivan Arapa, one of our scouts, is from the Matis tribe, who were first contacted by the outside world about 25 years ago. Ivan still remembers the wholesale death that accompanied these very first visits of Brazilian government officials to his village.

"Everyone was coughing, everyone was dying," he recalls. "Many, many Matis died. We didn't know why."

More than half of the 350 Matis living along the Ituí River inside the Javari reserve perished in the months following contact, officials say.

It's a dismal story that's become all too familiar to Possuelo during his 40-year career as

There are *indios bravos*, wild Indians, up there. That's their territory.

a *sertanista*, a uniquely Brazilian profession that folds all the skills and passions of a frontiersman, ethnographer, adventurer, and Indian rights activist into a single, eclectic vocation. That's why our mission is not to make contact with the Flecheiros but rather to gather information on the extent of their territory's boundaries, information Possuelo will use to bolster his efforts to protect their lands. In other respects, the Flecheiros are to remain, in large measure, a mystery.

As we passed through squalid Kanamari Indian settlements on our way up the Itaquai River a month earlier, villagers gave vague, contradictory tales of the Flecheiros—third- or fourth-hand accounts, translated in halting Portuguese, of sightings of the Indians and clashes between them and logging crews that once operated in the area. Some said the Flecheiros are tall and muscular with long, flowing hair. Others told us they paint their faces and bodies red and clip their hair in a classic bowl shape common to many Amazon tribes. But the Kanamari all agreed on this: The Flecheiros are dangerous, "untamed," they said, and villagers carefully steered clear of Flecheiros lands upriver. "We don't go there," said a Kanamari man we met one afternoon as he paddled a small dugout in the honey-colored waters. "There are *indios bravos*, wild Indians, up there. That's their territory."

These are stories Possuelo actually likes to hear. In his encounters with the Kanamari he actively nourishes an image of the Flecheiros as a deadly peril to be avoided. "I prefer them like this—violent," Possuelo says. Isolated tribes willing to kill intruders to defend their lands, or that have a reputation for doing so, make the most tenacious guardians of the pristine forest.

At the same time, isolation offers groups like the Flecheiros the best hope for maintaining their cultural vibrancy, even their very survival. This interplay between ecological preservation and the protection of uncontacted tribes lies at the heart of Possuelo's work. "In protecting the

Aerial view of the Amazon River. Leading the expeditions with missionary zeal, Possuelo is driven by a gospel of his own: "I don't need to know what language the Flecheiros speak or what gods they worship. I just want to protect them."

isolated Indian, you are also protecting millions of hectares of biodiversity," he says.

During the past few days we've found signs of the Flecheiros everywhere: crude blazes hacked into tree trunks, decaying old lean-tos, overgrown footpaths. All bear witness to an isolated, semi-nomadic people still living beyond the reach of our "civilized" world in a distant, virtually Neolithic past. Yesterday afternoon we broke through dense underbrush into a sunlit clearing to behold a cluster of low-lying palm-roofed huts that looked more like hobbit dwellings than shelters for full-grown human beings. It appeared to be an abandoned fishing camp. Two tapir jawbones, still filled with teeth, were slung from a small tree, some kind of totem, Possuelo surmised. A cone-shaped cage fashioned from sticks gouged into the ground sat nearby. Alongside it lay a perfectly round, soot-blackened clay pot. "These Indians are very close to the way Amerigo Vespucci

would have found them," Possuelo said with a touch of marvel and admiration in his voice. "They live by hunting, fishing, and gathering."

Most of the vestiges we have found are days, weeks, even months old—far enough away in time to presume a relative margin of safety in distance between the Flecheiros and our expedition. An experienced tracker like Possuelo can observe such signs and instantly date them. The fishing camp, Possuelo figured, was from the previous dry season, the time of year when floodwaters draw back from the forest floor, and animals as well as humans move toward the Amazon's larger rivers and streams in a primordial quest for food and water.

But shortly after we departed the camp, our scouts came upon fresh signs of the Flecheiros, a piece of coiled vine and a chunk of masticated sugarcane left on the path. "These are from right now!" Ivan Arapa whispered excitedly. Just ahead we found fresh footprints. Possuelo read the skid marks left in the mud and said: "He saw us and took off running." He raised his hand for silence and sent word for all to maintain visual contact with one another along our single column that stretched far back into the forest. For the first time since our journey began, Possuelo strapped on his pistol.

Minutes later, our trailblazers glimpsed a pair of naked Indians as they dashed across a log footbridge and vanished into closed jungle on the far side of the river. Possuelo tried to reassure them of our peaceful intent, calling out into the forest: "Whooo! Whooo!" Only the forlorn cry of the screaming piha replied.

And last night, another first: Possuelo posted sentries to keep vigil as we slept fitfully in our hammocks, straining our ears above an eerie, reverberating chorus of frogs for any snapping of twigs or rustling of leaves that could signal an approach by the Flecheiros. As we got under way this morning, Possuelo ordered the men to leave behind a machete and a knife as a peace offering. Does Possuelo suppose the Flecheiros will subject our campsite to the same sort of forensic scrutiny we have brought to bear on theirs?

"*Com certeza*," he replies. "You can bet on it." What might they be thinking about us? He looks me straight in the eye and answers with an edge of foreboding. "I imagine they're thinking that their enemies have arrived."

Now, having detoured around the strange Flecheiros roadblock, the men reach the embankment in groups of three and four, staggering under the weight of their backpacks overstuffed with provisions, collapsing around us on the damp forest floor. Among us there are a dozen Matis Indians, six Kanamari, two Marubo, and the rest mostly non-Indian frontiersmen. We guzzle water straight from the stream, but as the minutes wear on and Possuelo takes a head count he realizes that two of our Kanamari porters are missing. Laughter gives way to a tense silence. Possuelo

Imagine that they're thinking that their enemies have arrived.

paces back and forth, stealing glances at his wristwatch with a scowl. Though it's approaching midday and we're only a few degrees off the Equator, I've begun to shiver in my sweat-drenched fatigues.

"Damn it!" Possuelo snarls. "These guys are holding us up! A total lack of discipline!" With that, he dispatches a half dozen Matis to look for the stragglers. But when the Matis fail to return, an unspoken dread slowly creeps over all of us. Have our missing companions been captured, perhaps even killed, by the Flecheiros?

This certainly isn't the first potentially life-threatening crisis Possuelo has faced in his career. He was once held hostage by Kayapó warriors and on another occasion was pistol-whipped by white settlers seeking to invade Indian lands. He's had malaria 38 times and has received as many death threats. In the early 1990s as president of FUNAI, the Brazilian government agency that deals with indigenous peoples, Possuelo squared off with army generals, influential politicians, and a violent rabble of gold prospectors to win protection for the homelands of the Yanomami Indians, on Brazil's northern border with Venezuela. A few years ago Possuelo yanked 22 men on a FUNAI expedition by helicopter from the Peruvian border after they were surrounded by hostile, isolated Indians. This time he has assembled a large, well-armed contingent; the Flecheiros would have to think twice before attacking such a numerous force. But Possuelo has issued standing orders: If we are attacked, the men are only to fire warning shots in the air.

From the very moment I met Possuelo, I found him to be a man of boundless energy. Photographer Nicolas Reynard and I had joined him aboard the *Waika*, one of four vintage Amazonian steamers that was hauling us upstream toward the Itaquai's headwaters. He barked orders to the men while amiably fielding my questions without skipping a beat. Once we left the boats behind, we would spend nearly a month marching straight through the heart of unknown territory, he told me that first night. Eventually we would build our own dugout canoes to navigate down the Jutaí and back to civilization.

Our route would take us through the southernmost reaches of the Javari reserve, a vast wilderness area set aside by FUNAI in 1996, the year government agents under Possuelo's command expelled all non-Indian settlers and loggers from the territory. Picture the southern half of Florida, roughly the same size as the reserve, in pre-Columbian times: not a single road, a mere 3,900 inhabitants spread out over an enormous expanse of steamy woodlands, swamps, and alligator-infested rivers.

In fact, southern Florida 500 years ago hosted a much larger population than that, and ethnologists say it's certain the Javari drainage itself once did too. Archaeologists estimate that millions of indigenous people occupied the Brazilian Amazon at the beginning of the 16th century. Today there are some 350,000 in all of Brazil, including isolated groups like the Flecheiros whose numbers, along with many other things about them, are a matter of guesswork.

Not even Possuelo knows what language the Flecheiros speak, what their ethnicity is, or even what they call themselves. "It's not important to know any of that to protect them," he says. And anyway, it would be impossible to glean such information without exposing the Indians to deadly disease or a host of competing values that could erase their traditions. "Once you make contact, you begin the process of destroying their universe."

Possuelo didn't always think this way. Like other sertanistas, he once thrived on the excitement of contacting "wild" Indians. A FUNAI scout's professional reputation was built largely on how many first contacts he had notched. In all, Possuelo has been credited with seven since the 1970s. But in the course of making those contacts, Possuelo became disillusioned. The Indians began to visit the rough-and-tumble frontier towns, started drinking, and lost all sense of who they were. To meet new needs and wants created by the dominant white society, such as clothing, medicine, and consumer goods, they began selling off timber, despoiling their land in the process.

Possuelo eventually came to see contact as the undoing of once proud indigenous societies. "The curiosity I once had about uncontacted people has been subordinated by something else—the imperative to protect them."

Possuelo's last contact with an isolated tribe came with a group of Korubo in 1996, also within the bounds of the Javari reserve. But he undertook that initiative, he says, only to save the Korubo from increasingly violent clashes with logging crews. This position has placed Possuelo at loggerheads with a broad array of adversaries, including missionaries who, he says, have accused him of playing God with the Indians while shielding them from pastoral efforts to spread the Gospel and the word of everlasting life.

But now our own lives are at stake. Possuelo dispatches a second team, a dozen fully armed scouts, to look for the Kanamari and the missing Matis search party. One of our scouts finally returns with disquieting news. The tracks of our missing companions led straight past the Flecheiros gate—the broken sapling on the trail—then followed the path through a huge garden of cultivated manioc and plantains and into the clearing of a large Flecheiros settlement, about 14 huts in all.

The Flecheiros themselves had fled into the surrounding jungle, leaving behind prodigious heaps of smoked meats—monkey, tapir, turtle—and smoldering campfires.

"It's their system of security," Possuelo nods gravely. "They scatter into the forest."

The Flecheiros seemed to have been preparing for a feast, the scout reports. In the middle of the village, the scouts found several ceremonial masks made from long strands of bark, alongside ceramic vats filled with red urucú dye used to decorate faces and bodies. More ominously, the Indians took all of their weapons with them when they fled. But they left behind a sharp bamboo arrowpoint and the broken end of a blowgun, which the scout now holds aloft for all to see.

We thus learn for the first time that the Flecheiros have other weapons besides the bow and arrow. And they also left two large clay pots brimming with curare, the dark poisonous goop that they apply to their arrow tips. Most disturbing of all, the Kanamari's footprints vanished without a trace down a path on the far side of the village.

Now Ivan Arapa silently demonstrates, covering his mouth with one hand and drawing an imaginary vine around his neck with the other, how the Flecheiros could have jumped our companions from behind, gagging them and yanking them off their feet into the undergrowth.

"I'd say they've been taken by the Indians," Possuelo says. "Now we have to get out of here. Maybe the Indians will let them go." He looks out into the shadowy forest surrounding us. "But we can't wait for them here," he adds. "We're going to march to a more advantageous position. We'll camp by the river and see if they show up."

By now both search parties have come back, leaving only the two Kanamari unaccounted for. One of our lead scouts reports seeing footprints that match the Kanamari's rubber-soled sneakers farther ahead, spaced out in long intervals that would suggest the strides of men in panicked flight. Possuelo dispatches Soldado, his most dependable scout, with orders to overtake our fleeing companions and, if necessary, fire into the air to summon them.

Possuelo clamps his hands together as if beseeching God. But it is still another hour before Soldado and the two wayward Kanamari appear at the edge of the riverside clearing where we are preparing our campsite. The Kanamari bow their heads contritely as Possuelo glowers at them. But clearly he is more relieved than angry at the men.

It seems the two Kanamari thought the Flecheiros might be long-lost relatives separated from the main riverside settlements decades ago. They admit they ignored Possuelo's orders and ventured off to satisfy their curiosity. But fear washed over them when they got to the far side of the village. They leaped off the trail and took off running. Not until they heard the report of Soldado's rifle did they realize they were not being chased by the Flecheiros.

Possuelo seizes the occasion to call a kind of political pep rally around the campfire. "I'd say to our two Kanamari friends: You were born again today, because the Flecheiros could have killed you," he mildly scolds. "We're not here to get to know them. We're here to find out if the Flecheiros use this land."

Possuelo then reminds the Indians of the extraordinary things they saw today. Their incursion into the Flecheiros village amounted to a flagrant violation of Possuelo's policy to avoid making contact. Nonetheless, he is clearly elated by what he has learned from the unlikely visit.

"Here the Flecheiros live well," he says in slow, simple Portuguese, making sure his words sink in. "You could see it in their village. They hunt, they fish, and they grow food. They must be very healthy. Their babies must be fat; their mothers probably have lots of milk. They have parties. They are happy."

The last traces of daylight have faded from the sky, plunging the jungle into darkness. Luminescent moths zip through the trees overhead, and the nighttime chorus of trilling insects and croaking frogs has begun.

"The work we are doing here is beautiful, because they don't even know we're here to help them," Possuelo says. "We have to respect their way of life. We're not going to pursue them. The best thing we can do is to stay out of their lives."

Possuelo pauses to stare into the flames of the campfire. "Now we're going to continue our work and our journey," he says. "We're all going to get out of here alive."

> You were born again today, because the Flecheiros could have killed you.

Critical Responses

1. What is the lure of wilderness exploration? What kind of person does it take to be a wilderness explorer? What kind of person is Sydney Possuelo? How does he fulfill the functions of a *sertanista*?

2. What is the nature of Possuelo's mission? What makes it paradoxical? Given his views on contact with indigenous peoples, what do you make of his reaction to the discovery of the Flecheiros village?

3. What does Wallace's writing style contribute to the story? How would you characterize his prose? How does it affect your response?

4. What is the role of curiosity in this expedition? How does the narrative arouse the reader's curiosity? How are the two related?

Writing Topics

1. Considering the argument of this article, does the lack of visual evidence affect your reaction to the exploration? Do you think photographing indigenous people is a violation of privacy?

2. In what ways is Possuelo like a traditional missionary? How does he differ? What makes his mission antithetical to that of traditional missionaries? What makes it similar?

3. Compare Sydney Possuelo to Kira Salak, the explorer in the article on "Myanmar's River of Spirits," focusing on the role of each as an observer and on the way each sees indigenous peoples.

4. What leads Possuelo to conclude that in the village encountered, Flecheiros live happy, healthy lives? What if he is mistaken in reading the signs?

Further Explorations

1. It has been at least a decade since this expedition took place. Research what has become of the Flecheiros in the interim, as well as to the area of the Amazon they inhabit. Have Possuelo's goals informed what has occurred? If so, what is the effect? If not, why and what are the consequences?

2. While there is a medical justification for refraining from contact with hitherto uncontacted indigenous peoples, it is also possible to see a medical justification for making contact. Divide into groups to debate the question, and then write a paper persuading your readers of one or the other position.

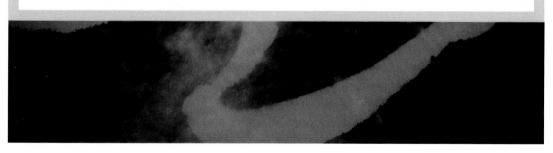

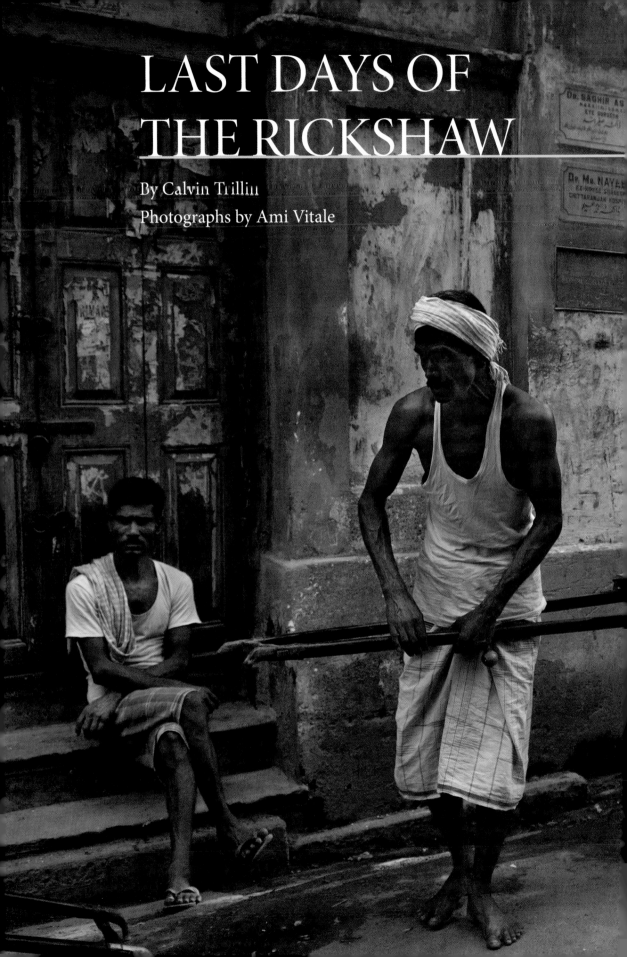

LAST DAYS OF THE RICKSHAW

By Calvin Trillin

Photographs by Ami Vitale

LAST DAYS OF THE RICKSHAW

Since the early 1960s, Calvin Trillin has been a regular contributor to *Time, The New Yorker,* and *The Nation,* and has written over two dozen works of fiction and nonfiction, bringing dry humor and wry wit to his observations of contemporary life. Here, he partners with Ami Vitale, an internationally acclaimed photojournalist, whose documentary images are known for their humanity and intimacy. Bringing together these distinct points of view in "Last Days of the Rickshaw," Trillin and Vitale provide a portrait of the cultural ambiguities and contradictions surrounding this mode of transportation and way of life in Kolkata, India.

S. K. Bikari regularly pulls a pair of girls to school in the city's fading historic center, yet he rarely sees his own five children back home in the state of Bihar.

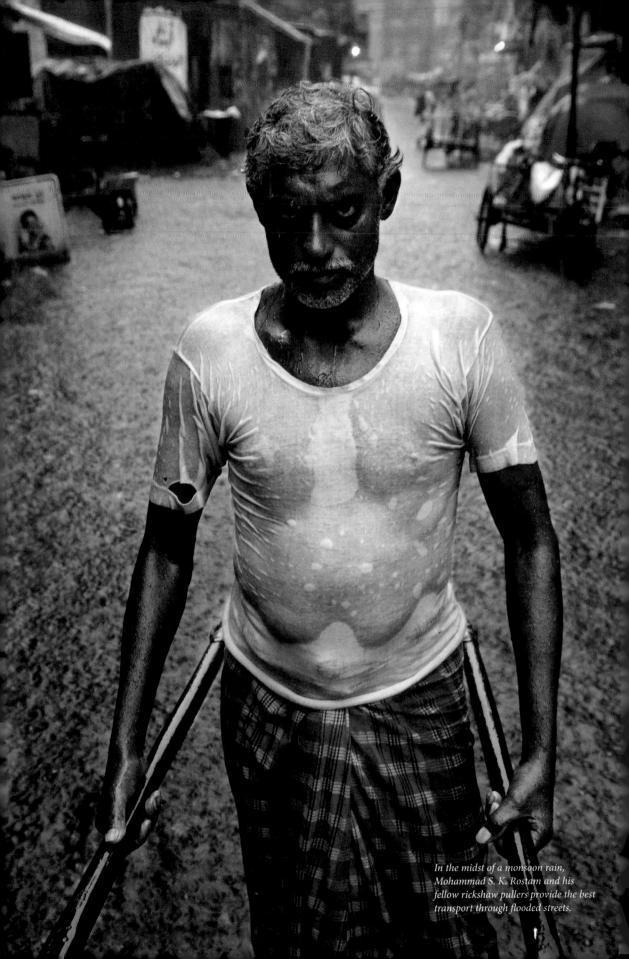

In the midst of a monsoon rain, Mohammad S. K. Rostam and his fellow rickshaw pullers provide the best transport through flooded streets.

KOLKATA IS BENT ON
BURNISHING ITS MODERN IMAGE— AND BANNING A POTENT SYMBOL
OF INDIA'S COLONIAL PAST.

The strategy of drivers in Kolkata—drivers of private cars and taxis and buses and the enclosed three-wheel scooters used as jitneys and even pedicabs—is simple: Forge ahead while honking. There are no stop signs to speak of. To a visitor, the signs that say, in large block letters, OBEY TRAFFIC RULES come across as a bit of black humor. During a recent stay in Kolkata, the method I devised for crossing major thoroughfares was to wait until I could attach myself to more pedestrians than I figured a taxi was willing to knock down. In the narrow side streets known as the lanes, loud honking is the signal that a taxi or even a small truck is about to round the corner and come barreling down a space not meant for anything wider than a bicycle. But occasionally, during a brief lull in the honking, I'd hear the tinkling of a bell behind me. An American who has watched too many Hallmark Christmas specials might turn around half expecting to see a pair of draft horses pulling a sleigh through snowy woods. But what came into view was a rickshaw. Instead of

> To a visitor, the signs that say, in large block letters, **OBEY TRAFFIC RULES** come across as a bit of black humor.

being pulled by a horse, it was being pulled by a man—usually a skinny, bedraggled, barefoot man who didn't look quite up to the task. Hooked around his finger was a single bell that he shook continuously, producing what is surely the most benign sound to emanate from any vehicle in Kolkata.

Among the great cities of the world, Kolkata, the capital of West Bengal and the home of nearly 15 million people, is often mentioned as the only one that still has a large fleet of hand-pulled rickshaws. As it happens, that is not a distinction treasured by the governing authorities. Why? It's tempting, of course, to blame Mother Teresa. A politician in Kolkata told me that the city is known for the three *m*'s: Marxism, *mishti*, and Mother Teresa. (West Bengal has had a government dominated by the Communist Party for 30 years. Mishti is a sweetened yogurt that Kolkatans love, though they're also partial to a sweet called *rössogolla*.) There is no doubt that the international attention given

---

Adapted from "Last Days of the Rickshaw" by Calvin Trillin: National Geographic Magazine, April 2008.

to Mother Teresa's work among the wretched and the dying firmly linked Kolkata in the Western mind with squalor—no matter how often Kolkatans point out that Mumbai, for example, has more extensive slums, and that no other city in India can match the richness of Kolkata's intellectual and cultural life.

The most loyal booster of Kolkata would acknowledge that the city has had some genuinely trying times in the 60 years since India became independent, starting well before the emergence of Mother Teresa. The partition that accompanied independence meant that, without substantial help from the central government, Kolkata had to absorb several million refugees from what became East Pakistan. There were times in the 1970s and '80s when it seemed Kolkata would never recover from the trauma of those refugees, followed by another wave of refugees who came during the war that turned East Pakistan into Bangladesh. Those were years marked by power outages and labor unrest and the flight of industry and the breathtaking violence unleashed by the Naxalite movement, which began with peasants demanding land redistribution in rural West Bengal and was transformed by college students into urban guerrilla warfare. In 1985 India's own prime minister, then Rajiv Gandhi, called Kolkata "a dying city."

There are still a lot of people sleeping on the streets in Kolkata, but there have been great changes in recent years. After decades of concentrating on its base among the rural poor and disdaining outside investment, the Communist Party of West Bengal has fiercely embraced capitalism and modernity. Although the government's symbols remain what might be expected from a party that still has a politburo—street-name changes have resulted in an American consulate with the address 5/1 Ho Chi Minh Road—the city regularly courts Western delegations looking for investment opportunities. Kolkata now has modern shopping malls and modern overpasses. Walking around the city recently for a week or so, often as the only Westerner in sight, I was approached by precisely two beggars.

Still, the image of any city has a half-life of many years. (So does its name, officially changed in 2001 from Calcutta to Kolkata, which is closer to what the word sounds like in Bengali. Conversing in English, I never heard anyone call the city anything but Calcutta.) To Westerners, the conveyance most identified with Kolkata is not its modern subway—a facility whose spacious stations have art on the walls and cricket matches on television monitors—but the hand-pulled rickshaw. Stories and films celebrate a primitive-looking cart with high wooden wheels, pulled by someone who looks close to needing the succor of Mother Teresa. For years the government has been talking about eliminating hand-pulled rickshaws on what it calls humanitarian grounds—principally on the ground that, as the mayor of Kolkata has often said, it is offensive to see "one man sweating and straining to pull another man." But these days politicians also lament the impact of 6,000 hand-pulled rickshaws on a modern city's traffic and, particularly, on its image. "Westerners try to associate beggars and these rickshaws with the Calcutta landscape, but this is not what Calcutta stands for," the chief minister of West Bengal, Buddhadeb Bhattacharjee, said in a press conference in 2006. "Our city stands for prosperity and development." The chief minister—the equivalent of a state governor—went on to announce that hand-pulled rickshaws soon would be banned from the streets of Kolkata.

Rickshaws are not there to haul around tourists. (Actually, I saw almost no tourists in Kolkata, apart from the young backpackers on Sudder Street, in what used to be a red-light district and is now said to be the single place in the city where the services a rickshaw *wallah* offers may include providing female company to a gentleman for the evening.) It's the people in the lanes who most regularly use rickshaws—not the poor but people who are just a notch above the poor. They are people who tend to travel short distances, through lanes that are sometimes inaccessible to even the most daring taxi driver. An older woman with marketing to do, for

Risking a fine, a puller takes a shortcut by traveling against traffic on a one-way street. With little education or professional training, the men who do this grueling work have few other job prospects. Many come from Bihar, one of India's poorest states.

instance, can arrive in a rickshaw, have the rickshaw wallah wait until she comes back from various stalls to load her purchases, and then be taken home. People in the lanes use rickshaws as a 24-hour ambulance service. Proprietors of cafés or corner stores send rickshaws to collect their supplies. (One morning I saw a rickshaw wallah take on a load of live chickens—tied in pairs by the feet so they could be draped over the shafts and the folded back canopy and even the axle. By the time he trotted off, he was carrying about a hundred upside-down chickens.) The rickshaw pullers told me their steadiest customers are school-children. Middle-class families contract with a puller to take a child to school and pick him up; the puller essentially becomes a family retainer.

From June to September Kolkata can get torrential rains, and its drainage system doesn't need torrential rain to begin backing up. Residents who favor a touch of hyperbole say that in Kolkata "if a stray cat pees, there's a flood." During my stay it once rained for about 48 hours. Entire neighborhoods couldn't be reached by motorized vehicles, and the newspapers showed pictures of rickshaws being pulled through water that was up to the pullers' waists. When it's raining, the normal customer base for rickshaw wallahs expands greatly, as does the price of a journey. A writer in Kolkata told me, "When it rains, even the governor takes rickshaws."

While I was in Kolkata, a magazine called *India Today* published its annual ranking of Indian states, according to such measurements as prosperity and infrastructure. Among India's 20 largest states, Bihar finished dead last, as it has for four of the past five years. Bihar, a couple hundred miles north of Kolkata, is where the vast majority of rickshaw wallahs come from.

continued on page 294

Live chickens ride on Gopal Shaw's rig from the wholesale New Market to a retail shop. A puller's day may begin with such early morning deliveries and end after midnight with passengers.

continued from page 291

Once in Kolkata, they sleep on the street or in their rickshaws or in a *dera*—a combination garage and repair shop and dormitory managed by someone called a *sardar*. For sleeping privileges in a dera, pullers pay 100 rupees (about $2.50) a month, which sounds like a pretty good deal until you've visited a dera. They gross between 100 and 150 rupees a day, out of which they have to pay 20 rupees for the use of the rickshaw and an occasional 75 or more for a payoff if a policeman stops them for, say, crossing a street where rickshaws are prohibited. A 2003 study found that rickshaw wallahs are near the bottom of Kolkata occupations in income, doing better than only the ragpickers and the beggars. For someone without land or education, that still beats trying to make a living in Bihar.

There are people in Kolkata, particularly educated and politically aware people, who will not ride in a rickshaw, because they are offended by the idea of being pulled by another human being or because they consider it not the sort of thing people of their station do or because they regard the hand-pulled rickshaw as a relic of colonialism. Ironically, some of those people are not enthusiastic about banning rickshaws. The editor of the editorial pages of Kolkata's *Telegraph*—Rudrangshu Mukherjee, a former academic who still writes history books—told me, for instance, that he sees humanitarian considerations as coming down on the side of keeping hand-pulled rickshaws on the road. "I refuse to be carried by another human being myself," he said, "but I question whether we have the right to take away their livelihood." Rickshaw supporters point out that when it comes to demeaning occupations, rickshaw wallahs are hardly unique in Kolkata.

When I asked one rickshaw wallah if he thought the government's plan to rid the city of rickshaws was based on a genuine interest in his welfare, he smiled, with a quick shake of his head—a gesture I interpreted to mean,

I refuse to be carried by another human being myself.

"If you are so naive as to ask such a question, I will answer it, but it is not worth wasting words on." Some rickshaw wallahs I met were resigned to the imminent end of their livelihood and pin their hopes on being offered something in its place. As migrant workers, they don't have the political clout enjoyed by, say, Kolkata's sidewalk hawkers, who, after supposedly being scaled back at the beginning of the modernization drive, still clog the sidewalks, selling absolutely everything—or, as I found during the 48 hours of rain, absolutely everything but umbrellas. "The government was the government of the poor people," one sardar told me. "Now they shake hands with the capitalists and try to get rid of poor people."

But others in Kolkata believe that rickshaws will simply be confined more strictly to certain neighborhoods, out of the view of World Bank traffic consultants and California investment delegations—or that they will be allowed to die out naturally as they're supplanted by more modern conveyances. Buddhadeb Bhattacharjee, after all, is not the first high West Bengal official to say that rickshaws would be off the streets of Kolkata in a matter of months. Similar statements have been made as far back as 1976. The ban decreed by Bhattacharjee has been delayed by a court case and by a widely held belief that some retraining or social security settlement ought to be offered to rickshaw drivers. It may also have been delayed by a quiet reluctance to give up something that has been part of the fabric of the city for more than a century. Kolkata, a resident told me, "has difficulty letting go." One day a city official handed me a report from the municipal government laying out options for how rickshaw wallahs might be rehabilitated.

"Which option has been chosen?" I asked, noting that the report was dated almost exactly a year before my visit.

"That hasn't been decided," he said.

"When will it be decided?"

"That hasn't been decided," he said.

Critical Responses

1. What is Trillin's attitude toward rickshaws? What is his attitude toward the government of West Bengal? What specific words, turns of phrase, and sentence constructions most reveal his views?

2. What do Vitale's portrayals of rickshaw pullers convey about her attitude? What details stand out most in her images? How do they affect how you see these people and their occupation?

3. What makes pulling a rickshaw demeaning labor? Would you ride in one yourself?

4. Who tends to use rickshaws for transportation? Should the types of passengers and the contexts in which they use rickshaws be considered when determining whether it is right or wrong to ban rickshaws?

Writing Topics

1. Compare the verbal and the visual representation of rickshaws in this article. How would you characterize each one? What are the similarities? What are the differences? How do the perspectives of Trillin and Vitale relate to and interact with one another?

2. Given both of these perspectives, would you argue for or against banning rickshaws? Why? What in the article—in the text or in the images, separately or together—do you find most persuasive and relevant for your argument?

3. If the government were to ban rickshaws, would it have an obligation to assist or compensate the pullers in some way? If so, what would be the most beneficial course of action? If not, what would be the consequences?

4. How would banning rickshaws affect the passengers who typically use them? What might be some of the broader social and economic repercussions? Could or should the government address these?

Further Explorations

1. Transport yourself, as it were, to a car in a traffic jam and write an essay detailing the experience. In the process, be attuned not only to how you are affected, but also to the effect you want your writing to have on your audience. Do you want your readers to laugh or to seethe with annoyance, to pass off traffic jams as just an inconvenience or to give up cars for bicycles and public transportation?

2. While rickshaws originated in Japan (as did the term for "human-powered vehicle," *jinrikisha*), they have also been used, and continue to be used, in many countries in Asia and Africa. Recently, they have also been introduced in some cities in the United States and Great Britain. Forming research groups by region, investigate the cultural contexts in which rickshaws serve as means of transportation and what their doing so implies.

CELT APPEAL

"Celtic of any sort" is "a magic bag into which anything may be put and out of which almost anything may come," observed J. R. R. Tolkein, the father of fantasy prose influenced by Celtic tradition. Looking at contemporary Celts through the lens of history and journalism, author Thomas O'Neill and photographer Jim Richardson document the facts that substantiate Tolkein's observation, and the fascination this fringe culture continues to exert in new age circles.

CELT APPEAL

By Thomas O'Neill

Photographs by Jim Richardson

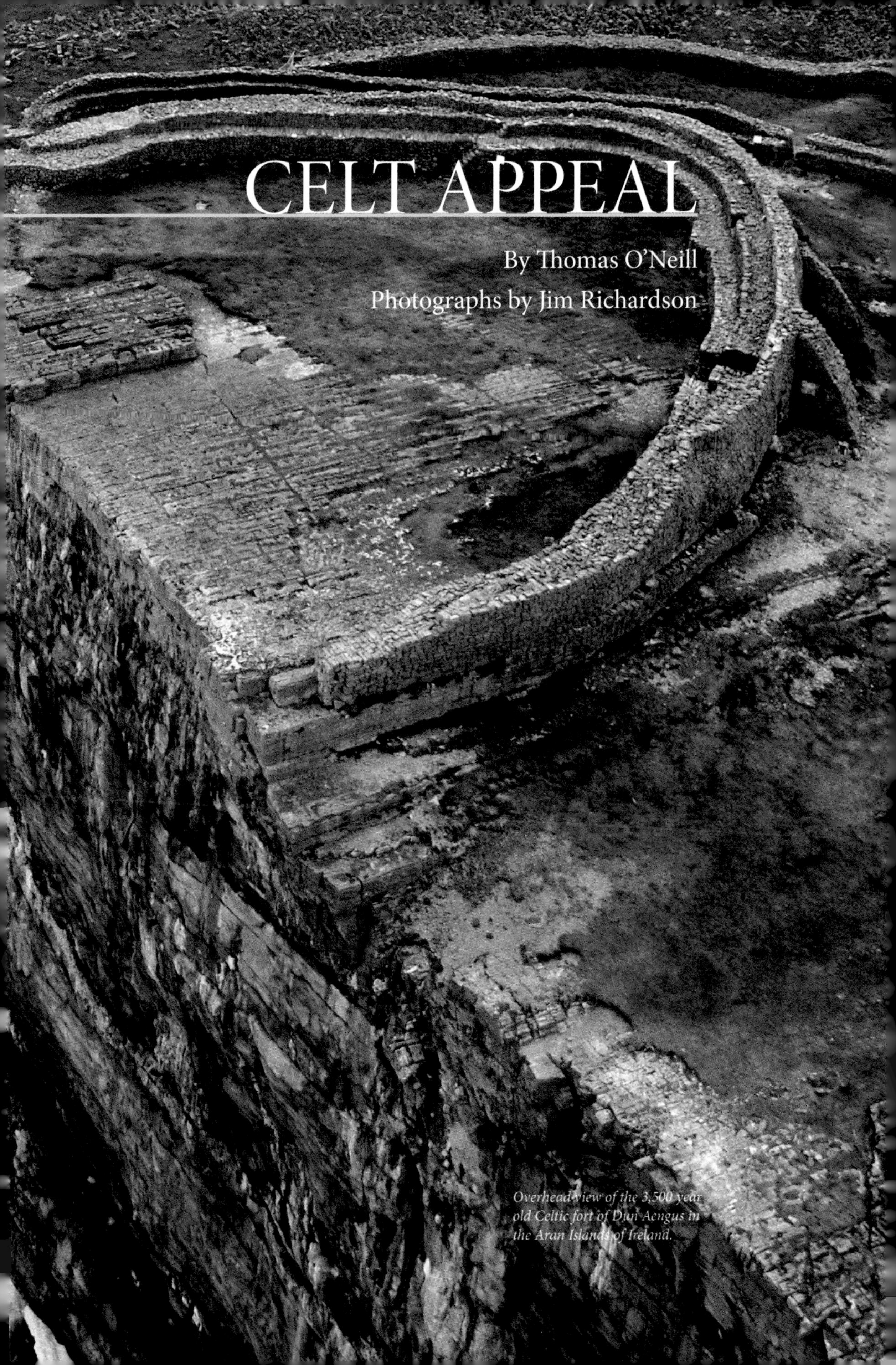

Overhead view of the 3,500 year old Celtic fort of Dun Aengus in the Aran Islands of Ireland.

Loyal to the Mother Tongue
Bannatyne MacLeod speaks the old language of Scottish Gaelic to his family and neighbors on Harris, in Scotland's Outer Hebrides. As everyday speech, the Celtic languages are most widely heard along the farthest western edges of the Celtic realm.

SO WHAT IF THE CELTS DISAPPEARED AS A CIVILIZATION LONG AGO.

THEIR LANGUAGES, MUSIC, AND DEFIANT SPIRIT STILL BURN BRIGHTLY

ALONG EUROPE'S ATLANTIC SHORES.

I felt as if I had stumbled upon a secret society.

Finding a Celt in 21st-century Europe isn't that difficult, though you may need a few ferry tickets, a good pair of boots, and a sharp set of ears before your search is done. Go as far west as you can, right up to the cliffs and coves of the Atlantic—it doesn't matter if it's France or England or Ireland or the outer islands of Scotland—and turn around. Odds are you'll see rocks, plenty of them, piled up in fences, shaped into houses, or lying like bare knuckles in scruffy fields. Probably it's raining. Your search is getting warm. To get warmer still, find a place like the Cross Inn on the windy, moor-covered Isle of Lewis in Scotland's Outer Hebrides. If you're lucky, you might hear a bagpipe or fiddle playing, and if you're luckier still, you might tune in to an unfamiliar sound: Celts talking.

The conversation might go:

"Hullo, Norman, how's your mother?"

"Great, she's visiting her grandchildren and planting flowers in the garden."

Except the speech is rhythmic and guttural, a back-of-the-throat performance, nothing like the rounded slip and slide of English. If there were sound balloons above their heads, they'd look like this: "*Hallo, a Thormoid. Ciamar a tha do mhàthair?*"

"*Gu dòigheil. Tha i a' coimhead air a h-ogh-aichean agus a' cur flùraichean anns a' ghàrradh.*"

The Sunday mates in the Cross Inn are speaking Scottish Gaelic. To them it's no big deal; it's the first language they learned at home. But to me, an American long intoxicated by Irish roots and curious whether an even wider and deeper kinship might exist, that of a Celtic identity, I felt as if I had stumbled upon a secret society. There was something thrilling, even subversive, about hearing an ancient Celtic language in the land of Shakespeare, where neither the Queen nor the Prime Minister would have the foggiest clue what these locals on Lewis were talking about.

When the men caught me listening, they switched to English. "It's rude, that's what we were taught, to speak our language in front of strangers," said Norman Campbell, a novelist and poet who publishes in Scottish Gaelic. I bought a round, and the men opened up, telling me how in their parents' time teachers

Adapted from "Celt Appeal" by Thomas O'Neill: National Geographic Magazine, March 2006.

would take a belt to students overheard speaking the native tongue. Now it's different, they said, and the government is promoting the language. More drinks, and Norman's brother Alasdair drops by and starts singing. The tune is "Gealach Abachaidh an Eòrna," or "The Moon that Ripens the Barley." It sounds sad, I remarked. "Well," Alasdair said, "that moon is huge, very yellow, and it breaks your heart."

Ah, the clues are adding up for identifying a Celt: the ancient language, an easily retrieved sense of historical grievance, a resort to song, and this bittersweet sentimentality. Less clear is how a fringe culture like the Celts managed to survive, even flourish, in a rapidly assimilating world. A brief detour into history begins to tell the tale.

Most of us are unaware that Celts once dominated the breadth of Europe from the Black Sea to the Atlantic—and for a long time. An early form of Welsh was spoken in Britain 1,500 years before Old English took root. The Celtic languages still spoken in Europe hark back to the Late Bronze Age (1200–800 B.C.) and a civilization of aristocratic warrior tribes. The word "Celtic" comes from the Greek *Keltoi,* first appearing in the sixth century B.C. to describe "barbarians" living inland from the Mediterranean Sea. Little suggests these people united or called themselves Celts. Yet there is no denying that these far-flung peoples spoke closely related languages and shared beliefs, styles of art and weaponry, and tribal societies. Trade, principally by water, connected them. Calling them Celts makes sense, if only to separate them from what they weren't: Roman or Greek.

All this categorizing might easily have become an arid academic debate about a lost

No one else wanted to live where the Celts did. Those places were poor and remote, and no one spoke their language.

people. Beginning in the second century B.C. Roman legions vanquished Celtic armies across Europe. Only the peoples of northern Britain and Ireland remained unconquered. In the fifth century A.D. the Anglo-Saxons invaded Celtic lands, followed by the Vikings, storming the coasts in their long warships, the Normans, who attacked from France, and finally the colonizing armies of the English and French crowns. From these wars of resistance came many Celtic heroes and martyrs such as the legendary King Arthur, the Irish High King Brian Boru, and Scotland's William Wallace, known as Braveheart.

By the end of the Middle Ages, Celtic culture was headed toward extinction, its remnants pushed to the very western edge of Europe. "No one else wanted to live where the Celts did," a Breton man said. "Those places were poor and remote, and no one spoke their languages."

Being ostracized to no-man's-land did not spare the Celts from further depredations. The English and French banned or restricted their languages, their instruments and music, their names, their right to own property, and in the case of the kilt-wearing Scottish Highland clans, even their clothing. It's a bit miraculous Celtic civilization survived in any form. By clinging to the fringes, geographically and culturally, Celts refused to vanish.

Now, in one of those delectable backward flips of history, Celts and all things Celtic suddenly seem omnipresent. "Europe's beautiful losers," as one British writer called them, are commanding attention as one of the new century's seductive identities: free-spirited, rebellious, poetic, nature-worshipping, magical, self-sufficient.

I first saw Fred Morrison onstage at the Festival Interceltique in Brittany, wearing a plaid kilt and a polka-dot tie, all sweaty

continued on page 302

The Celtic Fringe

Once spread across the breadth of Europe, Celtic culture, created by a loose-knit group of aristocratic warrior tribes, had shrunk to the edges of the continent by the late Middle Ages. Monuments to the glory days, like the 3,500-year-old, ocean-defended fort of Dun Aengus in the Aran Islands of Ireland, fell into ruin. But in isolation and poverty, Celtic society survived. Language anchors the current resurgence of Celtic identity: Some 2.5 million people claim to speak a Celtic language.

20° 15° 10° 5°W

Scottish Gaelic
Barvas
Outer Hebrides
Harris
Stornoway
Isle of Lewis
South Uist
Skye
Little Minch
Glenfinnan
SCOTLAND
Iona
North Channel
Edinburgh
Lindisfarne

Irish Gaelic
NORTHERN IRELAND
Croagh Patrick
Belfast
Stranraer
UNITED KINGDOM
Dun Aengus
Hill of Tara
IRELAND
Aran Is.
Clonmacnoise
Dublin
Irish Sea
Manx
Isle of Man
Glendalough
Anglesey
Liverpool
Welsh
Llanfairfechan
Machynlleth
ENGLAND
WALES
Coed Llathen
Llandovery

Celtic
Cornish
Glastonbury
Cardiff
London
Sea
Carn Euny
Cornwall
Stonehenge
Penzance

English Channel

Breton
Brest
Landévennec
Collorec
Brittany
Lorient

ATLANTIC
OCEAN
Paris
FRANCE

Bay of Biscay

A Coruña
Galicia
Asturias
Minho
Citánia de Briteiros
PORTUGAL
SPAIN
Numantia

SOURCE: JOHN HAYWOOD, *ATLAS OF THE CELTIC WORLD* NGM MAPS

Modern Celtic Realm

— Area of Celtic culture

◈ Historical site

⠿ Main concentration of Celtic-language speakers

Welsh Language

0 mi 100
0 km 100

SOURCE: JOHN HAYWOOD, *ATLAS OF THE CELTIC WORLD* NGM MAPS

continued from page 300

and solemn as he played Breton and Irish tunes on his bagpipes. Morrison ("the Jimi Hendrix of pipers!" a fan raved) is from the island of South Uist in Scotland's Outer Hebrides. When we met in a café late one morning, he had traded his kilt for blue jeans and looked like an off-hours traveling salesman with two attaché-size cases in hand. Inside were bagpipes. He said he'd learned the pipes from his father and in 1972, at 18, had headed to Amsterdam to play in the streets. Soon he hooked up with some Irish musicians and freed his style. "I learned to become a rebel musically," Morrison said. He went on to play for pathbreaking Scottish bands like Capercaillie and Clan Alba, and worked on the soundtrack for the movie *Rob Roy.*

For Morrison, like most modern-day Celts, the past became liberating; it was not some sacred, hands-off heirloom but a scuffed-up plaything, the more loved the more it's used. "I would never turn my back on tradition," Morrison said. "But I came to see that tradition can come with this straight face, allowing almost no freedom for improvisation. I decided it was cooler to break the rules." At that he set off to rehearse with a "killer bouzouki player," that being someone extremely handy with a mandolin-like instrument from the Balkans—sure to sound Celtic when Morrison is done accompanying it.

A similar sleight of hand is happening through- out the Celtic realm, from Scotland to Galicia in northern Spain, where anything goes and the definition of a Celt is as elusive and shifting as the coastal weather. There are "blood Celts," the several million people who were raised and still live in the surviving Celtic language territories. Then there is the growing tribe of "Celts of the spirit," who feel touched by the history, myths, and artistic expressions of beautiful losers. "Celtic of any sort," observed J. R. R. Tolkien, is "a magic bag, into which

> **C**eltic of any sort is a magic bag, into which anything may be put, and out of which almost anything may come.

anything may be put, and out of which almost anything may come."

Out of that magic bag drips water, the element that linked the Celtic lands in the past and now most often serves to separate them, for better or worse. Chugging across the Little Minch, the ferry remains the most practical way to reach Lewis and Harris, the northernmost of the Outer Hebrides. One Saturday night I caught the weekend's last sailing from the Island of Skye, the waves seemingly in sync with the churning vowels and consonants of the Gaelic onboard announcements. Ferries don't run on Sundays, a stone-quiet day when an austere form of Presbyterianism keeps shops shuttered and people inside their homes.

Driving down Lewis's empty roads, past stretches of gloomy bogland, through villages lined with houses the color of wet sand, I discovered a forgiven bustle of activity in the parking lot of the Free Church of Scotland in Barvas. A service in Scottish Gaelic was about to begin.

Lewis attracted me because of its isolation and because of its sounds. Many of its 18,500 inhabitants still speak Gaelic as an everyday language, a rare pocket considering that less than one percent of Scotland's population, or only about 30,000 people, are believed to be fluent in the language. An even rarer phenomenon awaited inside the bare-walled church: the singing of psalms in the local language, a musical form as unique and starkly sensual as the chanting of Tibetan monks.

Several dozen parishioners, mostly older folks, took their places on the hard pews, the gents in dark suits, the ladies a bit more daring in summer hats sprouting ribbons and bows. A well-freckled woman on my right shyly passed me a sweet. In a tradition going back to preliterate days, a precentor stood up and began singing solo, to imprint melody and words with the congregation. Soon everyone joined in. The voices didn't lift in ecstatic joy but keened and moaned. The singing conjured up worlds of lament and forbearance, a requiem for an island drifting away from its roots.

Services in English are outdrawing the Gaelic sessions, the minister said afterward. Other islanders told me they were worried that the toll of emigration—everyone had tales of relatives past and present leaving—and the decline of crofting, the family practice of raising crops and livestock on small plots, would finally bury the language. But the most pressing problem, it seems, is that for the younger generation, a whiff of country bumpkin rises off the ancient words. While I was interviewing Christina Morrison, 83, in her home, her middle-aged daughter interrupted from the kitchen. "It's not cool to speak Gaelic. The fancy people in town look down on us." The old woman nodded and admitted that even her grandchildren are a tough sell. "I give them ten pence if they answer in Gaelic."

Learning Gaelic does have economic benefits. In a cafeteria in Stornoway, the only town on the island, I met a dozen college-age islanders who through Comunn na Gàidhlig, a government-funded agency promoting Gaelic, worked at summer jobs using their bilingual skills. They were interning at places like the BBC radio station, which broadcasts 65 hours of Gaelic programming a week, and the local arts council. Most hoped to make a career out of teaching Gaelic, and all vowed to raise Gaelic-speaking children. "But amongst ourselves, we mostly speak English," confessed one young woman, Jayne Macleod. "Anymore, Gaelic is the language of schools and old people."

When I rode the ferry back to Skye, I noticed that the shipboard announcements were only in English. Christina should have been aboard with her change purse.

During the Celtic glory days of old, water routes converged on Ireland. From its shores came merchants, missionaries, soldiers of fortune, musicians, and in 1607, the last of the Gaelic aristocracy, including my ancestors, the Uí (Gaelic for "descendant of") Néill, who were fleeing English troops. Befitting this busy, water-coursed past, the ferry I took to Ireland was no slow boat to a rustic past but a high-speed catamaran rushing to a cosmopolitan future. For most of the passengers, crossing the North Channel from Stranraer, Scotland, to Belfast, capital of Northern Ireland, Celtic no doubt meant Celtic Tiger, a brand name of success given to the booming economy of the Republic of Ireland. Irish in both the north and south are gloating that—finally—they've caught up with England and the rest of Western Europe, embracing the one-size-fits-all notion of modern prosperity.

Poet Gearóid Mac Lochlainn, like a true Celt, resists the homogenizing forces of the time. He speaks and writes in the Irish language, which in parts of his native Belfast still comes across as fighting words. "Here the language itself is viewed as a taunt just by the fact that it's still spoken, that it's survived," said Mac Lochlainn, a thin, jeans-and-T-shirt guy with close-cropped hair.

Mac Lochlainn talked to me on safe ground, inside the Cultúrlann, a steepled red-brick church converted to an Irish-language center in the working-class Catholic neighborhood of Falls Road. He did not learn Irish from the cradle. He picked up threads of it from a Christian Brothers school and from family friends and visitors from the Gaeltacht, the areas in the republic, mostly on the western fringe, where Irish hangs on as a community language. His poems often marvel at the dissonance of sounds between the majority and minority languages, as when he flirts with an Irish-speaking woman whose "puckety-pocking words" show up his "sluppity-slip-slapping" drunken talk in English.

As Mac Lochlainn spun his past, people kept stopping by our table to say hello. He had caused a sensation with his book *Stream of Tongues (Sruth Teangacha)*—Irish poems side-by-side with their English translations. One called "Poet's Choice" laid out his fever dream:

"I want to speak, rant, rave / untie tongue till it blooms and bleeds / in seven shades of street rhythms." But it wasn't the printed page that caused the stir; tucked into the back of the book was a CD of Mac Lochlainn rapping his poetry to music. It was a mesmerizing performance. Admirers who turn out for his appearances probably think he shares turf with Eminem, but Mac Lochlainn points to a deeper influence, that of the Celtic bards. He likens his poems to *sean nós,* the traditional style of unaccompanied singing. "When I read my work, it's like a séance," he said. "I feel like I'm a vessel for past voices."

Soon he was off, a busy man, writing and recording a new book and preparing for performances in Liverpool, Slovenia, the Czech Republic. "It seems like everyone wants to be a Celt," he said. I dropped the bard off near his flat, somewhere in a tough-looking neighborhood of brick apartment blocks, a Celtic tiger on the loose.

Voyagers long knew the Celtic lands by their native names: Scotland was Alba; the Isle of Man, Ellan Vannin; Ireland, Éireann; Cornwall, Kernow; and Wales, Cymru. "kum-ree, kum-ree," I softly chanted aboard the *Jonathan Swift,* a ferry across the Irish Sea to the island of Anglesey in northern Wales.

As a nod toward their native languages, most modern Celtic lands put up bilingual town names. And as a nod toward independence, Celtic vandals just as regularly scratch out the English and French names, creating the sight of tourists standing befuddled beside their cars in places like northwestern Ireland and the western tip of Cornwall, a useless English-language map hanging from their hands. Memorizing a few pronunciation rules is almost mandatory in Wales. Try asking for directions to Machyn-lleth and Llanfairfechan.

Except for a few regions in Ireland, the Welsh stand apart in retaining their old unaccompanied, un-anglicized place-names, particularly in the north and west. Here is the best defended outpost of Celtic speech: Nearly 600,000 people, roughly a fifth of the population, can speak Welsh, the beneficiaries of a nationalist movement that has used language as a rallying cry since the 1960s. The old language bubbles up in schools, pubs, grocery stores, and on television. The English name for Wales comes from the Anglo-Saxon word *wealas,* meaning foreigners, a description many Welsh today would turn on its head and apply to the English themselves.

Besides language, what gives the Celtic Welsh a chest-pounding feel of home is heroic history—and Wales is thick with it: walled towns, roofless churches, spiral-engraved standing stones, holy wells, crumbling hill forts, all proclaiming a past age of Celtic dominance.

The history that stirs the hottest passions among Welsh Celts belongs to medieval times, when Welsh leaders resisted the ultimately successful invasions of the English kings. Those heroic days seemed as fresh as an open wound to David Petersen as he drove me through the Towy River Valley in southwestern Wales. I had met the ponytailed Petersen before at the Festival Interceltique, the pan-Celtic music event in Lorient, Brittany, where he headed the Welsh delegation. When I heard him call the Union Jack a "butcher's apron," I knew I'd found a Celtic troublemaker.

Petersen, a Celtic commentator and sculptor, wanted to show me one of the latest patriotic monuments to the Welsh cause. He was in a pugnacious mood, befitting the son of a former heavyweight champ. Jabbing his finger right and left as we sped through the mellow valley, Petersen bloodied the English face on the landscape. He angrily corrected a few anglicized names of towns; pointed out the ruins of Welsh castles while ignoring the bulkier, fixed-up English ones; and, slowing down beside a modest piece of pastureland, complained that no marker identified this ground as the site of the glorious Battle of Coed Llathen. Here, in 1257, Welsh troops crushed the invading English army of King Henry III. "A new map of this area has left the battlefield out," Petersen said in disbelief. "The effing nerve of the authorities to tell us that this has no historical value."

Holy Place
At monastic ruins in Ireland's Aran Islands, Dara Molloy, an ex-Catholic priest, marries the Yoshidas. The Japanese couple came for the atmospheric Celtic ceremony.

Wheeling into a car park in the center of Llandovery, an old market town, Petersen reached the point of his harangue: On a rise, sharing space with the broken walls of a castle, stood a warrior's statue. Helmet, spear, flowing cloak, shield, and broadsword—the costume of war gleamed in stainless steel. But where there should have been a face and a body inside the medieval uniform, empty space stared out.

The 16-foot-high statue represents Llywelyn ap Gruffydd Fychan, a "brave nobody," Petersen said. When English troops stormed the area in 1401, looking for the army of Welsh rebel Owain Glyndŵr, the local Lord Llywelyn led the enemy in the wrong direction, buying time for Glyndŵr to escape. As punishment for his subterfuge, Llywelyn was executed in the town square. "The English

took his stomach out and cooked it in front of him," Petersen said. The empty cloak symbolizes the horrific form of death.

Petersen knows the full story behind the raising of the statue on the 600th anniversary of Llywelyn's execution. His sons Toby and Gideon designed and built the locally commissioned monument. Back at the car we found a £30 ($50) parking ticket on the windshield. Petersen snatched it up, cursed the authorities, and vowed to fight the ticket. He had no choice: A Ghost of Wales Past was looking over his shoulder.

When I reached Cornwall at the southernmost tip of England by car—alas, no ferry— I drove from St. Just to St. Ives to St. Agnes to St. Austell. People joke that there aren't enough seats in heaven for all the Celtic saints. Wherever you are in Celtic lands, every day is a holy day. For the first week or so of September alone, I counted feast days for saints named Macanisius, Ultan, Rhuddlad, Disibod, Kieran, and Finian. The saints' names date to the time between the fifth and eighth centuries when Celtic Christian missionaries, most from Ireland, scattered along the Atlantic coast and beyond to establish monastic centers. The monks often located their sanctuaries at pre-Christian ceremonial sites, acknowledging their sacred significance.

This entwining of pagan and early Christian traditions today exerts a magnetic pull at the religious sites, luring pilgrims, tourists, spiritual groupies, and mystic seekers. Something about Cornwall, its woolly wet weather, its abundance of prehistoric sites, and its ties to the legend of King Arthur (local Arthurians locate his castle at Tintagel), draws the more mystical and pagan of the pilgrims.

One day while looking around the Iron Age village site of Carn Euny, I met Cheryl Straffon, a Cornish goddess worshipper. I first noticed her at the head of a group of American women coming out of an underground chamber. The early Celts may have used such subterranean rooms, called *fogous* in Cornwall, as ritual sites. "That room has great acoustics," I overheard Straffon saying. "Chanting sounds good in there."

Straffon is editor of a newsletter called *Meyn Mamvro* about sacred sites in Cornwall. Middle-aged with a mop of graying blond hair, she has been intensely drawn to the Cornish landscape since she was a schoolgirl here. "It's as if I had been born with memories of these places," she said. "It is not a cold remote past here. It's a warm immediate past."

To commune with that past, Straffon observes the pre-Christian Celtic calendar, conducting rituals on the season-turning feast days of Imbolc (February 1, to mark the lactation of ewes), Beltane (May 1, when flocks and herds were moved to summer pastures), Lughnasa (August 1, for the first harvest), and Samhain (October 31–November 1, when the world of the dead was believed to briefly open, inspiring the modern Halloween).

On each of these days Straffon and her fellow celebrants invite a Celtic goddess into their midst. Brigid, an Irish deity associated with healing, later absorbed by the church as a saint, is invoked on Imbolc when Straffon visits holy wells like Madron. We tramped one day through woods to the well, a pool of dark water seeping out of the ground. A fungus called stinkhorn gave off a piercing sour smell, and on the surrounding moss-furred trees, shreds of cloth and paper hung like ornaments off every branch. These were offerings, or "clouties," representing body parts that petitioners, Christians as well as pagans, wished to have healed.

When conducting a ritual here, Straffon said she and her friends decorate the well with candles and call in Brigid using Gaelic chants, just the way she imagines people did for centuries. "This gives us a sense of connecting with our ancestors who lived here," she said. "It allows us to relate to the land and give it thanks."

Pagans don't delight everyone in Cornwall. Some members of a local church have stripped the clouties at well sites, Straffon said, and a fundamentalist Christian farmer knocked down a standing stone on his land. But as we sloshed through mud back to the road and rain began to fall, Straffon remarked that, judging by the number of visitors from afar seeking out the local sacred sites, Celts must be everywhere. "I believe if you feel Celtic," she said, "you become Celtic."

In many ways the so-called Celtic spirituality has become as popular and marketable as Celtic music. People are embracing it for its aura of seeking the divine in nature and for treating women as the spiritual equals of men. They come to meditate and conduct rituals at early Celtic Christian centers like Iona in Scotland, Glastonbury in England, and Glendalough in Ireland. On Inishmore in Ireland's Aran Islands, I attended a "Celtic wedding." Dara Molloy, who had quit the Catholic priesthood ten years earlier to protest the prohibition against female clergy, read the vows inside the ruins of a 12th-century church—but only after he had led the

Unvanquished
Outfitted with kilt and shield and carrying the Scottish flag, a patriot climbs the hill at Glenfinnan, where in 1745 Gaelic-speaking Highlanders joined an uprising against the British king. The rebels lost, but now generations later, the underdog Celts insist their time has come again.

American couple to a fertility stone and holy well to pray.

The overnight ferry to Brittany across the English Channel probably follows a route similar to the one taken by Guénolé, a Celtic saint who sailed to "Little Britain" from England in the late fifth century to found a monastery. Driving through rolling farm country (finally, fertile, stone-free fields!), I stopped outside the village of Collorec, at a small fieldstone chapel named after the saint. A farmer was in the doorway, like Father Time himself, with a scythe on his shoulder, having just cut the grass around the building.

"When I was young, people would come to pray for the rains to stop," said Marcel Quéré, laying down his scythe and unlocking the chapel door to give me a look. "When a person died, someone would come ring the bell." Inside the dim interior I saw sculpted dragons swallowing the ends of the crossbeams and carved human heads where the walls met the ceiling. Tolerating these pagan symbols were sad-eyed wooden statues of the Virgin Mary and St. Guénolé.

One Sunday afternoon, a hundred or so people, almost all of them white-haired, gathered for Guénolé's pardon, or feast day. They sat on benches outside the chapel in the shade of pine trees. A mischievous breeze kept blowing the cross off the makeshift altar and onto the grass, until Father Pierre Mahé, smiling through his white beard, laid it flat on the table. Following custom, the priest, who serves 22 churches in four parishes, said the outdoor Mass in French, but the worshippers sang hymns in Breton, now spoken almost exclusively by the elderly. When Mass ended, two men carried the statue of St. Guénolé out of the chapel, hoisted him on their shoulders, and led everyone on a slow procession down the lane, past stone farmhouses, circling around to return the saint to the chapel.

For the rest of the afternoon, the congregants held a dance at a nearby crossroads.

Mostly the women danced, twirling and stepping in the crisp syncopation of Breton dance, while a pair of accordion players and someone on the bodhran, an Irish drum, made music under a hot sun. The men bowled in a grassy patch beside the road, tossing unpainted wooden balls at rows of pins. The priest, having replaced his vestments with blue jeans, stayed and drank beer. No one appeared in any hurry to leave.

I suspected that the Scots, the Irish, the Welsh, and the Cornish, the blood Celts among them anyway, would all feel at home here with these Bretons. There were no costumes or causes on display, nothing done to impress an outsider. The past danced into the present, and everyone, with a nod toward St. Guénolé, could feel thankful that on this day the world did not feel strange or hostile. It felt Celtic.

Critical Responses

1. How has Celtic culture been marginalized over time? How do Celts manage to continue to survive?

2. What does the description of Celts as "Europe's most beautiful losers" suggest? Is it applicable to other cultures as well?

3. What is the role of tradition for Celts encountered by O'Neill? What is the appeal of Celtic traditions and rituals for non-Celts?

4. What are some examples of marketing of Celtic culture in this article? Do they represent a violation or a cheapening? If so, why and to what extent? If not, why not?

Writing Topics

1. According to O'Neill, "clues to identifying a Celt" include "the ancient language, an easily retrieved sense of historical grievance, a resort to song, and ... bittersweet sentimentality." At the same time, he also refers to Celts' representing "one of the new century's seductive identities: free-spirited, rebellious, poetic, nature-worshipping, magical, self-sufficient." How can both be true at once?

2. What differing attitudes do various Celts have toward their language in relation to that of dominant cultures? What threatens Celtic languages? How, in general, is language crucial to Celtic identity?

3. Taking the point further, consider the role of language in relation to other essential aspects of Celtic identity. How do all these support and reinforce one another?

4. The theme of insiders and outsiders— or of insiders versus outsiders—is touched on in this article. Develop it further in connection with specific examples from the text.

Further Explorations

1. Of the Celtic qualities described in this article, which are the most appealing to you, and why? What, if any, values or ways of life are comparable from your point of view? And most appealing?

2. As a class, produce an inventory of the languages everyone in the room speaks. For each student, what language defines or contributes most to his or her identity? How is this language related to American culture? You may wish to consider regional accents and vocabularies in the process.

LONDON ON A ROLL

By Simon Worrall

Photographs by Jodi Cobb

LONDON ON A ROLL

London is the most populous city in the European Union, as well as one of the largest. It's been called a "Leviathan" and a "Babylon;" either way, its vitality is unmistakable. As Samuel Johnson said, "When a man is tired of London, he is tired of life; for there is in London all that life can afford." The observation holds just as true now as it was two hundred years ago. Produced by journalist Simon Worrall and photographer Jodi Cobb, both of whom might be termed world citizens, this feature article shows "London on a Roll," remaking itself as it always has as a world city and creating a thriving urban culture for the 21st century.

Aerial view of London showing Big Ben, the Houses of Parliament, and Westminster Abbey lining the banks of the River Thames. London is a "messy and confusing city," writes historian Stephen Inwood. Yet the disheveled grande dame of the Thames is enjoying a building boom unparalleled since recovery from World War II

Preening is a serious pastime for London's "It girls"—beauties like Alexandra Aitken who serve as fashionable and ubiquitous adornments on the party circuit. "They're world famous in London," jokes one public relations agent. In its way, the town Dickens quaintly called a "magic lantern" has become "It" among global cities, beaming with the intensity of a socialite's smile.

SUBLIME AND RIDICULOUS COLLIDE AT LONDON'S EXCLUSIVE HURLINGHAM CLUB, WHERE REVELERS DRIVE "DODGEMS" AFTER VIEWING ANTIQUE BENTLEYS AND OTHER REVERED MODELS AT THE LOUIS VUITTON CLASSIC CAR SHOW. GIDDY AS A REBORN SCROOGE, LONDON THRIVES AS A LEADER IN GLOBAL FINANCE, CULTURE, AND EVEN (GASP) CUISINE.

The last time London occupied center stage in world history was the "swinging sixties," when its music and fashion defined the look and sound of a generation. London is calling again. Its theater and music scenes are world leaders; its restored historic buildings and monuments glitter with gold leaf; its immaculate parks look better than ever. Most startling are the changes among its people. The millennium ended in Indonesia and the Balkans with ethnic cleansing and racial hatred. Londoners are moving in the opposite direction, making their city the world's greatest cosmopolis.

> The last time London took center stage in world history was the "swinging sixties."

for the past 30 years, keeping pace with all this is no small task. "To do the Knowledge now is taking up to three years," he said, recalling the exam that London cab drivers have to take before they can get their license, as we swept over Waterloo Bridge on our way to Peckham in south London, where he was born. "I left school at 15 and started work in the old Covent Garden flower market." A short, well-built man with a domed, balding head, blue-gray eyes, a close mustache, and a razor-sharp wit, John is one of those archetypal Londoners who seem to have stepped straight out of *Mary Poppins* or *EastEnders*.

For John Shepherd, a cabbie who has been threading his way through London's streets

Adapted from "London on a Roll" by Simon Worrall: National Geographic Magazine, June 2000.

"An old cabbie once said to me, 'John, my son, if you learn one thing a day while you're doing this job, by the end of your life'"—he paused meaningfully as a gray plaque marking the onetime home of Charlie Chaplin flashed by—"'your 'ead will be full of rubbish.'"

We pulled up outside a two-story house on Elmington Road. "See the different colored brick?" said John, pointing up at the wall. "That's where it was hit with a German bomb." From Brunswick Park, along the street, we could hear the sound of children playing. "I did the Knowledge in the afternoons while working at the flower market. In those days you had what was called the Blue Book, which had all the different runs in it. You would get a map, and you would study the route, with all the backstreets, and write them down. Then you would go out on your bike and follow the route. The hardest to remember were all the little alleyways and backstreets. We used to call them 'rat runs.'" He paused. "You can't use most of them now. They're closing them off."

Not closing, exactly; "calming" is the official term. The addition of speed bumps to London's side streets and alleys, many of which date back to medieval times, is one response to growth and traffic congestion. After decades of flight to the suburbs, London's population is expected to rise to 7.7 million during the next 20 years, approaching what it was at the start of World War II. "You've heard of road rage," said John. "Well, there's a lot of that now."

More than London's shifting topography, it is the shifts in the human landscape that bewilder Shepherd. "I feel like a dinosaur sometimes, as though they're just waiting for people like me to die out," he said, as we settled on a bench in Brunswick Park. As a child he had played a game called Knock Down Ginger in the streets and watched barrage balloons floating overhead to ward off the Luftwaffe's planes. Today kids play video games, and the Germans are allies. Gone too is the almost exclusively white community into which he

was born. The boys playing soccer in front of us were mostly of Pakistani or West Indian descent. When I asked John what he thought of mixed marriages, he paused and said with a wink, "A robin won't mate with a blackbird, will it?"

Daniel Shepherd, John's 21-year-old son, resembles John. He has the same slightly slanting, blue-gray eyes, prominent ears, and round face. But his attitudes couldn't be more different. "If I talk to someone, race is not the first thing I notice," he told me during his lunch break at Dorling Kindersley, the publisher, where he was doing a student internship. By coincidence his office is in Covent Garden, a few yards from where his father once worked and met Daniel's mother. "I have loads of friends who are black. I have got a lot of Indian friends at work. I don't see them as colored people. They're just my mates."

The whole world lives in London. Walk down Oxford Street and you will see Indians and Colombians, Bangladeshis and Ethiopians, Pakistanis and Russians, Melanesians and Malaysians. Fifty nationalities with communities of more than 5,000 make their home in the city, and on any given day 300 languages are spoken. It is estimated that by 2010 the population will be almost 30 percent ethnic minorities, the majority born in the U.K. Most of these Londoners are the children and in some cases the grandchildren of the many thousands who came here from the Caribbean and the Indian subcontinent during the 50s and 60s, after the British Empire imploded.

Annas Ali, a 17-year-old Londoner of Bangladeshi descent, feels deeply rooted in British society. "I have been here all my life," he told me, as we dodged our way through the festive crowds filling Brick Lane in the East End for Baishakhi Mela, the Bangladeshi New Year. The neighborhood is known as Bangla Town. Union Jacks fluttered next to the green-and-red flag of Bangladesh. Indian music echoed off Victorian brick houses. "I was born at Mile End hospital a half mile away and grew

Embracing the moment, Neil Williams and Joanne Evans enjoy a summer Sunday. "Mixed relationships are more accepted here than in the U.S.," says Evans.

up in Hunton Street. My father had a restaurant there."

Annas Ali himself is eclectic. With his dark skin, raven black hair, and lustrous brown eyes, he reminded me of Mowgli in the *Jungle Book*. But his hair was cut in the latest London style: short in back, long and slicked back with gel at the front. He is a devout Muslim, an Asian Londoner who talks Cockney English. The gold rings on his fingers were from India, his stylish, midnight blue cardigan—"pure wool," he told me proudly—from Prohibito, a clothes shop on Oxford Street popular among teenagers. "I want to go into fashion," he said. "I want to go to the London School of Fashion."

Two weeks before I met Annas, a nail bomb went off in Brick Lane—one of three that shook the city last year. The newspapers ran features about neo-Nazi groups with names like Combat 18 and speculated about a coming racial war. But the bombings last year were not part of a broader trend. They were a desperate attempt by a single individual pathologically at odds with his times to stop the racial mixing that, with a typically British lack of hype, has been going on for a generation.

"It's the holy grail of all societies to have the energy that hybridity brings without the distressing divisions," Trevor Phillips told me as we sat in the living room of his house in

continued on page 318

Pinstripes and polish mark Leadenhall Market in the City, London's square-mile financial district and the world's largest hub of international banking. "City men can afford the luxury of a shine," says Kathryn Ford.

continued from page 315

Stanmore, a leafy suburb on the northern fringes of the city. Born in London of Guyanese origins, Phillips is one of Britain's best known broadcasters and the chairman of the London Arts Board. "We're just reaching for it here. We're just on the edge of being able to do it."

Outside, a Volvo dozed in the driveway. Through a sliding glass door I could see a well-mowed lawn. It was every middle-class Englishman's idea of suburban comfort. What struck me even more was this black Londoner's ease in discussing a subject that in the United States can be fissile material.

"In America you always have to choose: I'm black, or I'm not black," he said. "When I go to New York to visit my sisters, I can, if I so choose, never speak to someone who is not black. Here that is not possible. There are so many different Londons that jostle side by side, and so many different kinds of people who live here, and we have a whole set of manners and ways of looking at people who are different from us that allow us to live right next door to them. To be cool about it."

It is this convivial mixing of the races, not just its diversity, that is so special about London. "There is a great amount of intermarrying here," says Sunand Prasad, an architect of Indian origin whose family emigrated to London 30 years ago. "The races used to be quite distinct, but rather than the edges becoming ever more sharply defined, as they are in France or the States, they are really beginning to blur."

Along with its cosmopolitanism and tolerance, London's surging economy is drawing a new wave of migrants—not from the Caribbean or Africa but from across the Channel. "London is very attractive to French people at the moment," said Christophe Beauvilain, a 32-year-old executive at Goldman Sachs, as we rushed across the fields of Picardy on Eurostar,

> **It's the holy grail of all societies to have that energy that hybridity brings without the distressing divisions.**

the high-speed rail link between Paris and London. It was Sunday night, and the train was packed with French returning to London after a weekend at home. "It is much more dynamic in terms of fashion or night life. And it's more entrepreneurial. All the headquarters of the big financial institutions are here. You make more money. The taxes are lower."

Since the 16th century London's financial district, known as the City or the Square Mile, has been one of the most powerful business centers in the world. Today, with 539 foreign banks, it is the most international: More than 437 billion dollars flows through its foreign currency markets every day, far more than anywhere else in the world. The value of London's economy—$162 billion—is larger than that of many countries, including Poland, Singapore, and even Switzerland.

Geographically and politically the United Kingdom may be on the fringes of Europe, but London has become, economically and culturally, the de facto capital of Europe. At the same time, it feels more European than ever. This can be seen in the way Londoners have discovered the street. When I was young, Soho was a backwater stalked by sleazy men in raincoats, but as I walked around late on a warm summer evening, there was a boisterous, carnival atmosphere. People spilled out of pubs with their pints; a young couple stood locked in a passionate embrace in an alleyway off Dean Street; gangs of girls with bare stomachs and studs in their navels sat at pavement cafés gossiping or ogling the boys.

"My picture of London before I came here was very old-fashioned—people drinking tea at 4 P.M. and everyone being very polite," said Ximena Cordova, a 24-year-old from Bolivia. With her Latin looks and azure blue sweater, set off by a white lily tucked into her hair, Ximena looked like one of those brilliant, exotic creatures you find in the rain forest. "But London is a very free place. I lived in Barcelona before, and London is much more tolerant, much more cosmopolitan."

London's broad-mindedness has made the city a magnet for homosexuals. "I feel like I'm part of the driving force of London," said Carl Gobey, 23, who is gay. A sociology student from Britain's second city, Birmingham, he is one of the 30,000 young people from other parts of Britain who pack a suitcase and, with a bit of money and a lot of hope, head for London each year to reinvent themselves. "Everything is here—different nationalities, different people, different styles and fashions. Anything you want to be, any life you want to lead: You can find it."

This golden age has a dark side. In a church graveyard in Brixton, I saw marijuana and other drugs being dealt among the tombstones. Across the road at the Fridge, 2,000 Generation Xers were dancing to the sound of Basement Jaxx, one of the hottest acts on the city's club scene. Many of the revelers were clearly high. A whole cottage industry of illegal drug factories supplies "dance drugs," such as ecstasy, amphetamines, and the anesthetic GHB. Hard drugs are also increasingly available. Last year some of London's poorest areas were flooded with three-dollar bags of heroin. "It's easier to get drugs in London than it is to get a taxi," John Ellis, a 24-year-old recovering addict, told me.

At last it is also just as easy to get good food. A journey to London used to be a gastronomic Calvary, but with more than 6,000 restaurants serving dishes from every corner of the planet, London may now be the most cosmopolitan culinary center anywhere in the world.

"The sea bass is the top bollocks today," said Steve Carter, the Yorkshire-born head chef at Bank, a huge—and hugely popular—new restaurant in the heart of the West End. I had signed up to be a sous-chef for a day, and now I was struggling into a black chef's jacket, a pair of black-and-white pinstripe cotton trousers, and an apron. It was nearly midday, and

the lunchtime rush was building. My fellow souschefs were from Sweden, New Zealand, Australia, France, and Italy. Steve strode up and down like Nelson before a naval battle, tasting sauces, checking ingredients. "I'm a bit worried about the langoustine," he said. "I have only a hundred portions. Let's just hope it's enough."

Bank is owned by Tony Allan, a working-class Londoner who took one of the city's oldest trades, fishmongering, and remade it. The fish served at his restaurants comes from sustainable sources, he says. Genetically modified food is prohibited—notices at each restaurant read, "This is a GM-free zone!"

"I was a chef originally," Tony explained, as Bank began to fill up. With his glowing tan, white jeans, denim shirt, and flowing locks, he looked like a pop star. "But I got the sack because I was always complaining about the quality of the fish. So I started going to the coastal markets, places like Hastings on the south coast, buying fish to supply to restaurants. One man with a van sort of thing."

Fourteen years later he supplies three-quarters of all fish used by London's restaurants, the van is a Ferrari, and Bank Group Restaurants is a publicly traded company worth 100 million pounds (160 million dollars). Such success stories have a long tradition; London's most famous bit of folklore tells of a poor country boy named Dick Whittington, who arrives with his possessions tied in a bundle at the end of a stick and ends up rich and famous. And though Allan isn't the mayor of London, as Whittington was, it is entrepreneurs like him—savvy, ambitious, quick to spot the main chance—who have always made London rich. Today he lives in a mansion in Kent and indulges his passion for falconry.

Like many of London's new restaurants, Bank has its kitchen in the middle of the dining area—a stage on which, twice daily, a noisy, olfactory drama is performed. Theater and spectacle have always been at the heart of London's life. Or, as Shakespeare put it: All the world's a stage. At Bank, the clank of pots and the billowing of smoke were the stage effects; my fellow sous-chefs and I, the actors. For maximum theatrical effect we bellowed each order at the top of our lungs and sprinkled our dialogue with French.

"105!" roared Steve Carter, spiking an order. "One chateaubriand! One calf's liver!"

"*Ca marche!*" came the answering cry from inside the kitchen.

My job was to see that each dish was accompanied by the correct side orders. By 1:20 P.M.

> London has become, economically and culturally, the de facto capital of Europe.

we were handling 55 main courses simultaneously, and I was sweating like a stevedore.

Through the plate-glass windows I could see the crowds surging along the sidewalks. Black cabs weaved through the cars and buses on their way to Trafalgar Square. As I watched them go by, I felt a wave of affection for this great city, which, like an ancient coral reef, has gone on shifting and growing, adapting itself to the needs and the dreams of each new generation for nearly 2,000 years.

Critical Responses

1. What is the focus of the text of this article? What is the focus of the photographs? How does each relate to the other—or not—and what are the implications?

2. What do the rigors of becoming a cabbie in London suggest about the city's values? What does the term for the course of study, "The Knowledge," itself imply?

3. How is London a "melting pot"? How, in this regard, does it compare to a major metropolitan U.S. city?

4. What, on the other hand, are some ways in which Londoners are divided? Are these unique to London? Or are they typical in modern cities?

Writing Topics

1. Though related, concepts such as "diversity" and "integration" are not quite the same. Defining each, and distinguishing between them, discuss ways in which London exemplifies the one and the other.

2. Taking this idea in a somewhat different direction, consider what "multiculturalism" means objectively as well as the values implied by the term. How does multiculturalism contribute to the overall culture of a specific place—whether it be a college campus or a city? Can it detract in any way?

3. Compare this depiction of London with that of New York in Joel Swerdlow's "Tale of Three Cities." What makes each a cosmopolitan city? How does each contribute to and expand your idea of what a cosmopolitan city is or could be?

4. How, according to Worrall, would Londoners view the couple embracing in Cobb's photograph? Do you agree that an American would have a different perspective? What about the observations about race and identity in London versus America? Does your experience bear them out, at least on the American side?

Further Explorations

1. Write a descriptive essay about a place you know well—whether it be a home town, a neighborhood, or a city—focusing on its demographic features. Does the demographic profile make it an attractive place? How and why, and, crucially, to whom?

2. What was London like in the 1960s? Research the question, whether individually or in groups. How do your findings illuminate points made in this article? How do they illuminate the character of the 60s in general? Are the themes of the period familiar to you? Or do they seem remote, in place and time?

DUBAI:
SUDDEN CITY

By Atshin Molavi

Photographs by Maggie Steber

DUBAI: SUDDEN CITY

What does it take to build a city from scratch? In the 21st century, what might be done when starting with a blank slate? Presenting just such possibilities, the development of Dubai also highlights one approach to modernization in the Middle East, as well as displaying spectacular shows of wealth and lifestyle attractions. Is Dubai a "glitzy anomaly," though, or a "model to be copied"? These are questions asked by acclaimed Middle East journalist Afshin Molavi, who, along with *National Geographic* photographer Maggie Steber, looks at the best and the worst of the city.

The Palm Jumeirah, a man-made island whose fronds offer beachfront lots for 4,000 villas and apartments, juts audaciously into the Persian Gulf. Dubbed the Eighth Wonder of the World, the development has doubled Dubai's 45-mile shoreline, but has also disrupted its coastal ecosystem.

Basking in the good life, expatriates watch a polo match at Arabian Ranches, a suburban-style development designed for moneyed foreigners drawn to Dubai by its well-paying jobs, social freedoms, and—until recent jumps in property values— its relatively low cost of living.

A FEVERISH DREAM OF THE FUTURE
SPRINGS FROM THE SANDS
IN DUBAI.

There once was a sheikh who dreamed big. His realm, on the shores of the Persian Gulf, was a sleepy, sun-scorched village occupied by pearl divers, fishermen, and traders who docked their ramshackle dhows and fishing boats along a narrow creek that snaked through town. But where others saw only a brackish creek, this sheikh, Rashid bin Saeed al Maktoum, saw a highway to the world.

One day in 1959, he borrowed many millions of dollars from his oilrich neighbor, Kuwait, to dredge the creek until it was wide and deep enough for ships. He built wharves and warehouses and planned for roads and schools and homes. Some thought he was mad, others just mistaken, but Sheikh Rashid believed in the power of new beginnings. Sometimes at dawn, with his young son, Mohammed, by his side, he'd walk the empty waterfront and paint his dream in the air with words and gestures. And it was, in the end, as he said. He built it, and they came.

His son, Sheikh Mohammed bin Rashid al Maktoum, now rules Dubai, and around that creek has built towering dreams of his own, transforming the sunrise vision of his father into a floodlit, air-conditioned, skyscrapered

Dubai is also a rare success story in the Middle East, a region with a history of failure and stagnation.

fantasy world of a million people. With its Manhattan-style skyline, world-class port, and colossal, duty-free shopping malls, little Dubai now attracts more tourists than the whole of India, more shipping vessels than Singapore, and more foreign capital than many European countries. The people of 150 nations have moved here to live and work. Dubai has even built man-made islands—some in the shape of palm trees—to accommodate the wealthiest of them. Its economic growth rate, 16 percent, is nearly double that of China. Construction cranes punctuate the skyline like exclamation points.

Dubai is also a rare success story in the Middle East, a region with a history of failure and stagnation. Whether Dubai represents a glitzy anomaly or a model to be copied by other Arab nations is a question worth asking these days, as the Islamic world struggles to cope with modernization. Abdulrahman al Rashid, a Saudi journalist and director of the Al Arabiya news channel, put it this way: "Dubai is putting pressure on the rest of the

Adapted from "Dubai: Sudden City" by Afshin Molavi: National Geographic Magazine, January 2007.

Arab and Muslim world. People are beginning to ask their governments: If Dubai can do it, why can't we?"

Dubai, it must be said, is like no other place on Earth. This is the world capital of living large; the air practically crackles with a volatile mix of excess and opportunity. It's the kind of place where tennis stars Andre Agassi and Roger Federer play an exhibition match on the rooftop helipad of the opulent Burj al Arab megahotel; where diamond-encrusted cell phones do a brisk business at $10,000 apiece; where millions of people a year fly in just to go shopping.

Over the past decade, I've traveled to Dubai often and grown to appreciate the quirky multiculturalism of a city where one can eat in an Italian restaurant run by an Egyptian, with an Indian head chef and Filipino waiters who break into operettas every half hour. Or watch, in the wee hours, a mob of English expatriates weaving home from a pub as the Muslim call to morning prayer echoes through the streets.

Many Americans first heard of Dubai, one of seven emirates that make up the United Arab Emirates (U.A.E.), when a state-owned company, Dubai Ports World, purchased a British firm that managed six U.S. ports. Some members of Congress reacted with alarm, charging, correctly, that the 9/11 conspirators used Dubai as a key financial transit point. Others supported the deal, noting that the U.A.E. had proved a staunch ally in the war on terror, and that U.A.E. ports host more U.S. Navy ships than any port outside the United States. In the end Dubai decided to pass on managing the U.S. ports. "We're too busy for politics," Sultan bin Sulayem, the head of Dubai Ports World, told me. "The Americans didn't want us on that deal. Fine. We move on. There's lots of business to be done."

Indeed. Dubai has created one of the most dynamic business environments in the world. "It's not just the buildings and the islands and the hotels," says Ali al Shihabi, the Princeton-educated director of a leading investment bank. "It's the soft stuff: the laws, the regulations, the liberal social environment." With no corporate or income taxes, a top-notch banking system, and a legal code that favors property and ownership, Dubai embodies old Sheikh Rashid's motto: "What's good for the merchants is good for Dubai."

And then there's his son, Sheikh Mohammed, the 57-year-old ruler of Dubai, whom Edmund O'Sullivan, editor of the *Middle East Economic Digest,* calls a "radical modernizer" and the "most significant figure in Arabia since King Abdulaziz"—the founder of modern Saudi Arabia who leveraged his country's oil reserves to become a major world player.

Unlike a traditional Middle Eastern autocrat, Sheikh Mohammed (known to many as Sheikh Mo) manages Dubai like a good CEO. Besides keeping a full schedule of public appearances, he's often seen driving himself around the backlots of Dubai, surveying his construction sites, as his father did, at the crack of dawn. He'll sometimes show up unannounced in the workplace to ask tough questions, fire poor managers on the spot, and reward the hardest workers. From these he handpicks Dubai's next generation of executives, including many women. "Hire the best women you can find," he told Anita Mehra Homayoun, the head of marketing for Dubai's airport, when he tapped her for the job in 1996. Mehra Homayoun herself rose through the ranks of the airport's dutyfree shopping operation and caught Sheikh Mo's attention by organizing car raffles and celebrity golf and tennis tournaments, and by attracting top retailers to the airport's dutyfree empire. "Sheikh Mohammed makes you believe you can do anything," she said. "His vision is contagious."

Another of the chosen, Mohammad Alabbar, grew up, like many Dubaians, in a tent made of palm fronds. His father supported a wife and 12 children with his fishing net. Then, in 1966, Dubai struck oil, and Alabbar went to college in the United States on a government scholarship paid for by oil revenues. (Though a windfall early on, Dubai's modest oil reserves now account for only 6 percent of GDP.) After graduation, he impressed Sheikh Mo during a six-year stint in Singapore, where he turned stagnant retail enterprises into thriving businesses. That led to a posting as Dubai's director of economic development, a role that showcased his ability to boost commerce by cutting red tape. As a reward, the government granted him land at little or no cost, and he started building.

Today he travels the world in a private jet and oversees Emaar, one of the richest real estate development companies in the world. "We have come a long way," Alabbar told me at the project site of the Burj Dubai, a towering, torpedo-like structure that will be the tallest building on the planet when it's finished in 2008. "But we must always remember where we came from. Our kids must know that we worked very, very hard to get to where we are now, and there's a lot more work to do."

Who actually does that work is a touchy subject. Dubai is not, demographically, an Arab city-state: Fewer than one in eight residents are citizens of the U.A.E., and South Asian guest workers make up more than 60 percent of the population. Many educated Indians live a comfortable life in Dubai, and a few have become rich. ("Dubai is the best city in India," quip the fortunate.) For others, however, Dubai is a dead end.

The local press had been reporting labor unrest the evening I visited one of the squalid neighborhoods where tens of thousands of guest workers live. The laborers' barracks stood among many battered, squat buildings along a dirt and gravel road littered with garbage. Hundreds of men with sun-soaked brown faces scuttled past in tank tops, baggy slacks, and torn flip-flops. Some of these workers joined in recent strikes, fed up with being treated as "less than human," in the words of Human Rights Watch. The average laborer makes about five dollars a day, working 12-hour shifts in scorching heat. (Human Rights Watch reported nearly 900 construction deaths in 2004, including deaths from heatstroke.)

Fewer than one in eight are citizens of the U.A.E.

Listen to their stories, and you learn that many workers are trapped here, mired in debt to unscrupulous agents back home who charged them exorbitant fees for their work visas. "If I didn't have to pay back my fee, I'd go home today," one man told me. "We have nothing," said Kutty, a short, sunken-cheeked 25-year-old from the Indian state of Kerala. "We are living a nightmare here, and nobody cares."

Reacting to such abuses—and the bad publicity they generate—the government recently announced it would allow workers to unionize, and ordered all contractors to halt work for four hours a day during the heat of July and August.

Dubai's troubles don't end there. Creating man-made islands offshore, for example, may have been a brilliant, if outrageous, business decision—waterfront properties sell for 7 million to 30 million dollars—but in the process, environmentalists say, Dubai has killed coral, destroyed turtle nesting sites, and upset the marine ecology of the western Persian Gulf. And behind the glittering skyscrapers lies a late-night world of fleabag hotels and prostitutes, Indian and Russian mobsters, money launderers, and smugglers of everything from guns and diamonds to human beings.

The night I stopped by the Cyclone Club, the prostitutes on hand hailed from Moldova, Russia, China, eastern Europe, the Caucasus, and various countries in East Africa. Their clients were Arabs, Europeans, Asians, and Americans. Music throbbed, drinks flowed, and soon the couples headed for the exits. I met a Chinese woman who goes by the name Muri. "I only go Cyclone two times a week," she said in halting English. During the day she works as a chef at a Chinese restaurant. Her clients, she said, tend to be Europeans or Americans on leave from the war in Iraq. "The Arabs like the European girls and Russians." I asked if she knew of trafficking rings that

continued on page 332

A guest at a mass wedding peruses the thick program, which lists 47 couples. Dubai's government bankrolls such events to encourage marriage of native-born couples. Most of the city's work is performed by foreigners, who now outnumber natives eight to one.

More than half Dubai's population lives in workers' camps like this one, where South Asian men sleep in crowded dormitories that open onto standing sewage. Most owe money for the cost of their trip to Dubai. Many wait months for wages; some never see them.

Jumeirah Beach Residence rose in just 36 months, its concrete poured by laborers working day and night. Some critics are questioning the speed of change and a lack of planning: The towering apartment complexes stand like a wall, cutting off the rest of Dubai from its coast.

continued from page 327

deal in Chinese girls. "Yes, of course," she said, wrinkling her eyebrows. "Very bad. Some girls very young."

A few days later I asked a top aide to Sheikh Mohammed whether Muri was right about the influx of Chinese prostitutes and traffickers. "It's not easy to stop the ones who come to Dubai by choice," he told me, "but we have no tolerance for traffickers." The U.S. State Department, however, reports that Dubai's efforts to curtail the trade fall short of even "minimum standards," and estimates that some 10,000 women in the U.A.E. may be victims of sex traffickers.

Dubai's relaxed approach to these and other problems does prompt criticism, though carefully muted. "We need to slow down, things are going too far," one prominent writer told me, referring to unrestrained development running roughshod over local culture. He asked that I not use his name. Said another native, "I know that some of my Arab friends only visit us because we have foreign prostitutes here. This is shameful."

Dubai's tolerance can also be a good thing. Alongside its bars and nightclubs, there are mosques and churches and Hindu temples, and, for a city with so many competing religions and nationalities, it is remarkably free of ethnic conflict. "I don't know who's a Sunni and who's a Shia, and I don't care," Sheikh Mohammed told me during a brief meeting. "If you work hard, if you don't bother your neighbor, then there is a place for you in Dubai." Even Israelis can do business (quietly) with Dubai.

While the Dubai model—built on freewheeling capitalism, entrepreneurship, and religious moderation—might be a blueprint for other developing nations, Dubai is uniquely positioned for the 21st century largely due to the vision and ambition of one man. Other Arab leaders might emulate Sheikh Mo or his methods, but in the end—and some would say thank goodness—there's only one Dubai.

Before I left the emirate, I decided to do what millions of visitors have done over the past decade: Go to a shopping mall. Dubai reportedly has more shopping malls per consumer than any other city in the world, and day or night they are packed with the kind of crowd one typically finds in Dubai: veiled Saudi women browsing Victoria's Secret; teenage Emirati boys in ghetto gear flirting with eastern European girls in black leather miniskirts; Senegalese and Egyptian and Iranian and Kazakh and Korean families, strolling amid the fountains and stores as Western pop music, globalization's soundtrack, plays over the loudspeakers. At one mall, the Hamarain Center, the theme song to *Titanic*, by Céline Dion, was played so often that local retailers complained.

I chose the Mall of the Emirates, one of Dubai's newest megamalls, a 2.4-million-square-foot behemoth that features an indoor ski slope. Entering is like crossing the threshold into an alternative reality: a lavish, artificial world of high-end clothing boutiques, edgy music stores, cafés, and restaurants that culminates at a massive, plate-glass window with skilifts in the distance. I joined the crowd at the window to watch skiers descending a snow-covered "mountain," children throwing snowballs at each other, and instructors guiding beginners through their first runs.

I spotted what looked to be a group of Dubaians on a family outing. A middle-aged Arab man in a rented overcoat walked gingerly through the snow in street shoes. Nearby, a woman in a black *abaya*, also wearing a rented coat, nervously held the arm of an Asian woman, perhaps her Filipina housekeeper. A teenage boy with a wispy mustache approached them, skis strapped to his feet. He chatted for a moment, then labored off toward the lift for another run. The woman let go of the Filipina and took a few steps. Then she smiled, squatted down, and picked up some snow, a small white miracle in the desert of Arabia. She seemed to be enjoying herself. The temperature of the real world outside was 110 degrees, but in the dream world of Dubai it was just about perfect.

Critical Responses

1. Starting with the question asked by Molavi about whether Dubai is a "glitzy anomaly" or a "model to be copied," consider how each position is illustrated in the article. Do you find an answer there, one way or another? Bearing in mind places like Las Vegas, what do you think?

2. What does each of the photographs say about Dubai? What picture do they create together?

3. "We have come a long way," says Dubai's director of economic development. "But we must always remember where we came from." Does Dubai encourage this kind of cultural memory—or does it wipe it out? Can it escape old problems? Does it exacerbate them?

4. How would you characterize the style and the tone of the opening of this article? What attitude does this opening convey and what expectations does it arouse? In what ways does it continue to inform the article? How, on the other hand, does the article diverge?

Writing Topics

1. What are some of the similarities between the laborers described in this article and those described in the article on "21st-Century Slaves"? To the extent that Dubai's laborers are enslaved, what should be done to ameliorate their condition? Should international sanctions also be brought to bear?

2. "What's good for the merchants is good for Dubai," says its ruler, Sheikh Mohammed. Evaluate this statement, both on its own terms and in relation to specific examples from the article.

3. Review the "winning formula" of Alexandria, discussed by Joel Swerdlow in "Tale of Three Cities," and consider the extent to which it does or does not apply to Dubai, and what it may or may not suggest about Dubai's future.

4. Compare Dubai as represented here to New York as represented by Swerdlow and to London as represented by Simon Worrall in this reader. In considering specific similarities and differences, consider whether and to what extent you could call Dubai a "cosmopolitan city."

Further Explorations

1. What is your favorite city, and why? Does Dubai have any similar features? Are there some that are unique to Dubai and enticing to you? What about aspects of the city that don't attract you? Would you want to go there? Why or why not?

2. Virtual tours of Dubai are readily available online. Dividing into groups, and selecting one such tour per group, analyze the representation of the city, considering what elements are highlighted, how their appeal is conveyed, what organization is responsible for creating the tour, and who the target audience is. What picture emerges from your collective inquiries? How does it compare with that given in this article?

POPULATION: SEVEN BILLION

By Robert Kunzig

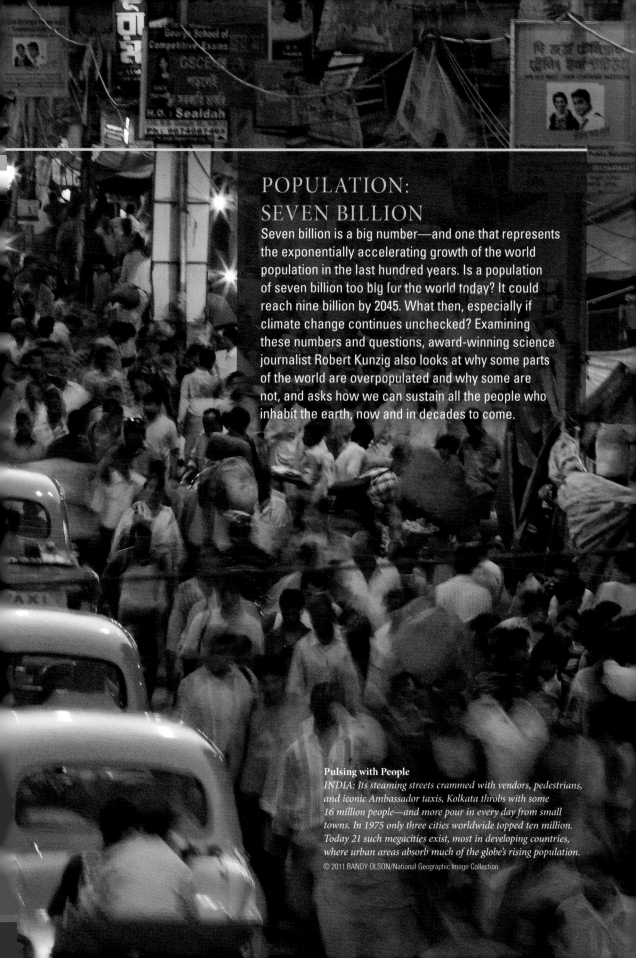

POPULATION: SEVEN BILLION

Seven billion is a big number—and one that represents the exponentially accelerating growth of the world population in the last hundred years. Is a population of seven billion too big for the world today? It could reach nine billion by 2045. What then, especially if climate change continues unchecked? Examining these numbers and questions, award-winning science journalist Robert Kunzig also looks at why some parts of the world are overpopulated and why some are not, and asks how we can sustain all the people who inhabit the earth, now and in decades to come.

Pulsing with People
INDIA: Its steaming streets crammed with vendors, pedestrians, and iconic Ambassador taxis, Kolkata throbs with some 16 million people—and more pour in every day from small towns. In 1975 only three cities worldwide topped ten million. Today 21 such megacities exist, most in developing countries, where urban areas absorb much of the globe's rising population.

Energized Landscape

ENGLAND: Glowing furnace bright at night, London became the world's largest city during the coal-powered industrial revolution, a tipping point for the steep rise of Earth's population. Wealthy countries use many times more resources per capita than poorer nations, but as global incomes rise, increased consumption may stress the planet more than population growth.

© 2011 HAWKES, JASON/National Geographic Image Collection

GLOBAL POPULATION IS PROJECTED TO REACH NINE BILLION.

CAN THE PLANET TAKE THE STRAIN?

How big will the population actually grow?

As we reach the milestone of seven billion people this year, it's time to take stock. In the coming decades, despite falling birthrates, the population will continue to grow—mostly in poor countries. If the billions of people who want to boost themselves out of poverty follow the path blazed by those in wealthy countries, they too will step hard on the planet's resources. How big will the population actually grow? What will the planet look like in 2045? The answers will depend on the decisions each of us makes.

One day in Delft in the fall of 1677, Antoni van Leeuwenhoek, a cloth merchant who is said to have been the long-haired model for two paintings by Johannes Vermeer—"The Astronomer" and "The Geographer"—abruptly stopped what he was doing with his wife and rushed to his worktable. Cloth was Leeuwenhoek's business but microscopy his passion. He'd had five children already by his first wife (though four had died in infancy), and fatherhood was not on his mind. "Before six beats of the pulse had intervened," as he

later wrote to the Royal Society of London, Leeuwenhoek was examining his perishable sample through a tiny magnifying glass. Its lens, no bigger than a small raindrop, magnified objects hundreds of times. Leeuwenhoek had made it himself; nobody else had one so powerful. The learned men in London were still trying to verify Leeuwenhoek's earlier claims that unseen "animalcules" lived by the millions in a single drop of lake water and even in French wine. Now he had something more delicate to report: Human semen contained animalcules too. "Sometimes more than a thousand," he wrote, "in an amount of material the size of a grain of sand." Pressing the glass to his eye like a jeweler, Leeuwenhoek watched his own animalcules swim about, lashing their long tails. One imagines sunlight falling through leaded windows on a face lost in contemplation, as in the Vermeers. One feels for his wife.

Leeuwenhoek became a bit obsessed after that. Though his tiny peephole gave him

Adapted from "Population: Seven Billion" by Robert Kunzig: National Geographic Magazine, January 2011.

privileged access to a never-before-seen microscopic universe, he spent an enormous amount of time looking at spermatozoa, as they're now called. Oddly enough, it was the milt he squeezed from a cod one day that inspired him to estimate, almost casually, just how many people might live on Earth.

Nobody then really had any idea; there were few censuses. Leeuwenhoek started with an estimate that around a million people lived in Holland. Using maps and a little spherical geometry, he calculated that the inhabited land area of the planet was 13,385 times as large as Holland. It was hard to imagine the whole planet being as densely peopled as Holland, which seemed crowded even then. Thus, Leeuwenhoek concluded triumphantly, there couldn't be more than 13.385 billion people on Earth—a small number indeed compared with the 150 billion sperm cells of a single codfish! This cheerful little calculation, writes population biologist Joel Cohen in his book *How Many People Can the Earth Support?*, may have been the first attempt to give a quantitative answer to a question that has become far more pressing now than it was in the 17th century. Most answers these days are far from cheerful.

Historians now estimate that in Leeuwenhoek's day there were only half a billion or so humans on Earth. After rising very slowly for millennia, the number was just starting to take off. A century and a half later, when another scientist reported the discovery of human egg cells, the world's population had doubled to more than a billion. A century after that, around 1930, it had doubled again to two billion. The acceleration since then has been astounding. Before the 20th century, no human had lived through a doubling of the human population, but there are people alive today who have seen it triple. Sometime in late 2011, according to the UN Population Division, there will be seven billion of us.

There may be some comfort in knowing that people have long been alarmed about population. From the beginning, says French demographer Hervé Le Bras, demography has been steeped in talk of the apocalypse. Some of the field's founding papers were written just a few years after Leeuwenhoek's discovery by Sir William Petty, a founder of the Royal Society. He estimated that world population would double six times by the Last Judgment, which was expected in about 2,000 years. At that point it would exceed 20 billion people—more, Petty thought, than the planet could feed. "And then, according to the prediction of the Scriptures, there must be wars, and great slaughter, &c.," he wrote.

As religious forecasts of the world's end receded, Le Bras argues, population growth itself provided an ersatz mechanism of apocalypse. "It crystallized the ancient fear, and perhaps the ancient hope, of the end of days," he writes. In 1798 Thomas Malthus, an English priest and economist, enunciated his general law of population: that it necessarily grows faster than the food supply, until war, disease, and famine arrive to reduce the number of people. As it turned out, the last plagues great enough to put a dent in global population had already happened when Malthus wrote. World population hasn't fallen, historians think, since the Black Death of the 14th century.

In the two centuries after Malthus declared that population couldn't continue to soar, that's exactly what it did. The process started in what we now call the developed countries, which were then still developing. The spread of New World crops like corn and the potato, along with the discovery of chemical fertilizers, helped banish starvation in Europe. Growing cities remained cesspools of disease at first, but from the mid-19th century on, sewers began to channel human waste away from drinking water, which was then filtered and chlorinated; that dramatically reduced the spread of cholera and typhus.

Moreover in 1798, the same year that Malthus published his dyspeptic tract, his compatriot Edward Jenner described a vaccine for smallpox—the first and most important in a series of vaccines and antibiotics that, along with better nutrition and sanitation, would double life expectancy in the industrializing countries, from 35 years to 77 today. It would take a cranky person to see that trend as gloomy: "The development of medical science was the straw that broke the camel's back," wrote Stanford population biologist Paul Ehrlich in 1968.

Millions of people in developing countries who would have died in childhood survived to have children themselves. That's why the population explosion spread around the planet: because a great many people were saved from dying.

And because, for a time, women kept giving birth at a high rate. In 18th-century Europe or early 20th-century Asia, when the average woman had six children, she was doing what it took to replace herself and her mate, because most of those children never reached adulthood. When child mortality declines, couples eventually have fewer children—but that transition usually takes a generation at the very least. Today in developed countries, an average of 2.1 births per woman would maintain a steady population; in the developing world, "replacement fertility" is somewhat higher. In the time it takes for the birthrate to settle into that new balance with the death rate, population explodes.

Demographers call this evolution the demographic transition. All countries go through it in their own time. It's a hallmark of human progress: In a country that has completed the transition, people have wrested from nature at least some control over death and birth. The global population explosion is an inevitable side effect, a huge one that some people are not sure our civilization can survive. But the growth rate was actually at its peak just as Ehrlich was sounding his alarm. By the

> When child mortality declines, couples eventually have fewer children—but that transition takes a generation.

early 1970s, fertility rates around the world had begun dropping faster than anyone had anticipated. Since then, the population growth rate has fallen by more than 40 percent.

The fertility decline that is now sweeping the planet started at different times in different countries. By the onset of World War II, fertility had fallen close to the replacement level in parts of Europe and the US. Then, after the surprising blip known as the baby boom, came the bust, again catching demographers off guard. They assumed some instinct would lead women to keep having enough children to ensure the survival of the species. Instead, in country after developed country, the fertility rate fell below replacement level. In the late 1990s in Europe it fell to 1.4. "The evidence I'm familiar with, which is anecdotal, is that women couldn't care less about replacing the species," Joel Cohen says.

The end of a baby boom can have two big economic effects on a country. The first is the "demographic dividend"—a blissful few decades when the boomers swell the labor force and the number of young and old dependents is relatively small, and there is thus a lot of money for other things. Then the second effect kicks in: The boomers start to retire. What had been considered the enduring demographic order is revealed to be a party that has to end.

In industrialized countries it took generations for fertility to fall to the replacement level or below. As that same transition takes place in the rest of the world, what has astonished demographers is how much faster it is happening there. Though its population continues to grow, China, home to a fifth of the world's people, is already below replacement fertility and has been for nearly 20 years, thanks in part to the coercive one-child policy implemented

continued on page 344

As we reach the milestone of seven
billion people this year, it's time to
take stock. In the coming decades,
despite falling birthrates, the
population will continue to
grow - mostly in poor countries.
If the billions of people who want
to boost themselves out of poverty
follow the path blazed by those
in wealthy countries, they too will
step hard on the planet's resources.
How big will the population actually
grow? What will the planet look like
in 2045? The answers will depend on
the decision each of us makes.

SOURCES: POPULATION REFERENCE BUREAU AND UNITED NATIONS

World population
200 MILLION
A.D. 1

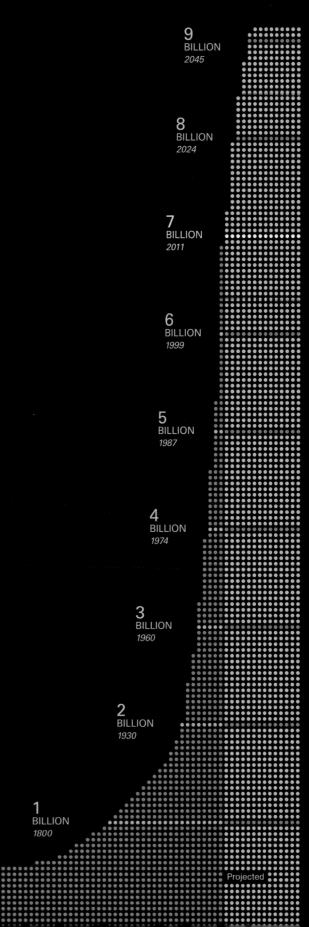

9
BILLION
2045

8
BILLION
2024

7
BILLION
2011

6
BILLION
1999

5
BILLION
1987

4
BILLION
1974

3
BILLION
1960

2
BILLION
1930

1
BILLION
1800

Projected

Agents of Change

SPAIN: Immigrants like these Indians at a Sikh festival in Barcelona are bolstering Europe's stagnant population growth rate. Around the world, the childbearing decisions of young women will determine whether global population stabilizes or not. Research shows that the more education a woman receives, the fewer children she is likely to have.

© 2011 RANDY OLSON/National Geographic Image Collection

continued from page 339

in 1979; Chinese women, who were bearing an average of six children each as recently as 1965, are now having around 1.5. In Iran, with the support of the Islamic regime, fertility has fallen more than 70 percent since the early '80s. In Catholic and democratic Brazil, women have reduced their fertility rate by half over the same quarter century. "We still don't understand why fertility has gone down so fast in so many societies, so many cultures and religions. It's just mind-boggling," says Hania Zlotnik, director of the UN Population Division.

"At this moment, much as I want to say there's still a problem of high fertility rates, it's only about 16 percent of the world population, mostly in Africa," says Zlotnik. South of the Sahara, fertility is still five children per woman; in Niger it is seven. But then, 17 of the countries in the region still have life expectancies of 50 or less; they have just begun the demographic transition. In most of the world, however, family size has shrunk dramatically. The UN projects that the world will reach replacement fertility by 2030. "The population as a whole is on a path toward nonexplosion—which is good news," Zlotnik says.

The bad news is that 2030 is two decades away and that the largest generation of adolescents in history will then be entering their childbearing years. Even if each of those women has only two children, population will coast upward under its own momentum for another quarter century. Is a train wreck in the offing, or will people then be able to live humanely and in a way that doesn't destroy their environment?

Dr. Chandra Bortamuly is on the front lines of a battle that has been going on in India for nearly 60 years. In 1952, just five years after it gained independence from Britain, India became the first country to establish a policy for population control. Since then the

China is already below replacement fertility, thanks in part to its coercive one-child policy.

government has repeatedly set ambitious goals—and repeatedly missed them by a mile. A national policy adopted in 2000 called for the country to reach the replacement fertility of 2.1 by 2010. That won't happen for at least another decade.

In the UN's medium projection, India's population will rise to just over 1.6 billion people by 2050. "What's inevitable is that India is going to exceed the population of China by 2030," says A. R. Nanda, former head of the Population Foundation of India, an advocacy group. "Nothing less than a huge catastrophe, nuclear or otherwise, can change that."

Sterilization is the dominant form of birth control in India today, and the vast majority of the procedures are performed on women. The government is trying to change that; a no-scalpel vasectomy costs far less and is easier on a man than a tubal ligation is on a woman. In the operating theater Bortamuly worked quickly. In less than seven minutes—a nurse timed him—the patient was walking out without so much as a Band-Aid. The government will pay him an incentive fee of 1,100 rupees (around $25), a week's wages for a laborer.

The Indian government tried once before to push vasectomies, in the 1970s, when anxiety about the population bomb was at its height. Prime Minister Indira Gandhi and her son Sanjay used state-of-emergency powers to force a dramatic increase in sterilizations. From 1976 to 1977 the number of operations tripled, to more than eight million. Over six million of those were vasectomies. Family planning workers were pressured to meet quotas; in a few states, sterilization became a condition for receiving new housing or other government benefits. In some cases, the police simply rounded up poor people and hauled them to sterilization camps.

The excesses gave the whole concept of family planning a bad name. "Successive

Time for Another Green Revolution
CHINA: Using every fertile inch, farmers harvest rice in the hills of Yunnan Province. High-yield seeds and ample fertilizer allow China to feed its billion-plus people on less than 10 percent of the Earth's arable land. Producing enough food as global population grows is possible, but doing so without exhausting finite resources, especially water, will be a challenge.

governments refused to touch the subject," says Shailaja Chandra, former head of the National Population Stabilisation Fund (NPSF). Yet fertility in India has dropped anyway, though not as fast as in China, where it was nose-diving even before the draconian one-child policy took effect. The national average in India is now 2.6 children per woman, less than half what it was when Ehrlich visited. The southern half of the country and a few states in the northern half are already at replacement fertility or below.

In Kerala, on the southwest coast, investments in health and education helped fertility fall to 1.7. The key, demographers there say, is the female literacy rate: At around 90 percent, it's easily the highest in India. Girls who go to school start having children later than ones who don't. They are more open to contraception and more likely to understand their options.

As an alternative to the Kerala model, some point to the southern state of Andhra Pradesh, where sterilization "camps"—temporary operating rooms often set up in schools—were introduced during the '70s and where sterilization rates have remained high as improved hospitals have replaced the camps. In a single decade beginning in the early 1990s, the fertility rate fell from around three to less than two. Unlike in Kerala, half of all women in Andhra Pradesh remain illiterate.

Amarjit Singh, the current executive director of the NPSF, calculates that if the four biggest states of the Hindi belt had followed the Andhra Pradesh model, they would have avoided 40 million births—and considerable suffering. "Because 40 million were born, 2.5 million children died," Singh says. He thinks if all India were to adopt high-quality programs to encourage sterilizations, in hospitals rather than camps, it could have 1.4 billion people in 2050 instead of 1.6 billion.

Critics of the Andhra Pradesh model, such as the Population Foundation's Nanda, say Indians need better health care, particularly in rural areas. They are against numerical targets that pressure government workers to sterilize people or cash incentives that distort a couple's choice of family size. "It's a private decision," Nanda says.

In Indian cities today, many couples are making the same choice as their counterparts in Europe or America. Sonalde Desai, a senior fellow at New Delhi's National Council of Applied Economic Research, introduced me to five working women in Delhi who were spending most of their salaries on private-school fees and after-school tutors; each had one or two children and was not planning to have more. In a nationwide survey of 41,554 households, Desai's team identified a small but growing vanguard of urban one-child families. "We were totally blown away at the emphasis parents were placing on their children," she says. "It suddenly makes you understand—that is why fertility is going down." Indian children on average are much better educated than their parents.

The annual meeting of the Population Association of America (PAA) is one of the premier gatherings of the world's demographers. Last April the global population explosion was not on the agenda. "The problem has become a bit passé," Hervé Le Bras says. Demographers are generally confident that by the second half of this century we will be ending one unique era in history—the population explosion—and entering another, in which population will level out or even fall.

But will there be too many of us? At the PAA meeting, in the Dallas Hyatt Regency, I learned that the current population of the planet could fit into the state of Texas, if Texas were settled as densely as New York City. The comparison made me start thinking like Leeuwenhoek. If in 2045 there are nine billion people living on the six habitable continents, the world population density will be a little more than half that of France today. France is not usually considered a hellish place. Will the world be hellish then?

Some parts of it may well be; some parts of it are hellish today. There are now 21 cities with populations larger than 10 million, and by 2050 there will be many more. Delhi adds hundreds of thousands of migrants each year, and those people arrive to find that "no plans have been made for water, sewage, or habitation," says Shailaja Chandra. Dhaka in Bangladesh and Kinshasa in the Democratic Republic of the Congo are 40 times larger today than they were in 1950. Their slums are filled with desperately poor people who have fled worse poverty in the countryside.

Eight billion corresponds to the UN's lowest projection for 2050. In that optimistic scenario, Bangladesh has a fertility rate of 1.35 in 2050, but it still has 25 million more people than it does today. Rwanda's fertility rate also falls below the replacement level, but its population still rises to well over twice what it was before the genocide. If that's the optimistic scenario, one might argue, the future is indeed bleak.

But one can also draw a different conclusion—that fixating on population numbers is not the best way to confront the future. People packed into slums need help, but the problem that needs solving is poverty and lack of infrastructure, not overpopulation. Giving every woman access to family planning services is a good idea—"the one strategy that can make the biggest difference to women's lives," Chandra calls it. But the most aggressive population control program imaginable will not save Bangladesh from sea level rise, Rwanda from another genocide, or

Emptied Countryside

RUSSIA: Traffic is light—a horse cart with grain, a puppy in pursuit—on a road passing an abandoned granary and church in Novotishevoye, one of thousands of Russian villages depopulating as people move to cities and have fewer kids. To combat a low birthrate, the government has promised to pay $11,500 to women who have a second child.

all of us from our enormous environmental problems.

Global warming is a good example. Carbon emissions from fossil fuels are growing fastest in China, thanks to its prolonged economic boom, but fertility there is already below replacement; not much more can be done to control population. Where population is growing fastest, in Sub-Saharan Africa, emissions per person are only a few percent of what they are in the United States—so population control would have little effect on climate. Brian O'Neill of the National Center for Atmospheric Research has calculated that

if the population were to reach 7.4 billion in 2050 instead of 8.9 billion, it would reduce emissions by 15 percent. "Those who say the whole problem is population are wrong," Joel Cohen says. "It's not even the dominant factor." To stop global warming we'll have to switch from fossil fuels to alternative energy—regardless of how big the population gets.

The number of people does matter, of course. But how people consume resources matters a lot more. Some of us leave much bigger footprints than others. The central challenge for the future of people and the planet is how to raise more of us out of poverty—the slum dwellers in Delhi, the subsistence farmers in Rwanda while reducing the impact each of us has on the planet.

The World Bank has predicted that by 2030 more than a billion people in the developing world will belong to the "global middle class," up from just 400 million in 2005. That's a good thing. But it will be a hard thing for the planet if those people are eating meat and driving gasoline-powered cars at the same rate as Americans now do. It's too late to keep the new middle class of 2030 from being born; it's not too late to change how they and the rest of us will produce and consume food and energy. "Eating less meat seems more reasonable to me than saying, 'Have fewer children!'" Le Bras says.

How many people can the Earth support? Cohen spent years reviewing all the research, from Leeuwenhoek on. "I wrote the book thinking I would answer the question," he says. "I found out it's unanswerable in the present state of knowledge." What he found instead was an enormous range of "political numbers, intended to persuade people" one way or the other.

For centuries population pessimists have hurled apocalyptic warnings at the congenital optimists, who believe in their bones that humanity will find ways to cope and even improve its lot. History, on the whole, has so far favored the optimists, but history is no certain guide to the future. Neither is science. It cannot predict the outcome of *People* v. *Planet,* because all the facts of the case—how many of us there will be and how we will live—depend on choices we have yet to make and ideas we have yet to have. We may, for example, says Cohen, "see to it that all children are nourished well enough to learn in school and are educated well enough to solve the problems they will face as adults." That would change the future significantly.

The debate was present at the creation of population alarmism, in the person of Rev. Thomas Malthus himself. Toward the end of the book in which he formulated the iron law by which unchecked population growth leads to famine, he declared that law a good thing: It gets us off our duffs. It leads us to conquer the world. Man, Malthus wrote, and he must have meant woman too, is "inert, sluggish, and averse from labour, unless compelled by necessity." But necessity, he added, gives hope:

"The exertions that men find it necessary to make, in order to support themselves or families, frequently awaken faculties that might otherwise have lain for ever dormant, and it has been commonly remarked that new and extraordinary situations generally create minds adequate to grapple with the difficulties in which they are involved."

Seven billion of us soon, nine billion in 2045. Let's hope that Malthus was right about our ingenuity.

Critical Responses

1. From the information provided in this article, does it appear that a global population explosion is occurring now or likely to do so in the near future? Is population growth in itself a problem?

2. It's one thing to look at population numbers on a global scale; it's another to do so within a given area. What are some advantages and disadvantages of focusing on absolute numbers? What is gained and lost by limiting investigations to specific regions?

3. What are some causes of overpopulation? What are some effects? What is the best way to prevent overpopulation? What is the best way to redress its consequences?

4. What attitudes toward population growth are represented by the sources Kunzig cites in this article? What does his own seem to be? How would you characterize his tone? How does it affect your own attitude toward the issue?

Writing Topics

1. Insofar as lower birth rates can be linked with higher literacy rates, what accounts for the correlation? What role does gender play, and how should the role of gender be addressed?

2. Looking at the issue of population growth from another perspective, consider which of the methods for curtailing population growth discussed in this article appears to be the most effective. Which of them is most consistent with democratic values? Least? What are some of the implications?

3. Compare the conclusion of this article with that of "The End of Plenty," and particularly with the way that Thomas Malthus figures in each. Which Malthusian vision does each author emphasize, and why?

4. What makes an assemblage of people a crowd? What makes a crowd a horde? What's the difference between a horde and a host? Between a mass and a mob? Work out distinctions among these words, using both dictionary definitions and your own concrete examples.

Further Explorations

1. If the growth trend illustrated by the graph in this article continues, what will the world population be by the time you are 65 years old? Where would you hope to be living then? And what effect would this population growth have on you yourself and on your children and grandchildren?

2. How can reducing the amount of meat in one's diet contribute to lessening the strain on global resources, according to Kunzig? After discussing this question as a class, divide into groups, decide amongst yourselves another simple personal action that could have similar far-reaching impact, and then resume your discussion.

© 1974 LLOYD K. TOWNSEND JR./National Geographic Image Collection

Studying the Image

1. The painting includes several types of indigenous people. Why do you think the artist includes so many instead of just one? What point is the artist making with this choice?

2. How does the picture depict the relationship between the people and their environment? What visual clues does the artist use to illustrate this relationship?

Writing Assignment

Many plants along the Amazon can be used for medicinal purposes and may lead to the discovery of new drugs. Write an essay explaining how you would weigh the rights of indigenous people against the medical benefits that could be gained from the exploration of this area.

© 1950 B. ANTHONY STEWART/National Geographic Image Collection

Studying the Image

1. The Confederate flag has become for many Americans a symbol of oppression, as has the rickshaw in Kolkata, which is pointed out in the article "Last Days of the Rickshaw." Do you think the photographer is making a political statement in this picture?

2. What period in American history does this picture represent? Do feel that the flag has the same meaning to people in the South today as it did when this picture was taken?

Writing Assignment

The Confederate flag has been removed from display in many public places in the South. Nikki Haley, however, the governor of South Carolina, refuses to take down the flag from the top of the state house despite strong protests against it. Write an argument supporting either the protesters or Haley, outlining your reasons for your position.

© 1961 MELVILLE B. GROSVENOR/National Geographic Image Collection

Studying the Image

1. Tintagel is considered to be either the site of King Arthur's conception or his birth. How does this picture help reinforce the mythological nature of Arthur's legend?

2. Essays, novels, and poems have been written and several film versions have been made about Arthur. He fits the description of a "beautiful loser" as outlined in the article "Celt Appeal," but his legend has endured more than that of any other Celt. How would you explain his popularity?

Writing Assignment

Research the origins of King Arthur's ascension to the throne of Britain. Then watch Excalibur, one of the film versions of the Arthurian legend, and write an essay analyzing how accurate you think the film is based on your research.

© 1983 O. LOUIS MAZZATENTA/National Geographic Image Collection

Studying the Image

1. Think about the composition of the picture. The photographer included the two boys in the foreground and the group of ethnically dressed people descending the steps in the background. What kind of statement do you think the photographer was making with this arrangement?

2. How does the clothing of the people in the picture help define them? Do you think they made a conscious choice to define themselves in this way?

Writing Assignment

Note the two boys' different facial expressions and body language as they look at the camera. Write a paragraph from each boy's point of view describing what he is thinking about at the moment the picture was taken. How aware is he of his surroundings? Of the camera/photographer?

© JODI COBB/National Geographic Image Collection

Studying the Image

1. Note the contrasting elements in the mural. What point is the artist making with these contrasts?

2. What kind of customer would this mural appeal to?

Writing Assignment

The article on Dubai notes that people in the Middle East are looking at the opportunities afforded by the success of that city and asking their governments, "If Dubai can do it, why can't we?" Research the Arab Spring and write an essay explaining whether or not you think the revolutions occurring in the Middle East have been influenced by the economic prosperity of Dubai.

© 2001 B. ANTHONY STEWART/National Geographic Image Collection

Studying the Image

1. How does this picture convey the destruction of the natural environment?

2. How should rich nations compensate poorer nations for their overuse and destruction of environmental resources?

Writing Assignment

Research the countries that are the top air polluters. Write an article outlining the impact an increased population in these countries would have on the trajectory of global warming. What regulations do you think should be imposed on these countries?

Index

Note: page numbers in **bold** indicate photographs